Night Creature

Books by Whitney Balliett

The Sound of Surprise
Dinosaurs in the Morning
Such Sweet Thunder
Super-Drummer:
    A Profile of Buddy Rich
Ecstasy at the Onion
Alec Wilder and His Friends
New York Notes
Improvising
American Singers
Night Creature

"Night Creature"
A Journal of Jazz, 1975-1980 ."

Whitney Balliett

New York
OXFORD UNIVERSITY PRESS
1981

Most of the material in this book
appeared in somewhat different
form in *The New Yorker* magazine.

Library of Congress Cataloging in Publication Data

Balliett, Whitney.
Night creature.

Includes index.
1. Jazz music—New York (City)   I.   Title.
ML3508.B34   785.42'09747'1   80–24678
ISBN 0–19–502908–9
Printing (last digit): 9 8 7 6 5 4 3 2 1

Printed in the United States of America

For Edith Oliver

Note

This book is a considerably revised selection from the critical and shorter biographical pieces on jazz that I have done for *The New Yorker* from the end of 1975 through the first half of 1980. The pieces are centered in New York City, and deal with jazz in night clubs, in concerts, on television and radio, on recordings, and in books. The title is borrowed from a Duke Ellington composition written in the fifties. I do not know what beautiful night creature Ellington had in mind, but mine is jazz itself.

East Orleans, Massachusetts   **W.B.**
1980

Night Creature

1975

September 26th

Paradox crisscrossed much of Mahalia Jackson's life. She became famous in her last fifteen years by singing black religious music before white secular audiences. She was a great jazz singer who never sang jazz. (One wonders whether she *really* believed that, particularly when the spirit was on her and she stomped up and down the stage, swinging unbelievably hard.) She was a black hero to many whites and a "white" traitor to many blacks. She was a conspicuously charitable woman who never lost her New Orleans "evil." (The New Orleans evil takes the form of outrageous perversity, secrecy, suspicion, and a high clannishness. So: in all the world, only New Orleans musicians are any good.) And now, she is the subject of a miasmic, six-hundred-page biography, *Just Mahalia, Baby* (Word Books), which was put together by a New Orleans newspaperwoman named Laurraine Goreau. The author hung around Mahalia for twelve or thirteen years, and she must have jotted down the comings and goings—even from room to room in Mahalia's Chicago house—of every person who came in contact with her. The result is a giant engagement calendar swarming with people

3

who are not always introduced and who do not always have
surnames. Once in a while, Mahalia's own voice comes
through, and we think, That must have been the way she
talked, the way she was—as in this passage about a transatlantic crossing:

> Even though the water made me sick, quite sick,
> I would find myself all day watching the sea, and
> the way the water would run. It never ran the same
> way; sometimes it was like this, and sometimes like
> that—sometimes like this—and like that. It keeps
> you interested all day long, watching which way
> the sea going turn—whether it's going spread out,
> or whether it's going drop; all these different forms
> that it takes. And the sounds it makes. There really
> is a song of the sea.

But much of the time the book drifts in and out of a synthetic
voice that is a queer attempt to make it seem as if Mahalia
were talking about herself in the third person. Hence:

> Right into running revival at Salem all week.
> Never mind tired—she promised God. Good she
> could tell Mildred to bring her singers one night.
> Let her be a part. Oooh, it's a small bed this week
> for Halie: Can't invite Rev. Bentley all the way
> from Philadelphia to preach and not give him the
> best, her queen-size; she sure wasn't going take
> Minnis's bed; got Laurraines in Sigma's or she
> wouldn't mind being in the little girl's. Anyway,
> Laurraines need to be there 'cause that's the closet
> where Allen keep the stationery and Laurraines
> writing the important people for her in India. Halie
> was ashamed to let it run this long. So *much!* But it
> was good to have people fill up some this space.

An outline of Mahalia's life eventually materializes. She was
born illegitimate and poor in New Orleans in 1912. Her
mother, Charity Clark, was a minister's daughter, who died

when Mahalia was five. Her father, Johnny Jackson, was also a preacher, whose attentions warmed in direct proportion to her fame. She was raised by an overbearing aunt, and when she was fifteen she moved to Chicago with another aunt. During the next twenty years, she worked her way up through the doctrinaire, jealous gospel world, changing the music as she went along. She freed it rhythmically, and she made commonplace such devices as blue notes and growls and abrasive shouts. By 1950, she had had her first hit record, and she was on her way. One suspects that she was never at peace for long. She was married twice—to an inveterate gambler and to a blowhard jazz musician—and divorced twice. She became encrusted with hangers-on and bullies and sycophants. Her weight weakened her health, and she was frequently bedridden during the last seven or eight years of her life. But by the time she died she was no longer just a gospel singer. She was a black American superstar. Goreau doesn't tell us whether, in reaching that eminence, she considered herself to have risen or fallen.

October 10th

Five important recordings:

It is rare when a recording of a jazz concert bears out what one thought one heard. Generally, the concern turns out to be neither as good nor as bad as it seemed. But the recording of the swan-song concert given by the Modern Jazz Quartet at Avery Fisher last November—"The Last Concert: The Modern Jazz Quartet" (Atlantic)—is an exception. It *was* a classic evening. The recording also proves that the group, which had actually given its final concert some months before in Sydney and had been defunct since then, was no longer the impeccable machine it had come to be. Indeed, the concert was not so much a celebration of what the group had achieved during its twenty years as it was a celebration of the new

freedom of its four members, and this shows in almost every
one of the fourteen numbers on the album, which is an edited
version of the original three-hour concert. The group's counterpoint is pretty much intact ("The Golden Striker," "Summertime"), but the solos, once so carefully balanced with the
ensembles, are long and almost aggressive. They are also
brilliant. Listen to Milt Jackson in "The Cylinder" and "Summertime," and especially in "What's New?" and "Django."
It's as if he were consciously knocking the stuffing out of
"Django," which came to be an M.J.Q. hymn. And listen to
Lewis's ascending opening phrase in his solo in "Summertime" and, midway, to its clusters of high notes. And to his
statement in "Skating in Central Park." Even Percy Heath
gets off two notable solos ("Blues in A Minor," "Bags'
Groove"), and throughout Connie Kay swings with an almost thundering precision.

Not long before the late Ben Webster left for Europe, in
1964 (for good, as it sadly turned out), he got together with
his old friend Milt Hinton at Hinton's house, in Queens, and
the two men made some music. Luckily, Hinton turned on his
tape machine, and four of the numbers they played have
been brought out on one side of "Here Swings the Judge:
Milt Hinton and Friends" (Famous Door). Two of the numbers—Webster playing vigorous amateur stride piano—are
indulgences, but the other two are invaluable. The first is a
very slow version of "Sophisticated Lady," in which Webster
plays the melody—a beautifully embellished, subtly altered
melody—for one chorus, gives way to a chorus of Hinton,
and returns for a chorus of serene and majestic improvisation.
Webster never played better, and one reason was the sheer
space at hand. There was no one to get in his way—no drummer, no pianist—and he soars. And the same is true of the
second selection—a short, graceful "All the Things You
Are." What a pity the two men didn't make a whole album!

During the forties, Lester Young made several dozen recordings for a small West Coast label, Aladdin, and a good proportion have been brought together in "Lester Young: The Aladdin Sessions" (Blue Note). His long and tortuous disintegration had begun, but he was still in superior form, particularly in such ballads as "These Foolish Things," "It's Only a Paper Moon," "You're Driving Me Crazy," "She's Funny That Way," "Sunny Side of the Street," and "I'm Confessin'." Young doesn't bother with stating the melody. He launches immediately into his improvisations, and they are such complete reworkings that sometimes it is impossible to tell what he is playing. He literally creates new and fascinating compositions out of the composer's chords. The album reminds us of how much his squadron of imitators learned from him, and, at the same time, how little.

Jim Hall's first new record in a couple of years, "Jim Hall: Concierto" (CTI), is a subtle, highly lyrical effort in which he is joined by Chet Baker, Paul Desmond (in just two numbers), Roland Hanna, Ron Carter, and the drummer Steve Gadd. There is a long, fast, inquiring version of "You'd Be So Nice To Come Home To" that is notable for Hall's spare solo, a brief bit of counterpoint between Desmond and Baker, and the first in the album of what turn out to be four first-class Baker solos. Baker has spent much of his career stepping on his own feet and obscuring the fact that, somewhat in Miles Davis's earlier mode, he is an intelligent, affecting player whose solos are often models of design and inflection and phrasing. They have a latter-day Beiderbecke quality. The second side is a fresh and eloquent study of Joaquin Rodrigo's mournful "Concierto de Aranjuez," which has been examined before by Miles Davis and the Modern Jazz Quartet. All hands (except the drummer) take forty-two-bar solos, and Baker and Desmond are excellent. And so is Hall, but his guitar is not favorably recorded. He uses a lot of low, reverberative notes, and they get entangled with the bass player, who is over-recorded, and with the pianist, who, though he plays well, is totally unneeded.

Anthony Braxton is a thirty-year-old saxophonist, clarinet-tist, and flutist from Chicago who, through no fault of his own, is being hailed as the new messiah, the new Charlie Parker-John Coltrane-Ornette Coleman. But Parker and Col-trane and Coleman were not nearly as wild-eyed as they first appeared; indeed, they turned out to be two-thirds conserva-tive, one-third rebel, and Braxton is no exception. He is an orderly musician, and he has taken the best of Coleman and Eric Dolphy and Miles Davis and Benny Carter and Paul Desmond and added his own curious, almost arithmetical way of phrasing. Braxton's music is small and confidential. It lacks Parker's ferocity and declamatory tone, Coleman's heedlessness, and Coltrane's zealotry. Now he has made his second record on a label of consequence—"Anthony Brax-ton: Five Pieces 1975" (Arista). There are four musicians (Braxton, trumpeter Kenny Wheeler, bassist Dave Holland, and drummer Barry Altshul), and the album consists of a straightforward and altogether admirable reading of "You Stepped Out of a Dream" and four of Braxton's politely shocking creations. These are identified only by mysterious formulas. Thus, the first number on Side 2 is

$$489 \text{ M}$$
$$70 - 2 - - (\text{TH} - \text{B})$$
$$\text{M}$$

All four numbers bear a melodic likeness to Coleman's com-positions, but they are arranged in a far more calculated manner. In "489 M" there is a long unison statement of the melody, and then Braxton improvises in quick succession on alto and sopranino saxophones, clarinet, flute, and bass clari-net. He plays straight and he moans and wails and makes

monster sounds, but in an unagitated way. The third number on Side 1 has a devious, irregular stop-time background
and a long section of solos, in which Braxton makes kissing
sounds on his alto and Wheeler suggests Rex Stewart. Holland is fashionably huge-toned and lightning-fingered, and
Altshul produces a soft, bonsai array of clicks, silken cymbal
sounds, and tap-tapping snare-drum and tomtom beats.

October 22nd

The revival, at the Uris, of Scott Joplin's "opera," "Treemonisha," is an altruistic act. "Treemonisha" was written
around the turn of the century and was not produced until
1972, and it is easy to understand why. It is—with the exception of the next-to-last number, in which Joplin finally sur-
faces—a dull and synthetic piece of work. It is also a sad one.
Joplin, in his rags, was a gifted and often stirring melodist,
but he did not know how to write opera. And the production,
done by the Houston Grand Opera Association, inadvertently
points this up at every turn. What Joplin wrote—a collection
of stiff, semi-operatic songs and a halting book that has to do
with a black Joan of Arc named Treemonisha—has been ob-
trusively fattened up with a kind of sub-ballet (choreographed
by Louis Johnson, who, oddly, leans on the cancan and the
Charleston), a huge chorus, symbolic sets, and so much stage
business (mock battles, dancing alligators, dancing swamp
grass, weeping, hugging, whispering, leering) that the music
becomes almost secondary. But the music gets through it all,
and even comes to life once—in "A Real Slow Drag." It is a
lyrical and graceful song, and it sounds exactly like a strain
from a Joplin rag. Most of the singing is done by Carmen
Balthrop, Betty Allen, Curtis Rayam, and Willard White,
and they handle Joplin's occasionally jagged melodies well.
Gunther Schuller's orchestrations are limber and apt, and he
is also conducting.

1976

January 14th

Until the mid-thirties, the only reference works jazz had
were the data banks that its most assiduous record collectors
carried around as heads. Then the first discographies appeared, and, after the war, were followed by more discographies and a still unabated flood of encyclopedias, histories,
picture books, glossaries, bio-discographies, and, lately, full-
fledged biographies. Two of the most recent reference works
are *Jazz Talk* (Bobbs-Merrill), by Robert S. Gold, and Brian
Rust's *The American Dance Band Discography, 1917-1942*
(Arlington House). Gold's work is a slightly revised edition
of his *A Jazz Lexicon*, first published in 1957. It is, though
far from complete and sometimes inaccurate, a fascinating
look into the spoken language that black jazz musicians have
invented to protect themselves from the white world, and
from their own square brethren. This inventiveness is not
surprising, for most jazz musicians tend, as informal court
fools, to be very funny people, whose humor ranges from excellent workaday hyperbole to the caperings of Dizzy Gillespie and Joe Venuti. Their comic inspirations also take the
form of reverse exaggeration (something marvellous becomes

"a mess" or "terrible"), synecdoche, and sheer poetic trans-
formations (to travel is to "broom"). This language changes
almost from day to day, and for good reason: since colloquial
language rises (and formal language sinks), it is constantly
being tapped by the world it is supposed to shut out. Some of
the expressions, long since turned to clichés, that have come
directly from jazz are:

cop-out	-ville (as in splitsville)
corny	uptight
hangup	kicks
the scene	square
shades	way out
to dig	to have a ball
groovy	freebee
to split	

Jazz musicians have smoked marijuana since the twenties,
and they have created endless euphemisms:

charge	pot
weed	vonce
Mary Jane	tea
muggles	stash
mootah	grass
boo	reefer
hemp	stuff
gage	roach
panatela	

Some of their inventions were never picked up by the
straight world and have become obsolete:

spots (written musical notes)
woodpile (xylophone)
hides (drums)
mice (violins)
dommy (apartment)
a fat man (a five-dollar bill)

a solid sender (a good record or performer)
a rug-cutter (a dancer)
reet (all right; yes)
bruz (brother)
hincty (suspicious)
a lane (a square)
to lay some iron (to tap-dance)

These are still inviolate and often choice:

to cop a nod (to sleep)
a crumbcrusher (a baby)
a fox (a girl)
to feel a draft (to sense hostility)
hame (an unpleasant job, after the actual word)
to make snakes (to have technical facility)
to woodshed (to practice)
a hawkins, or hawk (a cold winter wind)
to jump salty (to turn unpleasant or hostile)

So how many people would understand this: "Two things make me jump salty, man—when I feel a draft from a fox and when I take a hame"?

Brian Rust's dance-band discography comes in two big stubby volumes, and is over two thousand pages long. Rust has untangled the recording histories—dates and places, matrix numbers, labels, personnel, pseudonyms—of almost twenty-four hundred white dance bands (he has covered the black bands in another book, and has omitted Glenn Miller and Benny Goodman, each of whom already has his own definitive book), or presumably every dance band that recorded between the First and Second World Wars. Almost useless information is irresistible, and Rust's volumes are full of it. One learns that Bobby Hackett joined Horace Heidt in December of 1939 and left by July of 1941, and that during his tenure he worked behind such vocalists as Art Carney and Gordon MacRae and just missed Mary Martin, who recorded the "Pound Your Table Polka" on April 8, 1942. One can

follow Joe Venuti through his early labyrinthine recording
career—from 1924 to midway into the Depression. Here is a
chonology of the bands he recorded with (some names are
pseudonyms for Sam Lanin and Ben Selvin, who ran dance-
band cartels, and whose groups must have recorded every
day in the late twenties and early thirties):

> Jean Goldkette
> Roger Wolfe Kahn
> Deauville Dozen
> Irwin Abrams and His Knickerbocker Grill Orch.
> Broadway Bell-Hops
> Frankie Trumbauer
> Paul Whiteman
> Napoleon's Emperors
> University Orch.
> Ipana Troubadours
> Smith Ballew
> Chester Leighton and His Sophomores
> Rudy Marlow
> Dick Robertson
> The Cavaliers
> Jerry Fenwyck
> Phil Spitalny
> Rudy Vallée and His Connecticut Yankees
> Steve Washington
> Victor Young
> Adrian Rollini
> Dorsey Brothers
> Freddie Rich's Radio Orch.
> Russ Morgan

And one finds that Jerry Colonna, the pop-eyed Hollywood buffoon, played trombone briefly with Joe Herlihy and
His Orchestra, and in June and July of 1927 recorded three
numbers—"Cornfed," "State and Madison," and "Lighthouse
Blues"—on the Edison Diamond Disc label before moving on
to greater things.

January 18th

Eddie Costa was a small, wiry, intense pianist and vibraphonist, who was born in Atlas, Pennsylvania, in 1930, and
was killed in an automobile accident on the West Side Highway in the summer of 1962. Costa worked with, among others, Joe Venuti and Tal Farlow and Woody Herman, and he
reached a high mark in the mid-fifties, when he was in a trio
that was led by Farlow and included Vinnie Burke on bass.
Before it broke up, the group was recorded commercially,
but it was also recorded at its leisure in the apartment of Ed
Fuerst, a record collector, American-song authority, and one-
time road manager for George Shearing. The invaluable results of Fuerst's alertness have been issued as "Tal Farlow:
Fuerst Set" (Xanadu). Costa played with overwhelming
percussiveness. Each improvisation resembled an excellent
drum solo in its rhythmic intensity, pattern of beats, and elements of surprise. Costa liked to use octave chords in the left
hand and single-note lines in the right, and he liked to thunder endlessly down in the lowest registers of the piano. At
such times, he played chords in both hands and with stunning effect. He would let loose a staccato passage and then
an impossible two-handed arpeggio, or he would deliver on-
the-beat or offbeat chords—seesawing them, making them
into sixty-fourth notes, somehow slurring them, and develop-
ing great drive and momentum. But Costa had a good sense
of structure, for he dropped in frequent rests (he had clearly
listened to Basie), and after a prolonged period of subterranean rampaging he would float up a register or two on the
keyboard for several breathing, light-headed choruses. There
are four numbers on the album, and Costa is in fine form on
"Jordu," which lasts almost fifteen minutes, and in which
he plays low-register anvil music—offbeat chords, skidding
chords, pitching chords. And listen to the double-time chordal
dashes in his long solo on the pleasant "Out of Nowhere."

Farlow is in prime condition throughout (he went into semi-retirement two years later), and he takes an exceptional solo on "Opus De Funk."

January 25th

It is not clear why "Louis Armstrong—Chicago Style," a full-length television film shown tonight on ABC, was made, why it was shown, or what it means. Part fact, part fiction, it began in 1931. Armstrong (played by Ben Vereen) is entering his greatest period. He is finishing a gig in California (true) when a disgruntled would-be manager plants some pot in his jacket pocket (not true) and he is arrested and jailed (true, but for smoking his own pot between sets). He is quickly freed (true), and drives with his manager back to Chicago (probably not true, but inserted for a roadside scene with some rednecks), where he scuffles for a while (not true), visits his estranged wife, Lil Hardin (true, and a well-worked-out scene), and pursues his wife-to-be, Alpha. He is also offered a job by the syndicate and refuses (nonsense: the syndicate owned all the clubs and there was no choice), and, to escape a difficult situation, leaves for Europe and fame after turning down a lucrative job in New Orleans (not true: it was an enormously successful homecoming, and one that the late New Orleans trumpeter Manuel Manetta remembered with glee for Louis's failure while he was there to learn Manetta's trick of playing two trumpets at once). The moral? Stay cool like good old Pops and you'll make it. About half of Vereen's performance was right. He was too manic on the bandstand (Louis bowed and rumbled and smiled a lot when he was onstage, but when he played he rarely moved a muscle), his laugh was wrong, and his gravel voice was only fair (George Kirby does it a lot better). Yet Vereen had flashes—a concerned expression, a sudden twist of the head, a gesture of hopelessness—that were just right and almost justified the film. There was no Armstrong on the soundtrack, and the faithful, if rather frenetic, subbing was done by Snooky Young, Shorty Sherock, and Cappy Lewis, none of whom got credit.

January 26th

It has become plain in the three years since Jimmy Rowles emerged from his hibernation on the West Coast that, regardless of style or category or age, he is the most prepossessing jazz pianist we have. There are many reasons: the very way he addresses a piano (some pianists sit down at the keyboard as if they were depositing an invaluable work of art on the piano bench), without hesitation, announcements, or one of those radar, room-circling who's-here? glances; his originality, which draws largely on Art Tatum; his imaginativeness and variety, which enable him to play long, muscular studies of slow ballads or fast, driving blues that swing and swarm and swell; his technique, which is used only to say what he has in his head; his harmonic sense, which leads him to plumb the songs he plays as well as to add new levels that turn them into formidable structures; his unfailing taste; his humor, which is evident in his choice of songs, in his tempos and rhythms, and in interpolations from other songs; and his improvisational abilities, which are spelled out in endless ways—the short, bent runs, the funny, falling-away passages, some of them almost slithery, the chords that have a single-note spareness. Tonight, at Bradley's, he gave us a soft "Looking at You," Tom Satterfield's "Restless," a brazen, chattering "Brazil," an impressionistic "Skylark," a jumping "Dancers in Love," "My Funny Valentine" as a dirge, a casual, hats-off "Sweet Lorraine," Billy Strayhorn's "U.M.M.G.," complete with some Oriental closing figures, and an attractive waltz that sounded like Willard Robison.

Rowles is also highly visible in a fascinating recording, "A

Day in the Life of Billie Holiday" (Differant Drummer), in
which Billie talks, laughs, garbles, and sings her way through
a rehearal held in Los Angeles with Rowles and the bassist
Artie Shapiro not long before she died. Her voice is almost
leaden, but her intonation is fine, and on some of the numbers she is stunning—a fragment of "I Must Have That
Man," a swinging "Everything Happens to Me," a lazing
"Jeepers Creepers," a dreaming "Prelude to a Kiss," and two
versions of "Please Don't Talk about Me When I'm Gone."
In between, she swears, kids Rowles, and reminisces about
such things as the audition she had in a Harlem club at thirteen and was laughed out of because she had no idea what a
key was. Rowles plays sparkling piano behind her and gets
off such a beauty at the beginning of the last bridge of
"Everything Happens to Me" that Billie throws in a fast,
parenthetical "There ya go!" Her laugh, which is all through
the record, has a wild, scimitar quality, very bright and a
little dangerous.

February 4th

Ray Nance—cornettist, violinist, singer, dancer, high-jinks
person—died a few days ago at the age of sixty-two. Nance
was with Duke Ellington from 1940 until 1963, and he was
the epitome of what Ellington needed in his soloists. He was
never a star. He was a singular stylist: any two Nance notes
immediately identified him. He played with considerable
emotion, particularly on the blues. His cornet solos were
short, and he was not much of an improviser, but his fretting
vibrato and feminine, beseeching tone made them invariably
affecting. His solos preached and exulted. He was a good jazz
singer, with an easy rhythmic baritone. His violin was often
used for Billy Strayhorn's ballads, and it fitted their sheer
textures. Nance liked to horse around and do funny dances,
and, along with most of the musicians of his generation, he

liked to drink. He worked where and when he could after he left Ellington, and most of the time he still played well. His cornet playing summoned up his idol, Louis Armstrong; it also displayed an ardent, unplaned beauty that has almost gone out of the music.

March 8th

The Ruby Braff-George Barnes Quartet disappeared before it ever fully appeared. The group was formed in 1972 and dissolved in 1975. (In addition to the co-leaders, it consisted of Wayne Wright on rhythm guitar and John Giuffrida on bass; they were ultimately replaced by Vinnie Corrao and Michael Moore.) It worked less than half the time it lasted, and, as far as New York was concerned, didn't seem to exist at all, for, outside of random concerts, it played here only five weeks—three at the Rainbow Grill, where it shared billing with a singer named Damita Jo, and two at the old Buddy's Place, on Second Avenue. Yet the Braff-Barnes Quartet was one of the best small jazz groups ever put together. It was disciplined, it invariably swung, and it did superior songs. The sound was a treble-bass blend reminiscent of the classic Rex Stewart-Barney Bigard-Django Reinhardt-Billy Taylor pickup group of 1939. It was lyrical *and* funky. The quartet had an electric in-person presence, and always played at the top of its gifts—no loafing, no padding, no windiness. Most jazz groups are monochromatic, but Braff-Barnes ceaselessly changed color. Braff's dynamics have never been more agile. Within four bars, he would move from a low-register whisper to a barely tapped high note to a full, middle-register cello tone. Barnes stretched his dynamic sense to its limits, too. Dreaming, barely voiced notes gave way to wild high-register *twangs* that sounded like a clarinet, and these gave way to soft, wind-harp chords. All the while, whether the two were soloing, playing in unbreak-

able unison, or fashioning elbowing counterpoint, there was
the *whirr whirr whirr* of the rhythm guitar and the steady
poling of the bass. Luckily, the group was decently recorded,
and perhaps its truest record—with Wright and Moore—was
done at a concert in the spring of 1974: "The Ruby Braff-
George Barnes Quartet: Live at the New School" (Chiar-
oscuro). There are some true blue moments—the two long,
low Braff notes on "Solitude" that are indistinguishable from
cello notes; the sliding, unearthly sotto voce way that Braff
begins his solo on "Sunny Side of the Street" (it summons up
Louis Armstrong's supreme solo on his 1930 "Sweethearts on
Parade"); Barnes's ringing high notes on "Sugar"; Braff's
tough, swinging solo on "Struttin' with Some Barbecue"; and
the big-band ensemble effect the quartet achieves on "Rockin'
in Rhythm."

March 12th

A pair of musicians who should not be forgotten, and who
are fortunately celebrated in new reissues: Charlie Shavers,
trumpeter, composer, and arranger (1917–71), and Leo Watson, tiple, drums, trombone, and vocals (1898–1950).

Shavers was a highly gifted musician. A skilled arranger
(he did most of the tight, polite arrangements for the John
Kirby band, from 1937 to 1944), he wrote "Undecided," long
beloved by jazz musicians, and he was a whirlwind trumpeter. He came up with Tiny Bradshaw and Lucky Millinder, and after he left Kirby he worked on and off for eleven
years with Tommy Dorsey. He gigged away the rest of his
life—with Jazz at the Philharmonic, as an accompanist to
singers, and abroad. His death came two days after Louis
Armstrong's, and went almost unnoticed. Shavers was short
and roundish, and he had a cheerful, compulsive look. His
music buffeted him, and he was in constant motion. When
he was picking his way through a particularly dangerous ar-

peggio, he would lift his right foot and, completing the figure,
slam the foot down and follow through by pointing his trumpet at the floor and hunching his shoulders. Shavers was the
first virtuoso jazz trumpeter. He relished his powers. He had
a big tone, a rococo attack—often spelled out in excited runs
that matched Art Tatum's and Charlie Parker's—and he
liked to fool around in the highest register. The showoff quality in many of his solos was fully intended (he carried to perfection what Harry James only began in his display pieces,
and he paralleled in a less advanced harmonic way Dizzy
Gillespie's tarantellas, which, indeed, he may have inspired),
but every once in a while he set his fireworks aside and
played with simpleness and lyricism. The Bethlehem label,
which was around in the fifties and early sixties, is being reactivated, and one of its first reissues is "The Finest of
Charlie Shavers." The record was made late in the fifties,
and it provides Shavers with the setting every jazz horn
player dreams of—a large and bosomy string section. He
plays ten ballads and is in relatively calm form. He lolls
against the strings, letting loose broad lower-register figures,
quick high notes, gentle double-time figures, and Rex Stewart
half-valved notes. He embellishes and polishes each song until it gleams. Shavers the improviser is fully visible, though,
on seven tracks of "Sidney Bechet: Master Musician" (RCA).
These were made in 1941, while Shavers was with John
Kirby. He is very hot on "Twelfth Street Rag" and on
"Limehouse Blues," but on "I'm Coming Virginia," "Mood
Indigo," and a blues, "Texas Moaner," he is sorrowing and
elegiac. Listen to the way he repeats a two-note Louis Armstrong figure at the beginning of his solo on "Texas Moaner"
and then caps it with the proper blaring high note, and to
"Mood Indigo," where he discovers, both in his melodic state-
ment and in his solo, a rending blueness.

   In his special way, Leo Watson was a genius. He was little
known during his life, which was madcap and short. Much

of his career was spent in a swinging novelty group called
the Spirits of Rhythm, which flourished in the thirties and
forties and was made up of various combinations of tiples,
guitars, bass, and drums. Although he played the tiple (a
stringed instrument between the guitar and the ukulele),
trombone, and drums, he was primarily a scat singer. Scat
singers are human horns who improvise often wordless,
sometimes onomatopoeic songs, and the best of them have
included Ella Fitzgerald, Anita O'Day, Jackie Cain and Roy
Kral, Mel Tormé, and Louis Armstrong, who is said to have
accidentally invented the form in 1926 when he was recording "Heebie Jeebies" and dropped the music. But Watson
was the greatest of them all. His vocals contained long
phrases of quickly revolving vowels that were interrupted fe-
verishly with words used in a sly nonsense fashion. He had
a wild sense of time, and in the late thirties he got off passages that predated Charlie Parker and Dizzy Gillespie by
five years. His voice was harum-scarum. He growled, blared,
whined, chanted, shouted, crooned. The recording that has
brought Watson out of oblivion—"Pre-Bop" (Bob Thiele Music)—was made in 1946 and contains his last record date.
Four tracks were made—"Sonny Boy," "Tight and Gay,"
"The Snake Pit," and "Jingle Bells"—and with him are Vic
Dickenson, Leonard Feather, who was the A. & R. man as
well as the pianist, the bassist Vivien Garry, and the drummer Harold (Doc) West. The first three numbers are vintage
Watson, but "Jingle Bells" suggests "Finnegans Wake." It
begins in a slow tempo with ricky-ticky piano and Dickenson growling his way through the melody. Then West
abruptly doubles the tempo, and Watson is off. Here, in
rough transcription, is what he does:

babadeladabaaaaaaaaaohhhhhhhhhhhhhhhhdela
     (*pause*)
bells of the wedding of the wedding cake

cut the cake, cut the cake, cut the beyyaaaaaaaaaa-
   yehbedoooo
oooooloayyyyy bebop deyaeeeeeeeayo
jingle bells, jingle bells (*growls*)
snowbirds of Chicago (*pause*) Chicago Chicago
   (*singing the melody*)
ayeyiyiayeyiyibelopdeoooooooooyaaaaaaaaaa bebop
East Side West Side all around the town (*singing
   the melody*)
all the birds of snow of Chicago (*legato, then his
   voice falls away and into*)
aeyohhhhhhhhhhhhhhhhhh deum
(*Vic Dickenson solos, and Watson returns*)
didge-ye-everhear didge-ye-everhear didge-ye-everhear didge-ye-everhear
Alexander's Ragtime Band? Band playing (*pause*)
de-bing de-bing de-bing de-bing de-bing de-bing
the big bass drum de-bing bong bing
aaaaayaeeeeeeeeh (*and smoothly into a wordless
   closing duet with Dickenson*).

March 13th

The imaginative jazz repertory experiments carried forward
in 1974 and 1975 by the New York Jazz Repertory Company
and Chuck Israels's National Jazz Ensemble have been in
abeyance until tonight, when Israels's big band gave the first
of its four 1976 concerts at the New School. Most of the sixteen men Israels brought on tonight are carry-overs from the
excellent group he had last year. They include Ben Aronov
on piano, Bill Goodwin on drums, Tom Harrell, Jimmy Maxwell, and Dave Berger on trumpet, Joe Randazzo and the arranger and composer Rod Levitt on trombone, Dennis Anderson and Ken Berger on saxophone, and Steve Brown on guitar. The rewarding new members are Arnie Lawrence on
alto saxophone, Joe Romano on tenor saxophone, and Steve

Gilmore on bass. The band is the best collective group Israels
has had, and it offered faithful versions of Jimmy Lunceford's "For Dancers Only" and Duke Ellington's "Rockin' in
Rhythm" and "Bundle of Blues," the last marred only by an
out-of-sync reprise of Barney Bigard's solo. The other resto-
rations included "Two Bass Hit," a smooth-shelled arrangement by Gil Evans of Jelly Roll Morton's "King Porter
Stomp," and a properly tongue-in-cheek rundown of Charles
Mingus's funny Morton salute "My Jelly Roll Soul." The
rest of the evening was not as enterprising. We heard a per-
fervid "Body and Soul" and a fine Johnny Carisi number,
"Springsville," both done by Phil Woods, who appeared for
half a dozen selections, but we also heard lesser efforts by
Levitt, Woods, and Israels himself, who brought his wife,
Margot Hanson, out for some wordless Kay Davis coloratura.
The emphasis tonight had shifted from substance, which in
the past had been rare and often intricate, to the band itself,
which was precise and swinging. Bill Goodwin was especially
surprising. He has sometimes played ladyfinger drums, but
tonight he rocketed like the old Don Lamond.

Two independent repertory groups have also surfaced this
winter. One has just finished a month at Michael's Pub. Led
by Dick Hyman and including Bob Wilber, Pee Wee Erwin,
Milt Minton, and Bobby Rosengarden, it played easy and attractive updatings by Hyman of James P. Johnson ("Old
Fashioned Love," "Carolina Shout"), Jelly Roll Morton
("Buddy Bolden's Blues," "Fickle Fay Creep"), Scott Joplin
("Maple Leaf Rag"), and Louis Armstrong ("Cake Walking
Babies"). The second group, the New California Ramblers,
was named after the famous cornucopic dance band that recorded in New York in the twenties and thirties. The new
band was put together by a twenty-two-year-old bassist, tubist, and bass saxophone player named Vince Giordano, who
played the booting bass saxophone with Joe Venuti, Zoot
Sims, and Bucky Pizzarelli in the New York Jazz Repertory

Company's second Bix Beiderbecke concert in 1975. The New
Ramblers has nine members, among them Clarence Hutchen-
rider, the clarinettist of the Casa Loma band; Al Galladoro,
the virtuoso alto saxophonist; the guitarist Marty Grosz; a
fine reed player named Sam Parkins; and Richard Sudhalter,
the co-author of the recent Beiderbecke biography and a
graceful cornettist in the Buck Clayton-Ruby Braff mold. The
group mainly uses stock arrangements from the Ramblers'
period, and plays them as they were written, leaving their
eights and sixteenth undotted. In the course of a recent
evening, the band, which has been keeping its soul together
by playing alternate Thursdays at a Queens Boulevard bar
called Egbert's, went through a 1931 Archie Bleyer arrangement of "Business in F," Ellington's 1928 "The Mooche,"
Coon-Sanders's 1929 "Kansas City Kitty," a 1927 stock of
"Stardust," the Ramblers' 1925 "Charleston," the Trum-
bauer-Beiderbecke "Singing the Blues," a 1933 stock of "I'll
Never Be the Same," and the 1933 Dorsey Brothers' "Mood
Hollywood."

April 30th

Billie Holiday was an urban woman who sang urban (however silly) songs. Her successor, Ray Charles, raised on
church music in the lonesome Southern backwoods, is a primitive of the highest order, a shaman, a magic man, a hypno-
tist. He improvises constantly, and he will use any vocal
weapon—melismatics, yodels, growls, crooning, falsetto, whispers, shouts, chanting, blue notes, grace notes, retards. It no
longer matters whether he sings blues or country-and-
Western or standards or "Eleanor Rigby" or "America"; it
only matters how he sings. One waits for the shout that falls
in a beat to a whisper, the flashing falsetto, the pine-sap dic-
tion, the pained hoarseness, the guttural asides, the spidery
staccato sprays of notes, the polysyllabic explosions, the

faster-than-the-ear dynamics. Charles does not display his feelings; he gives them to his audience, experiencing cathar-sis and offering sublimity. His music courses through him, making him rock from side to side, making his hands spring from the keyboard and sculpt air, making his feet dance. He is a prism constantly refracting his music. Charles shies away from New York, and that made his two Carnegie Hall concerts tonight a treat. During the first, he gave us a minia-ture Charles retrospective. He sang the blues; "Busted," in which he manages to convince you he is destitute when you know he has a million dollars in the bank; "Georgia on My Mind," a masterly lullaby whose first word, sung sotto voce and behind the beat as "Chor-ja," takes you immediately into shuttered rooms and long-ago afternoons; the delicate, tea-cup "Am I Blue?" and the chanting "I Can't Stop Loving You"; the hurrying "You Are My Sunshine" and the fast, rocking "What'd I Say?"

June 1st

Milt Jackson is an improviser of the rank of Coleman Haw-kins and Charlie Parker and Teddy Wilson, and his years with the Modern Jazz Quartet suggested what might have happened if Joyce had joined the Bloomsbury group. The Quartet must have been a strain on Jackson. It confined his improvisational afflatus, imposed on him materials—some of them rather artificial and arch—that he would not otherwise have played, and demanded arduous and delicate ensemble work. He is a prolix, free-floating performer, and learning how to fit into the MJQ must have taught him a good deal about self-editing, a skill few jazz musicians learn. Jackson has rid himself of the MJQ, but he is still at the mercy of an-other burden—the very instrument he plays. The vibraphone is an electrified marimba, a streamlined xylophone, a four-legged metal piano. It has attracted some extraordinary musicians, but none has managed to circumvent entirely its neon tone, its hippy vibrato, and its science-fiction timbres. (Red Norvo has come closest; he approaches the clarity and tone of a piano.) Like the organ, the vibraphone constantly calls attention to itself. Its players must extract their solos from the instrument, and Jackson has become remarkably adept. He arrived at his preëminence in a roundabout way. He fell first under the stomping sway of Lionel Hampton (both Hampton's vibraphone and his mercurial two-finger piano playing, the latter having had more influence than has been acknowledged), and was then warmed by the suns of Charlie Parker, Dizzy Gillespie, and Bud Powell. The result is a performer of great fluidity and lyricism. Jackson's solos tumble and spill. They are full of hammered repeated notes (Hampton's piano), arpeggios, sudden rests followed by surprisingly accented behind-the-beat single notes, double-time dashes, legato chords, and an inventiveness that has rarely been surpassed in the music. Since the dissolution of the MJQ, Jackson's solos go on and on, shouting and whooping, and listening to him is an ecstatic business. Much of his new quality has been caught on "The Big 3: Milt Jackson-Joe Pass-Ray Brown" (Pablo). There are two strolling ballads, Jobim's "Wave" and Django Reinhardt's lovely "Nuages." There is a reshaping of "Moonglow," which is one of those curious songs that resist melodic improvisation because they are so well buttressed melodically. There is a fast "You Stepped Out of a Dream," in which Jackson starts his solo with a funny, jiggling, sidestepping passage that finally swings into his usual flow. And there is a gentle slow blues, "Blues for Sammy," in which he takes four choruses that both grieve and celebrate. The combination on the record of vibraphone and guitar and string bass works well. There are clearings in the ensembles, and each solo is well attended to by the two other players. It is a polite and brilliant coming-out party for Jackson.

June 8th

The inestimable cornettist-trumpeter Bobby Hackett died yesterday, at sixty-one, on Cape Cod, where he had moved five years ago. Hackett played his first engagement on the Cape at the Megansett Tea Room, in North Falmouth, almost forty-five years ago, and he played his last one at the Wequassett Inn, in East Harwich, this past Saturday. It had been his notion, after he finally settled on the Cape, to have his own club, where, except for occasional essential travelling, he would play most of the year, and where once a week his friends, professional and amateur, would be encouraged to sit in, for he believed there was little point in making music if it wasn't fun. But his club never came to pass, and he spent most of his time travelling all over the world to make enough money to live in a place he loved but really didn't live in at all. His whole life was that way—an endless parade of small disappointments, missed chances, broken promises, poor advice. He became a master scuffler, who endlessly patched and spliced and repainted, and somehow kept his modest ship afloat. Whenever one ran into him, he would be full of cheerful talk about new projects, but six or eight months later the projects had collapsed or vanished. Thus, his own record label, Hyannisport, only issued two records during its four-year life, and his ideal band (with his old friend Vic Dickenson and the pianist Dave McKenna, whom he considered nonpareil) only lasted a season. It was the same years ago when he missed the job of dubbing the soundtrack for Kirk Douglas in "Young Man with a Horn" (Harry James did it, for a figure that increased every time Hackett told the story), and when he reportedly took a flat fee instead of royalties after making his famous mood recordings for Jackie Gleason. Indeed, money appeared to conscientiously skirt him. (One of his most fervent admirers said of him despairingly, "Bobby couldn't stand success. Ever since he was a kid, he was bent on self-destruction.") The wonder is that Hackett survived as well as he did, for his gifts were unearthly. His playing threw angelic shadows, whether he was sailing through "Struttin' with Some Barbecue" or subtly recasting the melody of "What's New?" His tone was light and supple. His vibrato was reserved, and he had an impeccable rhythmic sense. He avoided the high and low registers, concentrating on the sunny middle octave. His solos had a prefigured design, a Greek Revival rightness. The excellence of his improvisations gave his solos a seeming sameness, but they were in fact full of fresh phrases and new turns. They also had a subtle wit, just as he did. He was small and trim, and had a small, laughing beaked face and glossy gangster hair. He sometimes wore a dime-size mustache, and he kept his eyes at a squint, as if what he saw out there should only be absorbed in small amounts. His voice was low, and he had a legato Providence accent. He prefaced almost everything with a long-breathed "Yehhh." He used it for both stoic and comic effect. Here are some of his mots:

On being asked how he liked his new bathtublike 1950 Hudson car: "Yehhh. I got to like it. I bought it."

On receiving no applause after completing a discreet dinner set in a noisy club: "Yehhh. I guess that was too confidential."

On a well-known virtuoso trombonist with whom he sometimes played: "Yehhh. Imagine his chops and my brains."

On seeing a couple of business associates of Irish extraction approaching on a Hyannis street: "Yehhh. Here come the Murphia."

When his work allowed him to stay on the Cape, one saw him everywhere—at Heinie Greer's celebrated Labor Day bash in Dennis, where Hackett, genuinely enjoying himself, would often be the only professional; at a concert held in a damp swaybacked hall in Provincetown; at a Chatham resort hotel, playing dance music for gazelles and hippos; at the

Columns in West Dennis, where he and Dave McKenna did
memorable duets; at the Olde Inn in Orleans, when he'd sit
in on Sunday afternoons with Marie Marcus and trade fours
with his friend Jim Blackmore, a Cape heating engineer, who
played one of Hackett's cornets, drove him to most of his gigs,
and, like the rest of us, cherished him.

June 10th

Benny Carter, the elegant instrumentalist-composer-arranger,
has begun edging back toward jazz, which he set aside for the
Hollywood studios in the late forties. He has been sampling
festivals, making records, teaching at Princeton, and accompanying Peggy Lee and the saucy Maria Muldaur, and now
he has taken an engagement at Michael's Pub, his first such
appearance in New York since 1942, when he had a group at
the Famous Door that included the greenhorn Dizzy Gillespie.
Carter was born in New York in 1907, and attended Wilber-
force University. In 1932, after stints with Duke Ellington,
Fletcher Henderson, Chick Webb, and McKinney's Cotton
Pickers, he formed his own band, hiring such superb neo-
phytes as Sid Catlett, Teddy Wilson, Ben Webster, Chu
Berry, Russell Procope, and J. C. Higginbotham. But it was
a bad time for big bands, and by 1935 Carter had gone
abroad, where he worked as a BBC staff arranger. He put together another big band in New York in 1938, gave that up,
organized several small groups, gave them up, and in the
mid-forties moved to the Coast, where he assembled a final
big band. The thirties were Carter's decade. He perfected his
alto-saxophone style as well as his trumpet and clarinet playing. His arranging bloomed, as did his special abilities as a
graceful and admired bandleader. (It was always a mark of
distinction to be hired by Carter.) By the end of the thirties,
he had developed an extraordinary persona. For a long time,

jazz was played by roustabouts and primitives. Carter was
one of the first jazz musicians to go to college, and he wasn't
expected to moan and shout and wear his blue notes on his
sleeve. He was expected to keep his emotional cards close to
his chest, and he did. He dressed flawlessly. His speech, possibly burnished by his BBC stay, was orotund. And he was a
handsome man, with intelligent, questing eyes and hundred-
watt teeth. He was a gentleman who, we were reminded
when he picked up one of his horns, also played music. To
be sure, Carter was the most admired alto saxophonist of the
thirties, but that was hardly surprising. Johnny Hodges
didn't draw himself to his full height until 1940, and such
colleagues as Charlie Holmes, Willie Smith, Tab Smith,
Hilton Jefferson, and Pete Brown, though absorbing in their
various ways, were not first-rank—which became startlingly
clear when Charlie Parker exploded several years later. Carter looks almost exactly as he did thirty years ago, and his
considerable gifts remain unimpaired. The arrangements he
played last year with Maria Muldaur had his customary un-
cluttered harmonies, his damask saxophone writing, and his
untroubled sense of space and structure. His alto-saxophone
playing has grown even statelier. The joyous, declamatory
tone has broadened, and the melodic lines have become longer
and more complex. Tonight at Michael's Pub (his accompanists are Ray Bryant, Milt Hinton, and Grady Tate), he
played custom versions of "Three Little Words," "Mean to
Me," "Body and Soul," and "Honeysuckle Rose." His saxophone solos gave the effect of skywriting: each hung complete in the air before being blown away by the succeeding
soloist. But the best part of tonight was Carter's trumpet playing. He doesn't take the instrument as seriously, and so his
playing is freer. He works in stone on the alto and in wood
on the trumpet. His phrases are short and judicious, he prefers a legato attack, and his lyricism is unstudied and airy.
He has not played trumpet much lately, and one had the im-

32   NIGHT CREATURE

pression of ideas highballing helplessly past unheard, but he
should soon be in good shape.

June 13th

The Sauter-Finegan band was put together in 1952 by the
arrangers Eddie Sauter and Bill Finegan both for kicks and
to show off their ingenious wares, and at the time it seemed
overripe and somewhat precious. It was a hybrid group that
had a six-man rhythm section and an odd instrumentation,
which consisted of a tuba, a harp, and a reed section that
doubled on piccolo, oboe, English horn, flute, kazoo, recorder,
clarinet, and bass clarinet. Voicings like these were common:
flute, two clarinets, two baritone saxophones; two flutes, two
clarinets, baritone saxophone; and clarinet, bass clarinet, flute,
two piccolos. The rhythm section gave off the sound of gongs,
vibraphones, chimes, big bass drums, tympani, gourds, wood-
blocks, sleigh bells, birdcalls, tambourines, and bongos. The
band was a sound factory, capable of producing everything
from a Bronx cheer to a hummingbird. It was Sauter and
Finegan's folly, and it was no surprise when the aggregation
finally sank of its own glittering weight. But this afternoon
the band was brought brilliantly back to life at the Ninety-
second Street Y.M.H.A. by Harvey Estrin, who was in the
original S-F band, and the Y's Studio Orchestra, and it was a
pleasure to discover that it had more substance and lyricism
than one had thought. The concert made it clear that some
of the Sauter-Finegan arrangements are easily up-to-date.
The voicings are choice and change continually within each
piece. The various sections do not bounce off one another but
intertwine or run parallel. Sometimes Sauter and Finegan
split up the sections vertically, putting half the reeds with
half the brass, and, by adding soloists, they sometimes produce half a dozen or more voices at once. The texture of the
arrangements is often elegant but rarely has the mandarin

effect of Gil Evans, and the rhythm section, despite its resemblance to a henhouse at midnight, is not nearly as cluttered as it once seemed. The Y's Studio Orchestra, which came into being this year, is made up of New York musicians, some of whom are students and some professionals, and who range in age from fifteen to the forties. It played Sauter and Finegan's material with even more dash and aplomb than the original band. One did not get much sense of the abilities of its soloists, outside of the startling trumpet work of Charles Miller. Sauter and Finegan are arrangers, and they assembled an arranger's band.

June 24th

In the late thirties, big bands, which had been prevalent in American popular music for over a decade, remembered that they had grown out of small bands, and, as a salute to their origins, many of them formed excellent small bands-within-bands. All these, lest they grow presumptuous, were given rib-tickling names. Tommy Dorsey had his Clambake Seven, Chick Webb his Little Chicks, Artie Shaw his Gramercy Five, Bob Crosby his Bobcats, Woody Herman his Woodchoppers (derived not from Herman's nickname, a corruption of Woodrow, but from the band's famous jump blues "Woodchopper's Ball," recorded in 1939), Dolly Dawn her Dawn Patrol, and Count Basie his Kansas City Seven. (Mundane old Benny Goodman, mindful that he might one day frequent the conservatory, simply had his trios, quartets, quintets, sextets, and septets.) But small working bands (as opposed to groups put together only for recording) also proliferated on their own in the late thirties, and perhaps the most famous was the John Kirby sextet, which flourished from 1938 until 1941, when its original personnel (Charlie Shavers on trumpet, Buster Bailey on clarinet, Russell Procope on alto saxophone, Billy Kyle on piano, Kirby on bass, and O'Neil Spencer on drums)

began to change. With the exception of Procope, the Kirby
band had passed through that invaluable Harlem kinder-
garten the Mills Blue Rhythm Band, which foundered in
1937. In the mode of the time, the Kirby band was completely streamlined. It had no edges or bulges, and it invariably pointed into the wind. It was witty and relaxed, and
it swung. The band mainly used unison scoring, which gave
it a single, direct voice. It was a treble band, made up of
high-pitched instruments—muted trumpet, clarinet, alto saxophone. And it was an ensemble band—its soloists jumped in
and got out, and their various timbres barely ruffled its silken
surface. (A startling exception: Charlie Shavers's *whap* open-
horn solo on the group's Vocalion recording of "Royal Garden Blues.") A typical medium-type Kirby number went
like this: Billy Kyle started flat out by playing a close variation on the melody for sixteen bars while the band supplied
organ chords behind him. The band took over the melody on
the bridge, and Kyle, the band again sailing along behind
him, finished the chorus. The second chorus was introduced
by an ad-lib four-bar unison flourish, and then the ensemble,
shifting into harmony, played a sixteen-bar variation of the
melody, gave way to an eight-bar Bailey solo, and resumed
its variation of the tune. Shavers, still muted, soloed for sixteen bars at the start of the third chorus. Kyle took the bridge,
this time without any organ chords, and the band played a
mock Dixieland ensemble for the final eight bars. Of the
band's four principal soloists (Kirby and Spencer rarely came
forward), only Shavers and Kyle were first-rate. (Bailey had
a reputation for being as schooled and fluid as Benny Goodman—they had the same teacher in Chicago—but his playing was academic and piping. Procope was simply a good
workaday alto player.) Shavers was only nineteen when he
joined the band, but his leaping baroque style was already in
place. Kyle also dazzled. He had grown out of Earl Hines,
and he used whipping single-note lines that were dotted with

finely accented on-the-beat notes. Kyle soloing at a fast tempo with the band humming along behind him was a V-8 miracle. The Kirby band was not perfect. Its tight, gleaming style precluded much texture or surprise, and it had a weakness, then shared by many jazz groups, for jazzing the classics. Doing variations on Tchaikovsky and Haydn and Grieg and Chopin was thought to be funny, and even somewhat heretical. It put those holier-than-thou longhairs in their place.

Columbia recorded the Kirby band at its height but hasn't put out a Kirby reissue for twenty-five years. A new release on another label, "The John Kirby Sextet" (Classic Jazz), gives a good notion of the band. Of the twenty-four numbers in the album, thirteen were made in 1941, when the original band was intact, and the rest were done in 1943 and 1944, when the personnel still included Shavers, Bailey, and Kirby as well as such newcomers as George Johnson on alto saxophone, Budd Johnson on tenor saxophone, and possibly Specs Powell on drums and Clyde Hart on piano. (The liner notes give no indication that the later tracks have different personnel, nor do they give the origins of the tracks. Are they studio transcriptions, air checks, Muzak, or V-discs? Whichever, the recording quality is adequate.) The early material is the best and is notable for sly and witty versions of the "Original Dixieland One Step" and "Bugle Call Rag" (here called "Bugler's Dilemma"), a long version of the group's slow blues, "Blues Petite," and exceptional Kyle on "Close Shave," "Move Over," and "Old Fashioned Love." And listen to O'Neil Spencer on the 1941 sides. He was a classy brush drummer, and he had perfect time.

June 25th

The first concert of the fifth Newport Jazz Festival-New York, given at seven-thirty in Carnegie Hall by Tony Bennett (accompanied by a thirty-odd-piece orchestra led by Torrie Zito) and the Bill Evans trio, was professional, succinct, and often inspired. The promotional matter was misleading, for it suggested that Bennett would sing with Evans, the two having made a successful duet album during the past year. Bennett sang the first number, a jumpy "My Foolish Heart," with Evans, and they did two closing songs, but that was all. In between, Evans was joined by Eddie Gomez (bass) and Eliot Zigmund (drums) for six rather spirited numbers. Evans doesn't tell his listeners what he is playing, which is doubly rude: the composer is erased and the audience is made to feel unworthy of such information. It's like a minister neglecting to reveal his chapter and verse. But there was a possible "Spring Is Here" (Rodgers and Hart), two definites—"Up with the Lark" (Kern and Robin) and "Some Day My Prince Will Come" (Frank Churchill)—and three blanks. Evans played almost aggressively. He got loose from his habitual middle octave and produced some scintillating upper-register figures, and he piled up a series of encyclopedic descending chords during a fast number made chiefly of eight-bar exchanges. He came close to emerging from the inner-directed improvisational fortress he sequesters himself in these days. Gomez is one of the young brilliants on his instrument, and Zigmund is fashionably busy and circular. Bennett, buoyed by Zito's exceptional arrangements—Benny Carter saxophone figures, single-instrument backing, deft, floating string passages—sang well over a dozen songs, among them "Just in Time," Fred Astaire's skimpy "Life Is Beautiful," " 'S Wonderful," "There'll Be Some Changes Made," "What Is This Thing Called Love?" and three Ellington numbers. He used dynamics and tempo changes, he belted and he sang

sotto voce, and he missed very few notes. But he needs a new
dance teacher. His onstage assortment of spins, one-arm
akimbos, salutes, marching steps, and waffling hands sends
up so much visual persiflage it obscures his singing.

June 26th

For a long time in the sixties, Charles Mingus was rudder-
less. But, having been encouraged in recent years by a Gug-
genheim Fellowship, the publication of his funny, scurrilous
autobiography, a university teaching job, and his realization
that he is a seminal bassist, he has taken on direction again.
At the first Carnegie Hall concert tonight, he was the roaring Mingus of the fifties and early sixties. He had with him
two of the best musicians who worked for him then—Dannie
Richmond (drums) and Jimmy Knepper (trombone)—and
he played two of his best older pieces, "Good-bye Pork Pie
Hat" and "Fables of Faubus." (The rest of his group was
made up of Ricky Ford on tenor saxophone, Jack Walrath on
trumpet, and Danny Mixon on piano.) He also played two
new compositions—the short, fast "Remember Rockefeller at
Attica" (sometimes the musical content of Mingus's jabs at
politicians has less satirical edge than their titles), and a long
lyrical piece, "Sue's Changes," which has a lilting, descending melody, tempo changes (double time, accelerando, decelerando), and brief, cacophonic ensembles. Mingus delivered short, fountainhead solos, but the best statements were
by Knepper. He is an improviser of the greatest subtlety and
invention. His phrases, set in a soft, scarfed tone, keep turning away from where you think they are going, and move in
an intricate, organic fashion. Each phrase develops from the
previous one, and each is stocked with surprising notes. They
are also replete with the warming shadows and forms of those
two great masters Dickie Wells and J. C. Higginbotham.
      Cobham/Duke, a jazz-rock group made up of Billy Cobham

(drums), George Duke (piano), John Scofield (guitar), and Alphonso Johnson (bass), gave the late concert at Carnegie Hall. They play look-at-me music. On the left side of the stage were Cobham's drums, an orchard of sound perhaps six feet high and twelve feet across, which included a dozen or so bass drums, tom-toms, and snare drums (most of them transparent and lit from beneath), seven or eight cymbals, and two bent-knee megaphones attached to the front of the set and feeding into microphones. The right side of the stage was filled with Duke's workshop, a towering collection of electronic keyboards and synthesizers. Johnson and Scofield, anchored by their amplifiers and delivering occasional solos, stood guard at either flank. Despite the electronic din, the music was old-fashioned and straight-forward (Duke even sang a falsetto ballad), and it was played with endless laughs and brilliant smiles, suggesting that it was all what it looked like—a cheerful put-on.

June 27th

As Confucius said: He who lives in the past walks backward into the future. Today, we had repertory in the afternoon, repertory in the evening, and repertory at midnight (all in Carnegie Hall). Taken chronologically, it began with Duke Ellington in 1927 and ended with John Coltrane in 1967. The Ellington repertory, the first of four to be given this week, consisted of twenty-two numbers from the twenties played by a New York Jazz Repertory Company group that was made up of, among others, Doc Cheatham, Dick Sudhalter, and Joe Newman (trumpets), Eddie Bert (trombone), Bob Wilber (reeds), Milt Hinton (bass), Panama Francis (drums), and Dick Hyman (piano), who was also the musical director. There were such monuments as "Rockin' in Rhythm," "The Mooche," and "Mood Indigo," "Creole Love Call," and "Black and Tan Fantasy" as well as the rarely heard "Harlem River

Quiver," "Jungle Nights in Harlem," "Blues I Love To Sing,"
"Doin' the Voom Voom," and "Stevedore Stomp." The band
acquitted itself pretty well. The trombonists had trouble re-
producing Tricky Sam Nanton, and Norris Turney's Johnny
Hodges was pale. There were constant rhythmic problems.
The Ellington band of the twenties hadn't begun to swing,
and it is almost impossible for present-day musicians to mimic
vanished rhythmic ineptitudes. The tempo went up and
down, and at times the rhythmic pulse died altogether. But
the trumpets, joined midway by Cootie Williams, were excellent, and so was Bob Wilber. It was eerie how he made Barney
Bigard's fifty-year-old improvisations sound like his own, how
he often gave them more feeling and éclat than Bigard himself had.

The afternoon concert was twenty-five years farther along.
The George Coleman septet, which included Harold Mabern
(piano) and Frank Strozier (alto saxophone), re-created the
hard-bop of the early fifties, with its long solos and stout
oaken ensembles. Another septet, led by the trumpeter Ted
Curson, who graduated over a decade ago from the Charles
Mingus Finishing School and then departed for a long European stay, played Mingus-type music of the fifties and early
sixties. The concert was closed by a quintet led by Anthony
Braxton, who recalled Stravinsky, the Dave Brubeck Octet,
and some of the mid-fifties experiments of Shelly Manne and
Shorty Rogers and Jimmy Giuffre. Braxton's pieces depend a
good deal on his ceaseless reed doubling. This afternoon, he
played alto, soprano, and bass saxophones and clarinet and
contrabass clarinet. His bass saxophone is an eight-foot-high
mastodon; if it were an inch higher Braxton would have had
to stand on tiptoe to reach the mouthpiece.

The Coltrane program started becomingly but turned to
sand. Elvin Jones' quartet played Coltrane's "A Love Supreme," and Jones revealed again that he is a master of poly-
rhythms and of the old business of keeping perfect time and

listening to the people he accompanies. McCoy Tyner's sextet offered one number that was enlivened by his percussionist's leaping-salmon motions and by some Tyner staccato arpeggios. Then another N.Y.J.R.C. orchestra, with Jones and Tyner sitting in, did Andrew White's hodgepodge tribute to Coltrane. White himself, a tall man with coat-hanger shoulders and short pipestem pants, raced through a couple of Coltrane's solos, but the arranged passages for the band had little to do with the dark, impassioned strivings of Coltrane, who by the time of his death had passed from mere musician to messiah.

June 28th

The pianist Keith Jarrett may become messianic if he persists in the course he took tonight at the late Carnegie concert. He appeared with the Norwegian saxophonist Jan Garbarek, who is making his first visit, and the bassist Charlie Haden and a large string orchestra. Jarrett played two of his own concerti grossi, each lasting over forty minutes. Both pieces were crowded, and some of those in the press were Chopin, Ornette Coleman, Alberto Arpeggio, Rachmaninoff, the blues, Tchaikovsky, Dmitri Tiomkin, gospel music, George Russell, and Cecil Taylor. In one passage, the strings went into a crescendo seesaw passage while Jarrett, a figure of ecstasy who often half stands and half sits, played jubilant chords, and we knew that the baby had been born and the mother would be all right. In another, with the strings humming and Jarrett throwing off legato, canoeing figures, the rains came at last and the crops were saved. Chopin didn't improvise, but Jarrett repeatedly showed us how he might have sounded if he had. Now and then it came off, particularly in short solos and in the passages, either in unison or in counterpoint, that he worked out with Garbarek.

June 29th

The second Ellington retrospective, given in Carnegie Hall, dealt with the thirties, the preparatory time for Ellington's 1940–42 period, when he and the band became an indivisible masterwork. In the thirties, Ellington wrote the beautiful melodies that paralleled popular songs and included "Mood Indigo," "Sophisticated Lady," "Solitude," "In a Sentimental Mood," "Prelude to a Kiss," and "I Let a Song Go Out of My Heart." He wrote his first longer works—"Reminiscing in Tempo" and "Diminuendo and Crescendo in Blue." And he wrote the first of the innumerable miniature concerti that he furnished for his best soloists during the next forty years— "Echoes of Harlem," "Boy Meets Horn," and "Clarinet Lament." At the same time, the personnel of the band became almost fixed, and it revolved around the nucleus of Cootie Williams, Rex Stewart, Lawrence Brown, Tricky Sam Nanton, Juan Tizol, Barney Bigard, Johnny Hodges, Harry Carney, and Sonny Greer. When Jimmy Blanton and Ben Webster joined at the end of the decade, the varsity was complete. The thirties were also the time when the band began to swing. Tonight, a N.Y.J.R.C. orchestra that included Jimmy Maxwell, Bernie Privin, Dick Vance, and Cootie Williams (trumpets), Jack Gale (trombone), Bob Wilber, Kenny Davern (baritone saxophone), Lawrence Lucie (guitar), and Bobby Rosengarden (drums) played twenty-nine numbers, and the best were "Slippery Horn" and "I'm Checkin' Out, Goom Bye," for their reed writing; "Boy Meets Horn," the oblique and funny Rex Stewart vehicle; "Echoes of Harlem," in which Williams excelled; "Drop Me Off in Harlem"; and good loose versions of "Stompy Jones," "Portrait of the Lion," and "Ring Dem Bells." Jimmy Maxwell's Cootie Williams was fine, and Bob Wilber's Hodges and Bigard were again first-class. Jack Gale came close to Tricky Sam, and Kenny

Davern to Harry Carney—at least in the section work.
Davern's solos kept sliding away from Carney's massive tonal
center. Yet how well the various Ellington soloists were re-
captured was only of passing interest. What matters in the
present Ellington retrospective is that many of his older
works, their scores long since lost, are being transcribed from
the records and put down once and for all on paper. Herewith some of the heroic ears who transcribed what we heard
tonight: Keith Nichols, Bob Wilber, Alan Cohen, Brian Priestley, David Hutson, Sy Johnson, David Berger, Fred Norman,
Jon Charles, and Dick Vance. Many of the same people also
arranged the compositions. That is, they have—when many
different versions of the same piece exist—worked out a final
representative score.

June 30th

The third Ellington program, given early tonight at Carnegie,
was half retrospective, half prospective. The program began
with a N.Y.J.R.C. orchestra giving the first complete public
performance of "Black, Brown and Beige" since its première
in 1943, and then offered the Duke Ellington Orchestra, conducted by Mercer Ellington. It was Ellington's oblique Jane
Austen way to write "Black, Brown and Beige"—which he
subtitled "A Tone Parallel to the History of the American
Negro"—at such a time; he knew that the war was a white
war and that the real conflict, the one that had been going on
in this country since the seventeenth century, was between
blacks and whites. "Black, Brown and Beige" was Ellington's
first "long" work, but it is, like all such Ellington compositions, a collection of short, intertwining program pieces. The
most famous, "Come Sunday," has become recognized as a
beautiful hymn, and it was sung with distinction tonight by
Carrie Smith. "The Blues," almost as well known, is at once
applause for and an affectionate sideswipe at a form he often

treated with mocking respect, and it was sung by Joya Sher-rill. The rest of the work is made up of marchlike pieces, a waltz, dances, and a mood piece. "Black, Brown and Beige" is primarily an ensemble work and is full of Ellington's unique voicings. The singer in "Come Sunday" is supported by pizzicato violin, bowed bass, and muted trombone, and earlier in the same piece the melody is stated by bowed violin, muted trumpet, and open-horn trombone. "Emancipation Celebration" has a plunger-muted trumpet and a plunger-muted trombone playing together and contrapuntally, and "The Blues" has a figure by three muted trombones. Although self-conscious and stiff in places, "Black, Brown, and Beige" is Ellington at the top of his bent; none of his later long assemblages were better. The performance tonight caps still another musical-archeological triumph. All that Alan Cohen and Brian Priestley, who did the transcribing, had to work with were fragments of the original score, poor record-ings made at the original concert and slightly later in Boston, and the recording of various parts of the work (it has never been properly recorded in its entirety) which Ellington him-self made throughout the years.

Pop, as Mercer Ellington calls his father, would have been both delighted and bewildered by what his son has wrought. When Ellington died, his band was almost moribund. The incessant travelling and incessant repetition of materials had driven some of its older members to the edge and had caused the younger ones to fall into accidie. Mercer Ellington has only Harold Minerve, Alvin Batiste, and Chuck Connors from the old band, and he has filled the rest of his seats with young musicians. He has also raised the decibel level about fifteen points and installed a drummer, Rocky White, who believes that power is rhythm. Tonight, the band played a *fast* "Sophisticated Lady," "Gong" and "Tang" from the "Afro-Eurasian Eclipse," "Caravan," "In My Solitude," "Harlem Air Shaft," "In a Sentimental Mood," and Elling-

ton's last multi-part work, "The Three Black Kings," which
has a funny gospel section, a form that Ellington mysteriously skirted. The band's prolonged roar obliterated Ellington's wit, subtlety, and delicacy. But he would have marvelled
at such pep.

July 2nd

The cool, pastel music extracted in New York in the late
forties from the inventions of Charlie Parker and Dizzy Gillespie by such as Lennie Tristano and Lee Konitz and Stan
Getz and Chet Baker and Gerry Mulligan eventually with-
ered in southern California in the late fifties. At its peak, it
formed little academies, and one of the best known was run
by Tristano, an autocratic blind pianist who had taken his
chief impetus from Art Tatum. He gathered about him young
players like Konitz and Warne Marsh, and they developed a
music whose intricate Charlie Parker-like ensembles were as
important as the solos. It was breathless, darting music, and
tonight, at the late Carnegie concert, it was brought back by
Konitz and Marsh and the rhythm section of Eddie Gomez
and Eliot Zigmund. (Tristano, long a self-appointed maestro,
retired from public view years ago and refuses to come out
again.) They played two of their oldies, "Wow" and "Sub-
conscious-Lee," and they also did "Body and Soul" and a
couple of originals. The best thing about their performance
was the ensembles, which were not set unison efforts but improvised counterpoint, and became dense and daring. Marsh
is another of the white Lester Young tenor saxophonists, and
Konitz absorbed both Young and Charlie Parker. Buddy Rich's
big band took up the last half of the concert, and it gave a
relatively subdued performance. It played ballads, a medium
blues, a couple of harmless flag-wavers, and Rich's set piece
"West Side Story," in which he delivered a long solo that was
closed with a delicate and succinct lesson on how to play a
true single-stroke roll. Here he is just before his solo:

July 4th

Two things were wrong before a note had been played at the highly anticipated fourth Ellington program, held in Carnegie Hall and dealing with his 1940–42 period. The N.Y.J.R.C. group for the evening had as its drummer David Lee, who is a gifted newcomer but has little conception of the drumming of thirty-five years ago. And its musical director was Joe Newman, who came up through Lionel Hampton and Basie and is not celebrated for his knowledge of Ellingtoniana, either as a player or as a leader. (Dick Hyman or Bob Wilber would, of course, have been just right.) Lee depended on a slogging snare-drum afterbeat—a device that Sonny Greer used crisply and with discretion. And he bungled the three great breaks in "Harlem Air Shaft," simply playing right

through the final one. (Would it have been so difficult for
him to learn from the original recording how Greer drove
Cootie Williams with his stampeding, double-time snare-drum
figures?) Beyond that, Newman almost invariably chose
tempos that were too slow. These numbers never recovered—"Chelsea Bridge," "Daydream," "Raincheck," "Subtle
Slough," "Blue Goose," "Across the Track Blues," "Warm
Valley," and "Main Stem." Selden Powell botched Barney
Bigard's solo in "Across the Track Blues," and Lee did the
same for Greer in "Jumpin' Punkins." There was no defini-
tion, no—*now!*—at the brilliant, leaping start of "Jump for
Joy," nor was there any in a laggardly "Jack the Bear." To
be sure, the beauties of Ellington's voicings came through
again and again, and Jimmy Maxwell and Butter Jackson
handled Cootie Williams and Tricky Sam Nanton with dis-
patch. Ellington's 1940–42 period is one of the high marks of
American music, and to re-create it for a generation that has
perhaps never heard it before demands taste and intelligence.

September 14th

It took the bass fiddle forty years to move beyond being a
timekeeper, a purveyor of quarter notes, a plugger of chinks
in the rhythm section. The first bassist to break this bondage,
to dare to improvise on his instrument (pizzicato and arco),
was Jimmy Blanton, who was born in Chattanooga around
1920 and died of tuberculosis in California in 1942. Blanton
was discovered by Duke Ellington late in 1939 and stayed
with the band until late 1941, when he could no longer play.
In that brief time, Ellington starred Blanton and his instrument in concerti like "Jack the Bear" and "Bojangles" as
well as in the highly unconventional duets that he recorded
with Blanton—"Pitter Panther Patter," "Mr. J. B. Blues,"
"Sophisticated Lady," and "Body and Soul." Ellington must
also have made sure that Blanton was properly recorded,

whether he soloed or not, for his big tone and easy, generous melodic lines move like rivers through every record they did together. Ellington handled Blanton's arrival in his customary things-will-work-themselves-out way. He writes of Blanton in his autobiography, *Music Is My Mistress:*

> He was a sensation. . . . We had to have him . . . although our bass man at the time [and for the previous four years] was Billy Taylor, one of the ace foundation-and-beat men on the instrument. So there I was with two basses! It went along fine until we got to Boston, where we were playing the Southland Cafe. Right in the middle of a set, Billy Taylor packed up his bass and said, "I'm not going to stand up here next to that young boy playing all that bass and be embarrassed." He left the stand, left us with Jimmy Blanton, and went on out the front door.

Despite Blanton's enormous tone, each note was complete and clear. His phrasing was spare, and his silences were as important as his notes. He adopted a hornlike approach to his instrument—that is, he no longer just "walked" four beats to the bar but also played little melodies—and suddenly the jazz orchestra had a new melodic voice. Blanton's accompanying was forceful; he pushed the band and its soloists by playing a fraction ahead of the beat. His measured hurrying had a beneficial effect on the Ellington band. Sonny Greer tended to play behind the beat, and a tension was created between Greer and Blanton which lifted the band and made it swing day in and day out. Blanton was felt far beyond the band. Bass soloists appeared everywhere, and within the decade a whole class had assembled, among them Oscar Pettiford, Wilbur Ware, Red Callender, Charles Mingus, Slam Stewart, George Duvivier, Milt Hinton, and John Simmons. (Blanton, of course, had been preceded by a host of strong bassists, known largely as accompanists, who included Billy

Taylor, Hayes Alvis, Artie Bernstein, Israel Crosby, John
Kirby, Pops Foster, and Wellman Braud.) Ray Brown and
the undersung Red Mitchell followed, and they were suc-
ceeded by an outpouring of bassists that continues to this day.
Among these are Richard Davis, Scott La Faro, Paul Chambers, Gary Peacock, Charlie Haden, Steve Swallow, Ron Carter, Eddie Gomez, Jay Leonhart, Lisle Atkinson, George
Mraz, Buster Williams, Dave Holland, and Michael Moore.

The stringed bass—the Fender bass is an electronic aber-
ration—has become the dominant instrument of the decade.
But it has done so in a melodramatic, and even bullying, way.
Stringed bassists, put off by the effortless BOOM BOOM BOOM
of the Fender bass, have taken to amplifying their instruments, but they haven't learned how to handle electricity any
better than electric guitarists, who had a thirty-five-year start.
Almost without exception, they turn the volume up too high.
The fibrous, twanging tones of the bass reverberate disas-
trously, and that causes the drummer and the horns to play
louder, while the pianist, locked in by an invariably weak
microphone and the decibel ceiling of the piano, disappears.
The new bassists have become hypnotized by technique.
They play dazzling runs, hammering double-stops, and en-
gulfing guitarlike chords (the influence of Ravi Shankar),
and they fool around ceaselessly with pitch, playing just
under or just over the note, which gives them a sour, freakish
sound. Their solos tend to be full of bravado and swagger
and, more often than not, hoodwink audiences in the way
that drum solos did when they were a novelty in the thirties.
A resounding eighth-note run is good for a hand, and a couple of fast triplets will bring down the house. Their accompaniment consists of counter-melodies whose off-pitch notes
and singsong, hand-over-hand attack detract rather than balance, distort rather than emphasize.

But several of the new bassists have avoided this narcissism,
and perhaps the best is Michael Moore. Moore came to New

York eight years ago from Cincinnati, where he was born and attended the conservatory, and he has listened to La Faro, Swallow, Peacock, Stewart, Brown, and Mitchell—the tradition of Jimmy Blanton. Moore has a half-moon smile and a Sunday-school mien, and he plays with great fervor. He hovers lightly over his instrument, closes his eyes, and slams the door of concentration. His virtuosity is subordinate to his invention. He has perfected what Blanton, and then Pettiford and Mingus and Mitchell, set out to do—improvise melodies of whatever length on the pizzicato bass. (Bowed bass is extremely difficult, and few jazz bassists have mastered it. Slam Stewart, who hums in octave unison with what he plays, is adept, but many others have been intimidated by intonation problems, by the very awkwardness of bowing the bass, and by the instrument's grave and almost immobile tonal qualities. Symphonic bassists are no better off, but for a different reason. Although they play a great deal in ensembles, the literature for solo bass, like that for solo tuba, has only begun to be written.) Without resorting to double-stops or guitar flourishes or tonal jokes, Moore constructs lyrical passages of the highest order. The new bassists, in attempting to transcend their instrument, make it obtrude; Moore lifts his listeners into the realm of pure melody, where one is conscious not of notes being plucked but only of new songs. Moore has an unfailing and always surprising rhythmic sense; he catches you by starting phrases in odd places and by suddenly doubling his time. Where another bassist would use a connective triplet or an arpeggio, Moore rests. Each solo gleams and multiplies, like sunlight on water, and each is important, in the way that Sid Catlett's and Sonny Rollins's and Jim Hall's are. You sit very still when Moore plays.

Moore is appearing at the Bemelmans Bar with Marian McPartland once or twice a week, and tonight turned out to be a brilliant and perhaps unwitting tussle. McPartland was in remarkable form; her runs were sheet steel, her single-note rhythmic passages cantered, and her harmonies were layered and tropical. Moore's accompaniment was model (if relentless), his solos (slightly louder than usual) were songs, and after a time intense competition took place. McPartland would solo, shaping a closing passage in which her chords revealed level after harmonic level, and Moore would come back with a four-bar arpeggio, a cluster of chattering staccato notes, and, before his next flash, a disarming legato melody. Eventually, they developed a stream of counterpoint that tilted only slightly when one or the other came to the fore.

September 26th

When the avant-garde brought forth in 1960 by Ornette Coleman and Cecil Taylor began, its banners shouted: Down with steady rhythm! Down with harmony! Down with conventional improvisation! Down with dynamics! Down with brevity! The avant-gardists proposed complete freedom, forty-five-minute solos, circular rhythms, and improvisations based on motifs, feelings, whims. For a time, these innovations were exciting, and even funny. Archie Shepp organized free-for-all bands that marched around and played excellent parodies of Ellington and brass-band music and bebop and Guy Lombardo. Coleman wrote harrowing anti-melodies and improvised with an ardor and thoroughness that suggested that he might be the first jazz musician to improvise on himself. Roswell Rudd made such unspeakable noises on his trombone that—in accord with the prevailing mood of perversity for perversity's sake—they completely hid his marvellous improvisational skills. John Coltrane began propounding an evangelical frenzy new in Western music. Jazz needed shaking up. It was harmonically and rhythmically pinched, and its musical rhetoric—witness hard-bop—had become humorless and bleak. But, having accomplished a general corset-loosening, the avant-garde (known first as "the new thing,"

then as "abstract jazz," and now as "free jazz") started
mindlessly repeating itself. It lost the intense little audience
it had won. It became a bore, and its black practitioners, sens-
ing a cul-de-sac, organized collective groups, like the Association for the Advancement of Creative Musicians, in Chicago.
They started wearing African clothes and took up African
instruments. They also studied music, and now a second generation, displaying a new sense and sensibility, is at hand.
Witness the delicate shadings of the Revolutionary Ensemble,
which made one of its rare appearances this afternoon at the
Tin Palace. The Ensemble, economics permitting, has been
together six years, and it includes Leroy Jenkins on violin
and viola, Sirone on bass, and Jerome Cooper on drums.
When the group is not fooling with gongs, temple blocks,
tympani, claves, thumb pianos, recorders, bells, saws, and
bugles, it plays modest pieces, perhaps eight or nine minutes
in length, which are generally made up of a comprehensible,
rather melodic theme; solos by Jenkins and Sirone that are
more like collective efforts, with first Jenkins turning to the
light, then Sirone; out-and-out group improvisation; and a
return to the opening theme. They carry their avant-garde
baggage lightly. Jenkins has a sweet, pleasing tone, and his
constant tampering with pitch is harmless. Sirone is zealous
and over-amplified, in the current mode, but his excursions go
no farther afield than Ron Carter's. Cooper, compared with
an early avant-garde drummer like Milford Graves, who altered all the conventional drum equipment, exhibits high de-
corum.

October 19th

Zoot Sims's head juts forward, his shoulders are stooped, he
has a small paunch, and his legs are bent from so many years
of hefting a tenor saxophone. But there is nothing decrepit
about him. His eyes are watchful, his porcupine hair crackles,

and his wit cooks. (He once described his difficult compeer
and sometime rival Stan Getz as "a nice bunch of guys.")
And he is playing with a vigor and inspiration that have
brought him to the front of the great movement of saxophonists founded by Lester Young. Sims is a cheerful man
who likes to play Ping-Pong, garden, make meat sauce, and
laugh, but he is surprisingly diffident. Not long ago, he talked
briefly of himself: "I was born in 1925 in Inglewood, California, which is south of Los Angeles, right by the airport. It
was all lemon groves and Japanese gardens then. I was the
youngest of six boys and one girl. My mother and father
were in vaudeville, and they were known as Pete and Kate.
He was from Missouri and she was from Arkansas. My
mother never forgot a joke or a lyric, and she performed at
the drop of a hat right up until she had a stroke a couple of
years ago. My father died in 1950. He spent his last years on
the road, scuffling, and he never sent any money home. It
was out of sight, out of mind for him. But there was never
any falling out among us. When he came for a visit, everybody forgave him, including my mother. I don't know how
we made it. The gas and water were always being turned off,
and we moved a lot. One move got me off the ground, though,
because we had to go to a new school where they were re-
cruiting kids for their band. They gave me a clarinet and my
brother Ray a tuba and my brother Bobby drums. I was
about ten. I liked the clarinet fine, even though it made my
teeth vibrate, which is why I don't play with a biting grip
today. Most sax players bite through their mouthpiece; mine
hardly has a mark on it. I played clarinet three years, until
my mother bought me a Conn tenor on time. I kept it through
my Woody Herman days in the late forties, and I finally sold
it for twenty-five dollars. I never had any lessons. I learned
by listening to Coleman Hawkins and Roy Eldridge and Chu
Berry, and later to Lester Young and Ben Webster and Don
Byas. My mind was elsewhere in school, which I quit after

one year of high. When I was fifteen or sixteen, I worked in an L.A. band led by Ken Baker. He put these supposedly funny nicknames on the front of his music stands—Scoot, Voot, Zoot—and I ended up behind the Zoot stand, and it stuck. Then, instead of joining Paul Whiteman, who invited me, I went with Bobby Sherwood. It was like a family, and Sherwood was a father image to a lot of us. Sonny Dunham was next, and after him it was Teddy Powell. I spent nine weeks on the Island Queen, a riverboat out of Cincinnati that had a calliope player who knew 'Don't Get Around Much Anymore.' In 1943, I joined Benny Goodman, and he had Jess Stacy and Bill Harris. I got along fine with Benny, and I still do, even though when I asked for a raise on a one-night gig a little while ago he said, 'Zoot, you hurt my feelings.' In 1944, Sid Catlett asked me to take Ben Webster's place in his quartet after Ben got sick, and we played the Streets of Paris, in Hollywood. I got drafted and ended up in the Army Air Forces later that year and fought the Battle of the South. I was stationed in Huntsville, Valdosta, Biloxi, Phoenix, Tucson, and San Antonio, where I played every night in a little black club. I got out in 1946 and rejoined Benny, and then I went with Woody Herman and became one of the Four Brothers, with Herbie Steward and Stan Getz and Serge Chaloff. I loved that band. We were all young and had the same ideas. I'd always worried about what other guys were thinking in all the bands I'd been in, and in Woody's I found out: they were thinking the same thing I was."

Sims's stay with Herman put him more or less on the map, despite the presence of Getz, whose Keatsian chorus on Herman's 1948 recording of "Early Autumn" made him famous. During the fifties and sixties, Sims worked in Gerry Mulligan's experimental sextet and in his staid "concert" band, and he teamed up with Al Cohn in a duo that still functions. Now he roams the world as a leader and sometimes as a sideman, and slowly he has built a stainless repu-

tation as a swinging tenor saxophonist. But Sims's eminence
has become unshakable only in the past several years—perhaps since the historic set at Richard Gibson's 1969 jazz party
in Aspen when Sims, teamed with Joe Venuti, whom Gibson
had just brought out of semiretirement, played an "I Found a
New Baby" with such concentration and swing and ferocity
that the event has become a Pinnacle of Jazz. (Sims's and
Venuti's performance was not recorded, and they have been
fruitlessly corralled into recording studios three times since
in hopes they would repeat their miracle.) Sims, as he suggests, is a compound of Coleman Hawkins, Don Byas, Lester
Young, and Ben Webster. Most of the white tenor saxophonists who stamped themselves "Lester Young" in the
forties—Getz, Cohn, Steward, Jimmy Giuffre, Buddy Savitt,
Bob Cooper, Bill Perkins, Allan Eager, Brew Moore—wor-
shipped Young's seeming languor and ignored his muscle.
Sims was an exception, and his early style had a tough,
bounding quality that has gradually been softened by Ben
Webster's rhapsodic approach to melody. But Sims's early
style has stuck in his listeners' heads, and he is praised too
much as a "swinger" and not enough as a lyrical player.
(Sims is deceptive. When his fount of invention is low, he
simply turns into a rhythm machine: his phrases rock, his
tone grows heated, and his notes swarm. He is swinging, but
that's all.) He should be studied at slow tempos, and particularly on the blues, where he is apt to coin phrases of such
lyricism and tenderness and grace that one goes back to them
again and again for sustenance and to quell disbelief. These
phrases, generally only a bar or two in length, have a beseeching quality, and rightly so. They have never been heard
before and, unless they are recorded, are likely never to be
heard again. But several instances of this eloquence have
been caught on five new recordings. These are "Nirvana:
Zoot Sims/Bucky Pizzarelli with Special Guest Buddy Rich"
(Groove Merchant); "Zoot Sims and Friend" (Classic Jazz);

and three releases on Norman Granz's Pablo label—"Zoot
Sims and the Gershwin Brothers," "Basie and Zoot," and
"Zoot Sims: Soprano Sax." Pay heed to the beginning of
Sims's third chorus on the slow "Blues for Nat Cole" ("Basie
and Zoot"), in which he plays a high, crooning phrase, and
to the bold total improvisation launching his solo on "Mean
to Me." And listen to the falsetto that states the melody on
"Gee Baby, Ain't I Good to You" ("Nirvana") and to the
opening of his melodic embellishments on "Wrap Your Trou-
bles in Dreams" ("Zoot Sims: Soprano Sax"). There are
other felicities in addition to Sims's lyricism: Basie's rollick-
ing stride piano on "Honeysuckle Rose," and his breeze-in-
the-elm organ on "I Surrender, Dear"; and much of the
"Nirvana" album, which has some unusually delicate Buddy
Rich drumming, beautiful husky Sims on "A Summer
Thing," and four Sims-Pizzarelli duets (of which there are
eight more on "Zoot Sims and Friend"). The album given
over to Sims's soprano, an instrument added to his stockroom
several years ago, is surprising. He stays in the lower register
and avoids much of the soprano's piping tendencies. He also
stays pretty much in tune. The Gershwin album is of note
only because it is a superb example of Sims's swinging hard
and becomingly (he is accompanied by Oscar Peterson, Joe
Pass, George Mraz, and Grady Tate) and saying almost
nothing.

October 21st

Marian McPartland's situation at the Carlyle began almost
two years ago, when the management moved her across the
hall from the Café Carlyle, where she had been subbing for
Bobby Short, into the Bemelmans Bar, where there had never
been live music. She was an immediate success, and has stayed
there off and on ever since. But it has not been easy. The
Bemelmans is a small, classic New York bar of the hideaway

kind that first appeared in the late thirties and early forties.
It has a twelve-stool bar, four horseshoe banquettes, and New
York murals by Ludwig Bemelmans, who liked to paint nurses
herding children across empty city spaces. The Bemelmans
is too small for a piano, but the Carlyle superimposed one,
and there it sits, like a stranded whale. Not only that. The
piano was tired, there was a rudimentary sound system, the
bar cash register hummed and crashed, and the patrons, un-
aware that they were in a mini concert hall, were noisy. But
Marian McPartland demanded and has finally got a new
piano and a proper sound system, and patrons now sometimes
remain ruly for a whole set. Her playing, often burdened by
prolixity and bravura when she is nervous, has become increasingly thoughtful. Her harmonies are orchestral but un-
sentimental, and her single-note lines cajole and startle. She
has discovered a pleasing laissez-faire on the part of the Carlyle and has begun a series of impromptu soirées to which
she invites singers and/or players. These have included Carol
Sloane, Teddi King, Susannah McCorkle, and Sylvia Syms;
the bassist Michael Moore, the cornettists Jimmy McPartland
and Richard Sudhalter, and the guitarist Gene Bertoncini.
There was a gathering tonight, and it included Jimmy McP.,
Bertoncini, and Moore. Jimmy McPartland is almost seventy
and has been battling indifference, weight, and embouchure
problems, but none of these got in his way tonight. Using a
Harmon mute or a piece of felt draped over his bell, he played
such non-Dixieland numbers as "My Heart Stood Still,"
"Thou Swell," and "This Can't Be Love" with freshness and
lilt. Bix Beiderbecke's jaunty attack was evident, but McPartland's phrasing was more adventurous. He held notes unexpectedly, and used big intervals, and substituted sudden
ascending figures for conventional fall-away runs. Marian
McPartland proved the truism that jazz pianists play better
in a crowd than by themselves. The four musicians, forced

by circumstances into a small space and seated in profile, resembled four men—persons—in a boat.

October 27th

Two disappointments: Allan Miller's hour-and-a-half film
"Amazing Grace—America in Song," shot for television and
shown on PBS tonight, and the "Porgy and Bess" recorded
by Ray Charles and Cleo Laine for RCA.

"Amazing Grace" is an instance of the odd and unintelli-
gent things that serious television does in the name of originality and under the indulgent banner of endowment money.
Here is some of what the film shows: a crowd in Fenway
Park singing "The Star-Spangled Banner"; a fourth-grade
class singing "Who Threw the Overalls in Mrs. Murphy's
Chowder?"; myriad folk singers singing Dust Bowl songs,
mining songs, union songs, sea chanteys, railroad songs, protest songs; Lena Horne singing Cole Porter's "It's All Right
with Me"; Billie Holiday singing her blues "Fine and Mellow"; Jack Teagarden and Louis Armstrong singing "Rockin'
Chair"; Bessie Smith singing "St. Louis Blues"; the Allman
Brothers singing "One Way Out"; white churchgoers singing
"Amazing Grace"; and Phyllis Curtin singing an Aaron
Copland song. "Amazing Grace" isn't even a good film. The
staged songs—a young man in an empty freight car singing
a railroad song, a young man standing on the Kansas plains
and singing "Starving to Death on My Government Claim"—
look staged, and in the chance sequences the subjects stare
at the camera or are caught just turning away. The film is
an anthology whose chief staple is variety itself. It could as
easily have shown Americans of every stripe tying their
shoes. Since "Amazing Grace" heads in the right direction in
its last half hour (Bessie Smith; Billie Holiday; Louis Armstrong and Jack Teagarden), what a shame that Miller didn't

go ahead and do the first good film on American singing. This might have entailed ten minute studies of Big Joe Turner, of Ray Charles, of Claude Jeter and Dorothy Love Coates, and of Frank Sinatra or Tony Bennett or Sylvia Syms or Mabel Mercer or Mel Tormé.

Norman Granz is an Idea Man. In the forties, he moved the jam session from the back room to the stage, and called the concerts Jazz at the Philharmonic. He recorded J.A.T.P. in action and, when the L.P. arrived, held studio jam sessions in which he gathered the kings of jazz (one record had Johnny Hodges, Benny Carter, Charlie Parker, and Ben Webster) and let them blow for a half hour at a time. He recorded nearly two hundred piano solos by Art Tatum, and he got Ella Fitzgerald and Louis Armstrong together. He put Fred Astaire, just starting his long and brilliant twilight, with a jazz rhythm section and had him sing and dance. And now he has persuaded Ray Charles to record excerpts from "Porgy and Bess" with Cleo Laine. There are seventeen vocal numbers. Laine and Charles collaborate on five, and each does six alone. There are also seven instrumentals, in which Charles, generally accompanied by a rhythm section, plays organ, celeste, and acoustic and electric piano. The album is a classy disaster. Frank DeVol's arrangements are unfussy, the accompaniment (eighty-odd musicians are used) is faultless, the recording is excellent, and the photographs in the album booklet are good. But Charles "sings" throughout the album, sounding proper and awed, and he takes off his shoes and lets go with his special whispers and falsettos and melismatics only on the gospel-like "Oh Lord, I'm on My Way," which happens to be the last number in the album. Cleo Laine misses notes, and when she rebounds through her high register in "Summertime" she is showing off, and the song remains untouched, as do all the songs she sings. Charles has never messed with "Porgy and Bess" before, and there are probably reasons. Perhaps he finds the songs highfalutin, or perhaps he considers them white man's black music. Perhaps they don't reach him, just as "Star Dust," which he has never recorded, doesn't. If Norman Granz had got Charles to record some blues and gospel songs, which Charles hasn't done in years and may never do again, the results wouldn't have been topical but they could have been classic.

October 28th

It wasn't easy to be an aspiring saxophonist in the early forties. There had been few choices until then about which way to go. Tenor saxophonists followed Coleman Hawkins or his best disciples (Chu Berry, Herschel Evans, Ben Webster, Illinois Jacquet, and Don Byas), and alto saxophonists studied Benny Carter or Johnny Hodges and checked out Pete Brown, Willie Smith, and Tab Smith. Then Lester Young appeared. Hawkins had championed an enormous cordovan tone, improvising on chords, and a foursquare rhythmic approach. Young, having learned a good deal not from Hawkins but, of all things, from three white saxophonists— Jimmy Dorsey, Frank Trumbauer, Bud Freeman—championed nothing. Indeed, his playing was almost anti-playing. His tone was light—it suggested soundless laughter—and he advanced a form of melodic improvising that, with its casual, long-held notes and easy selectivity, matched the new coolness of Billie Holiday and Teddy Wilson. No sooner had Young been absorbed than Charlie Parker appeared. Parker's tone fell between Hawkins and Young, and so did his improvisations. He worked with chords and melody, and eventually, as in his celebrated recordings of "Embraceable You," he passed through improvisation to the verge of a new *music*. Young had sidled into view, but Parker exploded. No one had ever heard such arpeggios on a reed instrument, such passionate, preaching blues playing, such avalanches of eighth notes. Faced with the totally dissimilar and equally attractive ap-

proaches of Young and Parker, what was a budding saxophonist to do? Tenor saxophonists followed Young and alto
saxophonists Parker; adventurous tenor players also listened
to Parker and adventurous alto players to Young. But a handful of saxophone players attempted to borrow a cup of this
from Young and a cup of that from Parker, and to find a way
between them. The most important was the tenor saxophonist
Dexter Gordon, who is now fifty-three. Gordon's tone is hard
and calculated, and resembles Parker's at its most careless, as
do his occasional rhythmically congested clusters of notes.
But Young has the upper hand in Gordon's work. Here,
transmogrified, are the long-held notes, the horizontal improvisations, the vibratoless attack, and the way of biting his
notes that Young developed in the forties.

Gordon came out of California, worked his way across the
country and through New York, and disappeared into Europe
permanently in the early sixties. He has become shadowy,
and even legendary, and his current quick American tour is
being greeted with reverence. Tonight the Village Vanguard
resembled the night in 1961 when Sonny Rollins returned
from his first and most famous retirement. Every handclap
was a genuflection. Gordon's appearance doesn't discourage
adulation. He is six and a half feet tall and has a long, Lincoln face. When he finishes a solo, he visibly withdraws from
the world of improvisation by grimacing and baring his
teeth, and he meets the applause by turning his saxophone
on its side and offering it to the audience with both hands,
like the country guitarist Ernest Tubb, who turns the back
of his guitar to the audience at the end of his performances,
revealing thereon the word "Thanks." Gordon's playing is an
extension of his stature. His sound is big and his notes are
big. He locks together giant cubes of sound in his solos, piling
one on another until he has constructed a gleaming amphi-
theatre. He builds these edifices in a determined, almost
harsh fashion, rarely missing a note, and finishes each phrase

so that it has a clear, sharp edge. He plays few arpeggios, and the only vibrato he allows himself is slow and broad and dramatic. There is a lot of musical and physical ritual in Gordon's onstage work, and it tends to obscure the fact that he is a transitional figure who in the fifties helped to invent a tenor-saxophone style that has come to be called hard-bop, and who helped get John Coltrane and Sonny Rollins going. Gordon's accompanists, all of them able and sometimes inspired, included Ronnie Matthews on piano, Stafford James on bass, and Louis Hayes on drums.

October 29th

Each generation throws off its own cultural hybrids. These tend to be pretentious, expert, topically ingenious, addictive, and—when their novelty wears off—of some artistic merit. The most recent in jazz has been the Stan Kenton band. Its immediate predecessor, the Paul Whiteman orchestra, thrived for a decade and slowly subsided five years before Kenton's arrival, in 1941. The two groups had a good deal in common. Both were bombastic, well drilled, aurally hypnotic, and eccentric. Kenton believed that he was changing the course of jazz, and perhaps of American music itself, when what he was principally doing was providing dozens of jazz musicians with a unique finishing school, many of whose graduates would end up pumping away in Hollywood studios. His "innovations," as he called them, were overblown and humorless variations of earlier big bands, Jimmy Lunceford's in particular, and of the driest atonal music. Whiteman also attempted to be a cultural pivot, but in a far subtler way. He built a dance band into a first-rate orchestra of nearly thirty pieces, capable of playing symphonic music, light classical music, dance music, and big-band jazz. He didn't altogether satisfy the various musical communities—the classical boys found him "jazzy" and the jazz people found him starchy and unswinging—but he changed American music. He commissioned George Gershwin's "Rhapsody in Blue," and got Gershwin off to a start as a "serious" composer, to say nothing of helping to bring into being the best piece of music ever written about New York. He hired arrangers like Bill Challis and Tom Satterfield, who evolved pioneering harmonic patterns and instrumental combinations that were almost certainly studied by Duke Ellington and Don Redman and Benny Carter. And he gave a leg up to jazz soloists by exposing within the stately confines of his band Jack Teagarden, Mildred Bailey, Bing Crosby, Frank Trumbauer, Bix Beiderbecke, and Tommy and Jimmy Dorsey.

Gershwin has been thoroughly considered in the past five years and has reached an apogee with the uncut production of "Porgy and Bess" (he still needs a good, literate biographer, though), and now it is Whiteman's turn. Richard Sudhalter, the thirty-eight-year-old cornettist, Beiderbecke biographer, and jazz archivist, began reactivating Whiteman in England two years ago, with his New Paul Whiteman Orchestra, and he continued tonight at Carnegie Hall, with a concert called "Paul Whiteman Rediscovered." There were twenty-five musicians and six singers, and they performed "Rhapsody in Blue" and a couple of dozen of Whiteman's jazz-oriented numbers, among them "Sugar," "China Boy," "Changes," "Mississippi Mud," "Oh Miss Hannah," and "Happy Feet." Nine arrangements were by Challis and the rest by Satterfield, Lennie Hayton, Matty Malneck, and Ferde Grofé. The evening contained surprises. The "Rhapsody" heard was the original 1924 version done by Whiteman at its Aeolian Hall première, and it had an attractive leanness and directness. Three of the other numbers—"Singin' the Blues," "Runnin' Wild," and "Hallelujah"—were never recorded by Whiteman. The reed scoring during the evening was often astonishing: three alto saxophones on "Singin' the Blues"; four clarinets and a baritone saxophone on "Runnin'

Wild"; and *two* baritone saxophones and a *bass* saxophone
on "Changes." The band was admirable—the reed section
had to double and redouble every four bars—and so were the
soloists. Johnny Mince played Trumbauer with a jiggling intensity, and the old virtuoso Al Gallodoro did Jimmy Dorsey's circus alto-saxophone number "Oodles of Noodles" with
a creamy brilliance that demonstrated what a beautiful instrument the alto saxophone is when played properly. Sudhalter handled Beiderbecke's solos with a combination of
Beiderbecke's tone and logic and his own more modern
phrasing and rhythmic attack. Larry Carr handled the Bing
Crosby vocals with plenty of glottal stops, and the Rhythm
Boys and the Whiteman Trio were done by Keith Nichols,
Norman Fields, Bob Lenn, Art Lambert, and George Mac-
Donald, who, sedate and furbished-looking, was with Whiteman in the early thirties. An unavoidable distraction: on
numbers like "From Monday On" and "Happy Feet" the
band tended to swing far harder than the original band
could or would have. Most jazz musicians in the twenties
hadn't learned to swing that way, and even if they had,
Whiteman would have considered such abandon indecorous.

November 26th

The Jazz Program at the Smithsonian is headed by the critic
Martin Williams, who organizes concerts and issues records.
The records are on the Smithsonian Collection label, which
was initiated three years ago with a six-record history of jazz,
"The Smithsonian Collection of Classic Jazz." That history
brought together for the first time material from many different labels—a feat that no private company had been able
to legally manage. The same anthology technique has been
used to great effect on a two-record Dizzy Gillespie album,
"Dizzy Gillespie: The Development of an American Artist."
The album follows Gillespie from the Roy Eldridge imitator

he was to the baroque wonder he became, and it contains thirty-three selections, five of them excerpts, recorded between 1940 and 1946. Most are drawn from the invaluable storefront labels that filled the vacuum created by the major labels, whose interests were elsewhere. Four selections are from Columbia subsidiaries, and one is from Decca, but the rest came out on Esoteric, Hit, Apollo, DeLuxe, Continental, Manor, Black & White, Guild, and Dial.

Gillespie fell under the sway of Roy Eldridge around 1936. Although Louis Armstrong was still playing well, Eldridge had come up with a style that suddenly made Armstrong sound old-fashioned. Eldridge's playing *hurried;* he used crackling high notes, falling-downstairs arpeggios, and a searing tone. He had immediate authority, and trumpeters everywhere began studying him. (The rapidity with which jazz sometimes moves is indecent. Only four years before, Armstrong had recorded his celestial thoughts on "Basin Street Blues" and "I Gotta Right To Sing the Blues" and "That's My Home.") Gillespie straightaway began adding his own touches—unlikely notes and rhythmic patterns. These can be heard on the four 1940 Cab Calloway sides included and on the excerpts from on-the-spot recordings made in 1941 by Jerry Newman at Clark Monroe's Uptown House. And they are clear on the numbers that Gillespie recorded with Les Hite and Lucky Millinder in 1942, especially on Hite's "Jersey Bounce," in which Gillespie plays a descending run that is an announcement of what is just around the corner. But, of course, we never get around the corner, because of a union recording ban that went into effect in mid-1942. The next records in the album, "Woody 'n' You" and "Disorder at the Border," were made in 1944 with a Coleman Hawkins group, and there, fully formed and fully packed, is the Gillespie we have had for thirty years. During the ban, Gillespie had worked in the Earl Hines big band with Charlie Parker, and it was then that he—and Parker—put his final

style together. The two men had been moving in the same
musical direction for years, Gillespie experimenting with expanding the chordal side of improvisation and Parker bent
on expanding it melodically and rhythmically. Gillespie is
quoted in the liner notes:

> I learned rhythm patterns from Charlie Parker.

> My association with Charlie Parker would have
> to be far above anything else that I have ever done
> musically in my career.

> Charlie Parker, the other side of my heartbeat.

Gillespie consolidates himself during the rest of the album,
and is particularly imposing on "Good Bait," "Salted Peanuts," "Be-Bop," and "March of the Boyds." Williams says
at the beginning of the liner notes, "We have carefully
avoided here all the recorded collaborations with Charlie
Parker. They have often been collected and reissued and,
more important, Parker's brilliance has sometimes clouded
the issue of Gillespie's own." A mistake, I think. Gillespie
and Parker were like Ellington and Strayhorn, Bob and Ray,
Rodgers and Hart. Each activated the other, and I recall no
recording where Parker ever edged Gillespie. Indeed, since
Parker did help assemble Gillespie, it is essential to hear
them side by side—say, on any of the four great Red Norvo
1945 Comet-label recordings, where they were set off by such
swing musicians as Teddy Wilson, Slam Stewart, J. C. Heard,
and Flip Phillips. These certainly have more importance
in the Gillespie canon than the Billy Eckstine and Sarah
Vaughan and Joe Marsala numbers that have been included.

1977

January 3rd

Erroll Garner last appeared in New York at the Maisonette Room of the St. Regis in May of 1974. His playing was effulgent, and he looked as he always had—a short, gleaming, funny, cooking man, his black hair a mirror, his great parrot nose pointed into the winds of his invention. He rocked and grunted and hummed at the keyboard, and his astonishing hands—he could span thirteen notes—went like jackhammers. The ad-lib whirlpool introductions to his numbers, sometimes eight bars and more, seemed to have spread and deepened, to be complete manic compositions, and his four-four improvisations were joyous and intense. Not long after the Maisonette gig, Garner fell ill with pneumonia, complicated by emphysema, and, never having fully recovered, he died yesterday at the age of fifty-three.

Garner was an anachronism, for he was a true folk musician, who belonged with the great jazz primitives of the twenties and thirties. He was self-taught, he never learned to read music, and, like all masterly folk artists, he developed a style of such originality and presence that it became nearly autonomous. One bar was enough to identify him, and his style was so persuasive, and pervasive, that he influenced older pianists (Earl Hines), pianists of his own generation (Oscar Peterson, George Shearing, Red Garland), and pianists of the next generation (Cecil Taylor). Garner never finished high school, and he was untroubled by the lapses of confidence and invention which academic training often instills. Indeed, he was embarrassingly confident and inventive. The critic and record producer George Avakian describes a Garner recording session for Columbia in 1953: "Erroll rattled off thirteen numbers, averaging over six minutes each . . . with no rehearsal and no re-takes. Even with a half-hour pause for coffee, we were finished twenty-seven minutes ahead of the three hours of normal studio time—but Erroll had recorded over eighty minutes of music instead of the usual ten or twelve, and . . . his performance . . . could not have been improved upon. He asked to hear playbacks on two of the numbers, but only listened to a chorus or so of each, before he waved his hand." And Garner appeared equally at ease in night clubs and on concert stages. He became the first wholly successful solo jazz performer. (Although he often appeared with a bassist and a drummer, they were extraneous.) This was startling and brave, but it was unfortunate, too, for his rare collaborations with horn players were enthralling. In the fifties, Garner had been almost underfoot; in the seventies, he seemed to have receded from view. So this dazzling, unique performer was all but lost to a generation. Mary Lou Williams has said of Garner, "Erroll came from my home town of Pittsburgh, and I first heard him there in a little joint when he was fifteen or sixteen. One of my nieces went to Westinghouse High School with him, and she'd told me about him. He was like Art Tatum—all over the keyboard. He started coming to New York, which scared him at first, in the late thirties or early forties, and he was always in my house. When I was at Café Society Downtown, I'd get home at four in the morning and Erroll would arrive at five and start playing my piano. One time, I took him to a symphony, and he loved what he heard so much that he rolled on the floor when he got back to my place, and then he sat down and played the whole thing. He had that kind of ear. Another time, he was playing here and he shouted suddenly, 'I got it! I got it!' What had happened was he'd found that bum-bum-bum-bum four-beats-to-the-bar left hand that he used the rest of his life. I tried to teach him to read once, but it didn't work. After a while, he said, 'Ooooooh, Mary. I can't cut that,' and he never learned. I also tried to get him to slow down and forget about Art Tatum when he was starting out, and he did. Nobody influenced his playing after that, and his style was completely his own, just like his fingering, which was built on a love of the piano keys. Partly, he worked his style out so that he would never need bass and drums, which he didn't, and partly so that he could reach the public easily, which he did. But the style he played in your house was wild and totally different. Erroll liked to laugh. He was so comical you'd have to break down. He didn't like statics or arguments. If you asked him about another musician, he always had a nice word. He never said anything disagreeable about anybody. He was like a little boy, like a jolly kid of seven or eight playing baseball. And he was like Art Tatum, because he liked to hang out and play any raggedy old piano in any club or in anybody's house. He influenced a lot of piano players, and I think a lot of musicians were jealous of him for his success and all the money he made on songs he wrote, like 'Misty.' But Erroll didn't have time to let that bother him. He was too busy writing his songs in his head and playing the piano."

January 14th

The arpeggio became fashionable in jazz in the forties. Propounded by Art Tatum and Charlie Parker and Dizzy Gillespie, the teeming run, ascending or descending, was taken up by every pianist, guitarist, trumpeter, and saxophonist. Some players used so many notes their solos resembled enormous glissandos. The individual note was sacrificed for babble, and silence, which allows music to breathe, vanished. Jazz began to sound harebrained. For a time, the trombone, alone among jazz instruments, resisted each baroque behavior. One of the most vulnerable of instruments, because of its technical oddities, its edgeless tone, and its lyrical propensities, the trombone had been a musical clown before being turned in the thirties into a poetic voice by Dicky Wells and J. C. Higginbotham and Lawrence Brown. But the young trombonists of the forties, envious of Parker's cascades, decided that the only way to get into the Bebop Club was to be a virtuoso. So they adopted an icy, nasal tone, stuffed their phrases with notes, and ran up and down their registers as if they were pianists or saxophonists. The grandeur of Wells and Higginbotham gave way to the cul-de-sac skating of J. J. Johnson, and then of Jimmy Cleveland, Urbie Green, Carl Fontana, and Bill Watrous. The new trombone virtuosity obscured the fact that the proper next step after Wells and Brown and Higginbotham *had* been taken. This was done quietly in the fifties by the brilliant and still largely unappreciated Jimmy Knepper.

A tall, diffident man with a small, closed face, Knepper was born in Los Angeles in 1927 and was playing the trombone by the time he was nine. He had some college training, and passed through the big bands of Charlie Barnet, Charlie Spivak, Claude Thornhill, Woody Herman, and Stan Kenton, and played in small groups with Charlie Parker and Gene Roland and Art Pepper. In 1957, he joined the first, and in

many ways the most important, of Charles Mingus's semi-
nars, and it was immediately clear that he had absorbed Higginbotham and Wells and Brown as well as the rhythmic and
harmonic advances of Parker and Gillespie. Knepper had,
and has, none of the dandyism of J. J. Johnson and his fol-
lowers, nor does he blare or whine or shout. He has a loose,
warm tone and a way of easing out his notes—even his occasional arpeggios—with an over-the-shoulder offhandedness.
He seems to lounge when he plays. But his serenity is deceptive, for he is a subtle and complex trombonist. He is an epi-
grammatist of a high order. His phrases, choice and balanced
and to the point, are smoothly linked so that entire solo
choruses form an uninterrupted melodic line. His gentle tone
resembles Lawrence Brown's, but he also shares Dicky Wells's
delight in the inherent heresies of his instrument. Knepper's
low notes are sometimes rude, his high notes wild. Plain in
every phrase are the practices of Parker and Gillespie: the
eighth notes, the ninth chords, the short, meteoric runs that
start a split second late, the quirky bittersweet notes. Parker
loved to open his blues solos with quick, shocking phrases,
and Knepper will do the same. He will fashion a six- or
seven-note announcement, its notes spread unevenly over an
octave, so that they seem to bob and weave as they go by, and
then pause, repeat the phrase, but with most of its notes altered a tone or half a tone, pause briefly again, and swing
into an ascending passage topped with a small, high yell, followed by two low closing notes. He will start the second
chorus with a double-time variation of his first-chorus announcement, pass through a low-curving note that ends in
congested eighth notes, and, after a brief connecting slur,
start a blue note, cut it off, drop in a couple of triplets, and
plane into his third and final chorus with a series of ascending and descending notes, which he carries, with infinitesimal
breaks, to the end of the chorus. His volume has risen and
fallen almost imperceptibly all through the solo, and one

realizes only at the end the urgency propelling each phrase. Some soloists wait for their notes; Knepper pursues his. The best improvisers of Knepper's generation are delicate and thoughtful, and demand close attention. Knepper's solos are propositions of musical beauty, not face-to-face pronouncements, and if you turn your ear they're gone.

Knepper's career has been evanescent, but he has been appearing every Wednesday and Thursday at Stryker's, where he is playing with Lee Konitz's Nonet. The group uses ensemble devices ranging from complex Lennie Tristano unison passages to mock-Dixieland tuttis, and it has a good, plunging full-voiced attack. The best thing about the group, aside from Konitz's marvellous fusion of Lester Young and Charlie Parker, is Knepper, who solos a lot and is wholly relaxed. He was especially commanding tonight on his own blues, "Birth of a Nation," on Konitz's arrangement of "Without a Song," and on a Tristano melodic line that, used as an opener, caught everyone with cold chops and sounded like an old Archie Shepp bee.

January 28th

One of the incidental acts of the avant-garde in the sixties was the rediscovery of the soprano saxophone, a difficult instrument (pitch problems, mostly) that fell into disuse after Sidney Bechet's death, in 1959. John Coltrane is generally credited with bringing it back, but he probably took it up because of Steve Lacy, a modernist who began playing it while Bechet was still alive. In 1967, Lacy moved to Europe, and now—a forty-two-year-old with a delicate, almost transparent handsomeness—he has returned for a short visit, and appearances downtown at The Kitchen, Environ, and Ali's Alley, where he played tonight.

Before Lacy went abroad, he gave an interview that was printed in *The Jazz Review* and reprinted in *Jazz Panorama*, a book assembled from that magazine by Martin Williams in 1962. Lacy said:

> [Music] can be regarded as excited speech, imitation of the sounds of nature, an abstract set of symbols, a baring of emotions, an illustration of interpersonal relationships, an intellectual game, a device for inducing reverie, a mating call, a series of dramatic events, an articulation of time and/or space, an athletic contest. . . . A jazz musician is a combination orator, dialectician, mathematician, athlete, entertainer, poet, singer, dancer, diplomat, educator, student, comedian, artist, seducer . . . and general all-around good fellow.

Lacy practices what he preaches. His playing tonight was excited, bucolic, abstract, emotional, intellectual, seductive, dramatic, and spatial. It demonstrated that the jazz avant-garde is refining itself. The relentless roars and screams and shrieks of the sixties—purposeful rude black jungle noises—have been muted and clarified, or simply discarded. The avant-garde has brought back some of the old verities of jazz in new dress: lyricism, form, the domestic emotions. Like the trombonist Roswell Rudd, Lacy came up in Dixieland and swing bands and then passed through the nimbuses of Cecil Taylor and Thelonious Monk. Lacy has a full tone, his pitch is steady, and he is facile. (Staying in tune doesn't mean much in Lacy's music, because keys and tonal centers have all but vanished. However, one can judge pretty well after a time whether or not a musician is playing what he wants to play.) Most of the first number consisted of long stretches of semi-atonal ensemble, in which Lacy and the alto saxophonist Steve Potts played rough unison or antiphonal figures. The second piece had a steplike theme, and Lacy soloed ruminatively and at length. He began in the middle register and then moved up, revealing a sweet tone, and passed into a series of falsetto figures, sprinkled with squeaks and trills. The third number opened as if the two horns were warming up, and for a minute or so one didn't realize that they had begun. After a windy alto solo, Lacy put forth his musical credo. We heard dogs, birds, anguished abstractions, throat-clearings, squeals, blips, and quacks. His work has a double effect. Its surface is resolutely amusical in the conventional sense. It offers a series of semi-abstract sounds, repetitive circular rhythms, and obscure thematic materials. It is a self-centered music that sometimes seems to move wholly through shrouded inner landscapes. Yet Lacy plays with a fervency that carries within it the lyricism and daring we sensed when Armstrong and Parker and Taylor first arrived.

February 11th

Bobby Short is between stints at the Carlyle, and tonight he talked about his friend Nat Cole. "Nat was a nice man, a most amusing man," he said. "He was much given to the wisecrack, and he was irresistible to the ladies. You could see the humor in those strange Oriental eyes. I worked in a club with him in Omaha in 1943, when his records were just beginning to catch on. He had at least temporarily gotten himself out of Los Angeles, where he had been a fixture for years on Eighth Street in the Negro section and where he was all but taken for granted. He was married first to a chorus girl named Nadine, then to Marie Ellington—no relation to Duke, with whom she sang. They bought a big house in Hancock Park, which was all white, and they had the usual threats and had to hire police guards. Marie brought in Tom Douglas, the best decorator around, and they lived in grand style. Nat's old friends thought he was putting on the ritz, but he had simply found a new way of life, because of commercial success. He was living up to that image and enjoying it, and I can understand that. You can't hang on to the old gang forever. He bought a house in Palm Springs, too, and became a part of the Sinatra scene and such, and eventually he was surrounded by songwriters and song pluggers. We were very different singers, but he invariably came to see me when I was in L.A. He never said anything about not being a jazz pianist any longer, but there's no question that he was very, very perceptive about music, and that he was one of the best pianists we have ever had."

Cole belonged with Earl Hines and Art Tatum and Teddy Wilson, from all of whom he learned, and if he had concentrated on playing rather than on singing he might well have outclassed them all. He was born in Montgomery, Alabama, and raised in Chicago, where Hines, a fixture at the Grand Terrace, put his mark on him. Cole worked in his brother's jump band in the mid-thirties, and got together his trio in Los Angeles in 1939, with Oscar Moore on guitar and Wesley Prince on bass. Jazz fans considered Cole's occasional agreeable vocals an excusable intrusion, but they became more and more frequent, and in 1943 his vocal version of "Straighten Up and Fly Right" was the trio's first hit. He gave up the trio in 1950, and five or six years later he was the most important popular singer in the country. Fortunately, Cole was well recorded as a pianist. He made a hundred and fifty trio sides, and he sat in on recording sessions with Buddy Rich, Lester Young, Charlie Shavers, Lionel Hampton, Coleman Hawkins. Cole's style was based on stunning single-note melodic lines. Their inventiveness and freshness beat Wilson's chaste phrasing and undercut Tatum's fat. Cole was slick in the best way: his effortlessness hid content. (It also hid the fact that by the early fifties, when he made his last piano records, he had easily absorbed the prophecies of Charlie Parker and had become as *modern* a pianist as we then had.) He swung no matter what the tempo, and there was a you've-never-heard-*this*-before newness about every solo. Twenty-two radio transcriptions by the trio have

been brought out as "Nat King Cole: Early 1940's" on the
Mark 56 label. Fourteen have vocals and brief Cole solos, but
eight are instrumentals, and they have some jumping moments. Note how Cole states the melody of "Indiana," using
empty space and a back-porch legato approach, and then how
he snaps into his improvised chorus. He does the same on "I
May Be Wrong," and on the very fast "After You've Gone"
he shows off his technique. There are two Basie numbers—
"Lester Leaps In" and "Miss Thing"—that don't quite jell,
but "I Can't Give You Anything But Love" is a wonder. Its
lazybones melodic statement is followed by a passage where
he drops in a couple of triplets and a dancing double-time
figure. The gap Cole left when he pulled out of jazz has never
closed.

February 14th

Originality is a benevolent dislocator. It forces us outside ourselves, and it makes us work. It rearranges the past, alters the
future, and agitates the present. The thirty-three numbers
that Louis Armstrong recorded for RCA on its Bluebird label
between December, 1932, and April, 1933, must have performed such services for those lucky enough to buy them
when they first came out. They have at last been reissued by
RCA in one place, on "Young Louis Armstrong." Armstrong
had been preparing for a decade. He completed his tutelage
with King Oliver in 1924, and spent most of 1925 with the
Fletcher Henderson band, which he converted from a dance
band into a jazz band. He thereupon made a lot of records on
his own, and became one of the first unmistakable jazz improvisers. By 1931, he had given up the New Orleans small-
band framework for ready-made big bands, he was recording
pop music, and he had begun investigating the high register
of his instrument—an area that was still largely closed to
trumpet players. He took his first European trip in 1932 and

was ecstatically received; in 1933 he went back and stayed a year and a half. But in between he made seven marathon trips into Victor's recording studios. On January 26th and 27th alone, he set down nine numbers, and on April 24th and 26th he set down eleven more. He did not record again at any length until the end of 1935, when he went with Decca records. There was nothing prepossessing about the furnishings of the Bluebird records. The tunes were a polyglot that included Armstrong novelties, a pair of Harold Arlens ("I've Got the World on a String," "I Gotta Right To Sing the Blues"), an early Hoagy Carmichael ("Snow Ball"), a Fats Waller ("I Hate To Leave You Now"), a couple of Reginald Forsythes, and "St. Louis Blues," "Sweet Sue," "Dinah," "Nobody's Sweetheart," and "High Society." The bands behind Armstrong were led by Chick Webb and the trumpeters Charlie Gaines and Zilner Randolph, and the gummy arrangements were of their time. There were some good sidemen, among them Teddy Wilson and Budd Johnson and his brother Keg, and they occasionally surface. But all this is painted scenery for Armstrong, who dominates every record with his singing, clowning, and playing. It is impossible to know now what suddenly possessed him on these records. Perhaps it was the impetus of the European trip, perhaps it was his baby stardom, perhaps it was sheer thirty-two-year-old bravado. Max Jones and John Chilton say in their book "Louis":

> In 1932, all the physical parts of his technique were in miraculous working order. He was the possessor of lung-power and throat, jaw, teeth and lip formation which seemed to be ideally suited to the production of trumpet tone. With these natural attributes went a control of the instrument giving him ease of performance in every department of the art. His mastery was matched by superior stamina, also by an artistic adaptability which was to be thor-

oughly tested on his first British tour. As a jazz
player he had it all.

Both his singing and trumpet playing have a quality they
had not had before and would not have again. His voice was
capable of great flexibility and daring, as in his double-time
passages in "When It's Sleepy Time Down South" and the
blue notes in "Hobo You Can't Ride This Train" and "I'll Be
Glad When You're Dead, You Rascal You." (These must
have been among the Armstrong vocals that Billie Holiday
grew up on.) His phrasing was adventurous and his rhythmic sense impeccable: he could put the beat anywhere he
wanted. He swung even when he breathed. He had perfect
intonation, and his scatted breaks were model improvisational
bursts. Armstrong's trumpet playing on the Bluebirds is su-
pernal. He wheels around in the high register like a gull, he
uses sorrowing middle-register blue notes no other trumpeter
has matched, he performs incredible rhythmic tricks, he
plays with an exalted lyricism. He is majestic and simple and
elegant. He invents a generation of trumpeters.
    The RCA reissue is not perfect. Armstrong grandstands,
albeit spectacularly, on "St. Louis Blues," "Sittin' in the
Dark," and "High Society," and not much happens on such
numbers as "Honey Don't You Love Me Anymore" and "Tomorrow Night." But "Basin Street Blues" and "That's My
Home" (two takes) and "I Hate To Leave You Now" (also
two takes) and "I've Got the World on a String" and "I Gotta
Right To Sing the Blues" are remarkable. And "Laughin'
Louie" is a wonder. After a lot of preliminary horsing around,
Armstrong suddenly plays a cappella a melody he remembered from his childhood, and, in its stark, effortless way, it
is one of the most beautiful happenings in jazz.

February 18th

Grass will never grow on Anthony Braxton. Tonight, the clarinettist, saxophonist, and elaborate, revolving composer-arranger appeared in a concert at Town Hall in the new ingenuously egoistic mode: by himself. He came on after an hour and five minutes by the Revolutionary Ensemble, which was in a fragmented, doubling mood, and he blew six nameless alto-saxophone "numbers," each differentiated from the last only by texture, dynamics, and levels of intensity. One febrile number was based on two notes, short and long. Another had a gliding melody knotted with staccato dissonances. Still another was sub-toned. Braxton toyed with breath, exuding notes that remained zephyrs or that crystallized briefly before becoming breath again. It was an intense piece, and suggested a man trying to move a piano silently through a sleeping house. The last number started as a formal exercise full of trills and high, bowing notes and turned into a parade of squeaks, quacks, grindings, clicks, grunts, and shrieks. Here and there, Braxton sounded exactly like Benny Carter. He displayed the same thoroughbred tone, the same slightly stiff rhythmic approach, the same high-collared intensity, but he did it without any of the conventional musical devices (keys, harmony, time).

Braxton has been turning out albums, too. The most recent are "Anthony Braxton: Duets 1976 with Muhal Richard Abrams" and "Anthony Braxton: Creative Orchestra Music 1976" (Arista). The duets are lyrical, spiky, conventional, disturbing, and funny. "Miss Ann," by Eric Dolphy, "Nickie," by Braxton and Abrams, and Scott Joplin's "Maple Leaf Rag" are nearly straight readings, with Braxton playing the melody on clarinet and alto saxophone and Abrams pumping chords. But

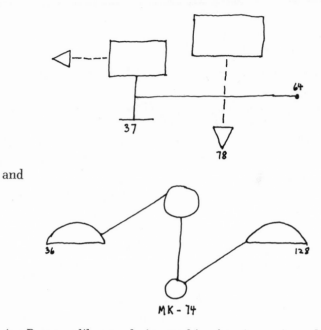

and

(as Braxton likes to designate his pieces) are jagged exercises, full of Cecil Taylor musings by Abrams, Braxton's Benny Goodman-toned clarinet, and carpenter noises.

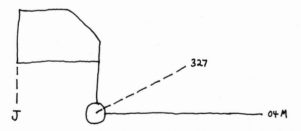

is taken up for the most part with a single note repeated five times: one one one one-one. Braxton plays the figure on his contrabass saxophone, which has a palatial bottom range that he barely taps, and Abrams is in unison. Braxton improvises while Abrams continues the figure. Abrams solos, using long melodic lines that keep running off the edge of his solo, and

Braxton huffs in the cellar. Little bits of melody appended at either end of the piece offer some relief, but the rest of it recalls the boogie-woogie "train" pieces minus their lyricism.

There are six numbers in the "Creature Orchestra" album, all titled with Braxton's geometric devices, and they are done by slightly different big bands, which include such avant-gardists as Dave Holland, Kenny Wheeler, George Lewis, Roscoe Mitchell, Leo Smith, Abrams, and Warren Smith as well as such older-styled men as Seldon Powell, Cecil Bridgewater, Jack Jeffers, and Jon Faddis. Fletcher Henderson's concept of the big band as an augmented New Orleans ensemble of trumpet-clarinet-trombone-rhythm playing syncopated riffs and antiphonal passages broken by short solos lingers on, but Braxton is doing some serious tinkering. (So is the tenor saxophonist Sam Rivers, who likes ensembles in which the sections war harmonically while sliding back and forth in overlapping layers, and likes double—or simultaneous—improvisation, an attractive practice that has frightened improvisational egos for decades.) On the second track of the first side, Braxton breaks the band up and sends it wandering, but we always know pretty much where everyone is from the periodic gongs, bass pluckings, bells, cymbals, mosquito sounds, synthesizers, and wind sounds. On the last track of the same side, the band plays a medium-tempo march that goes awry about a third through. The rhythm disintegrates, the key center slides away, a piccolo trumpet solos, and ostinato figures chase each other. There is a stop-time section; then a clarinet and an alto saxophone improvise together and are followed by a trombone that sounds like Kid Ory. The clarinet reappears against a background riff, and the piece shifts back into a straight march, with Faddis soloing above the ensemble. The best effort on the second side of the album was apparently inspired by Duke Ellington. It is latter-day Ellington seen in a distorting glass. The sections are quavery and discordant, and the rhythmic emphases stagger. A contrabass-saxophone solo pitted against an ostinato piano figure echoes, however surrealistically, Harry Carney's and Ellington's duet on "La Plus Belle Africaine," and a good rangy Kenny Wheeler trumpet solo soars appropriately over Braxton's kindly, lumbering Ellington devices. Good parody is an exercise in waspishness. But it is also a way of saying goodbye with affection and humor.

March 1st

Two superior pianists grew in Art Tatum's garden in the late forties. They were the Canadian Oscar Peterson and the Englishman George Shearing. Peterson developed a technique, which eventually became his very style, just as Buddy Rich's had become his. Peterson exploded into his solos from his opening melodic choruses. The "virtuoso" sign flashed incessantly, and it hid the fact that the chief content of his solos was packed into their first eight or ten bars; what came after was largely ornamentation and hyperbole. Shearing took a subtler course. He put together a succession of exceptionally smooth quintets, made up of vibraphone, guitar, bass, and drums, and he continually stepped back for his sidemen or melted into the creamy ensembles. After a time, one listened to the quintet rather than to Shearing, compelling though his bits of icing were. Peterson, framed only by his various loose trios, swelled, while Shearing, embedded in a suave collective of first-class musicians, receded.

Shearing, who is at the Café Carlyle with the bassist Victor Gaskin, was born blind, and he has developed agile defenses. Among them is a sense of humor that includes practical jokes, nonsense, and puns. He explained tonight at the Café that Bach, of whom he is exceedingly fond, had twenty children, and Mrs. Bach, in order to circumvent having so many children home from school for lunch, had invented the "Bach lunch." Later, he announced that he had grown tired of song

titles with the word "love" in them, and had taken to mentally substituting the word "lunch," which resulted in such
pleasant turns as "Lunch Walked In," "Feel Like Making
Lunch," and "Lunch Is Everywhere." He is a tough, delicate,
intelligent man, and during the silent minute when he sizes
up his audience from the piano just before his first set one
can almost hear his senses moving through the room. Such a
man would not be apt to lay his piano playing on. Indeed, his
style, quintet or not, is elusive. He came to attention in the
mid-forties, when no fewer than five pianists held the stage—
Art Tatum, Teddy Wilson, Nat Cole, Erroll Garner, and Bud
Powell—and he is forever tipping his hat to them, whether
in a clump of Garner chords, a sixteen-bar Nat Cole melodic
line, or a Tatum arpeggio complete with at least two keyboard sweeps. Shearing has a rich, harmonic sense, and his
single-note melodic lines are crisp and exhilarating. His
touch is feathery, bright, gentle. And he has one possibly
unique quality. Jazz improvisers tend to re-create their materials in their own image. A classic example is Coleman
Hawkins's 1939 record of "Body and Soul." Before Hawkins,
it was simply a torch song left over from 1930. But Hawkins
filled it with his special urgency and eloquence. He blew the
song tight, and one can no longer hear it without also hearing Hawkins's version in the background. Shearing, his improvisations notwithstanding, finishes what a song's composer set out to do. Tonight, he played John Lewis's "Django"
so that its stubborn, complex melodic structure took on—for
the first time in memory—a melancholy, lullaby quality.
He made "Django" an evening meditation on the great guitarist. He did the same thing for Garner's "Misty." It became a cheerful ballad, and three-dimensional Garner—not
a parody but a distillation. One was surprised to look up midway and discover not Garner but Shearing, with his big,
swinging face, his dark glasses collecting the light, his chin
plunging down-right, down-right, down-right.

March 6th

No two singers are more unalike than Bobby Short and Mabel Mercer. Short's origins are in jazz—in the singing of Ethel Waters and Ivie Anderson, and in the music of Duke Ellington. But he has also listened to Hildegarde and Billie Holiday and Stella Brooks and Mildred Bailey and Mabel Mercer. His light baritone has grown in resonance in the past six or seven years, and he has become a complex and sometimes overly forceful singer. He has developed an affecting lyricism. His rhythmic techniques have set. He never chooses a poor tempo, and his ad-libbing and time are flawless. Short's singing was once rather flossy, but it now has a smooth, carved permanence, no matter how often he dips his head, flicks a high C on the piano to punctuate a verse, or arches an eyebrow. Mabel Mercer, who is seventy-seven, transcends mere singing. She sits in her chair, folds her hands in her lap, lifts her chin, smiles, and unfurls her songs. She is regal, wry, homey, and bemused. Each song is a watercolor: the paints are soft and light, the colors flow, the textures are edgeless. Her origins are motley and somewhat mysterious. She began as a dancer in English vaudeville, had some formal training as a singer, and by the thirties was working in the Paris boîtes, where she came in contact with Cole Porter and Django Reinhardt and Bricktop. Somehow, she learned to phrase a thirty-two-bar song better than anyone, and she has radiated that knowledge for forty years. But ten years ago the cabaret business slumped, and the results were disastrous for Mabel Mercer. She lost her confidence, and her voice suddenly rusted through. She could no longer sustain notes, and she resorted to parlando. Then, somewhere around the celebration for her seventy-fifth, her voice returned. Now she can hold notes, bend them, and move them, and when a lyric seizes her she can belt it for a bar. She did tonight in Carnegie Hall, where she and Short—he was accompanied by Beverly Peer on bass and Gene Gammage on drums, and she by Jimmy Lyon on piano—gave their first joint concert in eight years.

It took Short four or five of his seventeen songs to settle down. He did a cheerful "Paradise," which Rudy Vallee used to moan; George Gershwin's "Innocent Ingenue Baby"; and a triumphant "I Can't Get Started," using its rarely sung verses. Mabel Mercer appeared in a homemade lime-green gown, and kept a gold brocade shawl about her while she sang. And how she sang! Song after resplendent song, each easy, lucid, and exact. She sang for nearly an hour and a half, and she sang well over twenty songs, until she finally came apart. It was an indelible demonstration, both of sustained singing and of her musical tastes, which have steered her to the best songs of her time. Some of them tonight included Joe Raposo's "Bein' Green," Bart Howard's "Walk-Up," Cole Porter's "Where, Oh Where," Kurt Weill's "Little Grey House," Noël Coward's "Chase Me, Charlie," Loonis McGlohon's "Grow Tall, My Son," Jobim's "Someone to Light Up My Life," and Stephen Sondheim's "Send In the Clowns," which she converts into a rueful one-act play. Mabel Mercer summed herself up tonight, and in doing so told us as much as we need to know about life to get gracefully by.

March 16th

Marian McPartland gave her old friend and former husband Jimmy McPartland a surprise seventieth-birthday party at the Café Carlyle a few days ago. McPartland put the gathering in focus when he and Marian cut his birthday cake and he said, "I suggest that all married people get divorced and begin treating each other like human beings," which is exactly what the McPartlands did seven years ago. He lives on the south shore of Long Island in a salt-box full of cats, and she lives a few miles away, in a red brick house. They talk on the telephone every day and see each other a couple of times a week. They discuss problems neither would discuss with anyone else. McPartland does errands for Marian, and she sometimes borrows his car. They go to the beach, and they play gigs together. "Unfortunately, these tributes are almost always paid posthumously," Marian said before the party. "So why not do it properly this time—when the old man is alive and can enjoy it?"

The old man, who actually became seventy the day after the party, is not only alive but jumping. He has shed a lot of weight, and his eyes are clear and quick. His voice, always of hog-calling dimensions, is strong, and he still enters rooms at about sixty miles an hour. When he talks, he rocks from side to side, like a boxer, which he was, and he frequently punctuates what he says by biffing the air with a good one-two. He likes to stir things up, whatever way. His Scottish face, with its long nose and broad forehead, is handsome and firm, and his gray hair has its Scottish curl. The party was scheduled for eight, and McPartland drove Marian in from the Island an hour before. He was wearing his uniform: a blue blazer, a blue-and-white striped shirt, a four-in-hand foulard tie, and trousers of a dark-green-and-red tartan. Marian had told him only that they would be playing a private party in the Café. When they arrived, she deposited him in the cubicle that the Carlyle lets her use as a dressing room, and told him to wait there until she called. He had his horn and two thermoses, one of hot tea and one of hot coffee. He carries them in a black bag everywhere he goes. They are his comfort and his crutch, for after struggling with alcohol much of his life he stopped drinking nine years ago. He has discovered that he plays better, feels better, thinks better, and looks better. "The drinking was just kidding myself," he said in Marian's dressing room. "It didn't help a thing, it only aggravated it. I started going to A.A. in 1947, and I've slipped six times, the last nine years ago. I've learned to be completely honest with myself." McPartland was sitting in a corner of the room, which was furnished with a clothespress, a bureau, two chairs, and a telephone. A thermos top of tea was by his right foot, and he had his cornet in his right hand. He likes to talk, and between conversational bursts he worked on his embouchure. Five years ago, when a front tooth began mysteriously receding, he started moving his embouchure slightly to his right, and he is still getting used to the change. He placed the mouthpiece slowly and precisely, as if he were affixing a stamp to a document, and blew: *"pew pew pew."* He took a breath, recemented the horn, and blew again. "You have to work on your embouchure every day," he said. "You blow five or ten minutes, and have a cup of tea, than you blow five or ten minutes more, and have another cup of tea. Keeping your chops in shape is an athletic business. It's like being a ballet dancer. You lay off one day, it's bad. Two days, it's worse. Three days, forget it. These muscles"—he pointed to the muscles on either side of his mouth—"give out, and everything goes blah. It's distressing. But when my chops are in shape and I'm playing with four, five, six musicians who have empathy, it's like a fine conversation. We're listening to each other, and we're talking in between, and it's no place for a loner. This perfection doesn't happen often, but it's a lovely and gratifying experience. Whatever emotions you have that day go right to the edge, and then come out. You forget about yourself, because you're too busy treating the other musicians like gentlemen and artists, which they are. Before I improvise, I just listen, and that triggers me. I don't see anything, and nothing goes through my mind except the melody, which I keep way at the back."

McPartland has been improvising professionally since 1923, the year before he replaced Bix Beiderbecke in the Wolverines. Alec Wilder has said: "There is a treasure there behind

the banner of age and the assumption he is too old to do anything different from what he did with the Wolverines. All
kinds of lovely sounds come out when he is relaxed and playing with non-Dixieland musicians. I heard it when he played
with Marian and Bertoncini. I didn't see any relationship to
Bix. It was simply the sound of excellent music." McPartland
at his best plays with a wild-kid lyricism, a singing, pursuing
quality, as if jazz were a race instead of a form of meditation. His playing rounds its shoulders and runs. It suggests
an admiration for the Louis Armstrong of the early thirties,
and it suggests Beiderbecke's tone and bemused legato attack.
When McPartland met Beiderbecke, who was his idol, Beiderbecke produced a nicely shaded mot, which McPartland has
probably repeated a thousand times. "I like you, kid," Beiderbecke said. "You sound like me, but you don't copy me."
Beiderbecke, his feet already on Olympus, was twenty-one
and McPartland seventeen. The school of playing that Beiderbecke unwittingly founded—Bobby Hackett, Red Nichols,
Rex Stewart, and McPartland are its best-known graduates—
has unswerving characteristics: a beautiful tone, a fondness
for big intervals and small, curling connective runs, a
straightforward rhythmic attack, a holding up of handsome
melodic mirrors. It is an attractive way of playing the cornet,
but it has been dismissed as a minor strain of jazz brass playing. Armstrong has long been regarded as king, but the truth
is that Armstrong and Beiderbecke each thought the other a
nonpareil in their day and they played together every chance
they got.

McPartland made several "*pew*"s, and poured himself another cup of tea. Marian called to say that it would be half an
hour before they were ready. They had to move the piano,
she said. "Move the piano, my eye," McPartland boomed.
"I think she has something in mind down there, but I don't
want to ruin her fun. Anyway, it takes me a while to get my
chops ready. It's not like the old days, when you just picked

up your horn and—bam!—you were ready to blow, which is
what we were crazy to do. When I was thirteen or fourteen,
we moved to Austin, on the west side of Chicago, and after I
graduated from the John Hay grammar school, I went to
Austin High, where I met Bud Freeman and Frank Teschemacher and Jim Lanigan. We all played the violin, the way
kids play the guitar now, and we hung out after school in the
Spoon and Straw, where there was a table covered with records that you could play on a windup. There were Paul
Whitemans and Rudy Wiedoefts, but one day a new record,
by the New Orleans Rhythm Kings, appeared, and we went
nuts. Lanigan took up the bass and Teschemacher the clarinet and Freeman the C-melody saxophone and me, the loud-
mouth, the cornet, and we also had my brother Rich on guitar, Dave North on piano, and a kid from Oak Park High
named Dave Tough on drums. We'd get together and play
the New Orleans Rhythm Kings' records and the Creole Jazz
Band and Bix and the Wolverines, and we'd play them two
bars at a time and try to memorize them. Not their solos—
no, sir. Everybody had to do his own solos. When we got
good enough, we played anywhere for anybody, and we got
to be known as the Austin High gang. I was apt and got better faster, I guess. When I was sixteen and in my second
year of high, I worked for a boxer named Eddie Tancil, who
had a saloon near Hawthorne, the race track. It was six
nights a week, and fifty-five dollars. The trombone player
Joe Quartell told the leader he'd heard a kid clarinet player
who was sensational. I had just gone into bell-bottoms, but
when this kid showed up he was still in shorts. He played
'Rose of the Rio Grande,' and I was flabbergasted at the way
he got around the instrument. His name was Benny Goodman, and we started running together. That New Year's Eve,
Vic Moore, who'd just left the Wolverines, heard me and
said, 'Christ, you sound just like Bix.' Then Dick Voynow, of
the Wolverines, sent a wire asking me to join the band at the

Cinderella Ballroom, in New York. Bix had been hired by
Jean Goldkette, and they wanted me. The telegram offered
eighty-seven-fifty a week, but I thought it was all a gag. I
wired back for transportation money, to see what would happen, and they sent thirty-five dollars. Everybody saw me off
at the La Salle Street station in Chicago. It took me three
days to get to New York, via Buffalo, because I'd taken some
sort of milk train. I met Bix after my first rehearsal. He'd
been sitting there the whole time and I hadn't recognized
him. Voynow put me in a double room at the Somerset with
Bix, and we stayed together eight days while he showed me
the fine points.

"The bouncer at the Cinderella was Frankie Fleming, and
I got to know him by knocking a guy cold who pulled a knife
on him. Fleming found out I was a boxer—my father had
taught me—and he took me to Philadelphia Jack O'Brien's
gym and had me work out, and he was all ready to book me.
I asked Voynow what he thought, and he told me that I must
be crazy even to think about it, that I'd have to be one or the
other—a cornet player needs all his teeth and a boxer doesn't.
When the Wolverines got back to Chicago, we went to work
at Barone's. I brought Jim Lanigan and Freeman and Tesch
into the band, along with my brother Rich and Dave Tough,
who became one of the great drummers. He would get a beat
going that pushed you so hard you couldn't help yourself—
you could ask anybody, including Sid Catlett. Husk O'Hare
took over promotion and the band became Husk O'Hare's
Wolverines under the direction of Jimmy McPartland. I was
nineteen, and making good money and behaving myself. I
had quit high school after two years, so every chance I got at
college gigs I sat in on classes and was given books and point-
ers and every sort of kindness. We worked the White City
Ballroom, on the South Side of Chicago, and Louis would
come by all the time. He wouldn't play. He'd just sit at
the back of the bandstand and listen. After hours, we'd go to

the Nest, where Jimmie Noone was, or to the basement of the
Three Deuces, and sit in with Louis and Bix and Pee Wee
Russell and Frankie Trumbauer. Which reminds me of when
I ran into Louis in Philadelphia in the fifties, and he said, his
voice down in the coal cellar"—McPartland makes an excellent Louis Armstrong voice—" 'Hey, McPartland! I been listening to that album you made, that "Shades of Bix." Man,
you blow the hell out of that horn!' That set me up for about
a decade. One morning, back in Chicago, Bix and I left the
Nest, and three tough guys were standing in front of a bar-
bershop, and one of them tried to grab my horn. I set it down
and—bang!—he was gone. And then—bang!—the second
guy was gone. Bix took care of the third. He could really
hit. He was a hell of a tennis player and a good ballplayer,
but you never would have known, because he didn't talk
about it. In fact, he didn't talk much at all unless he was
around musicians."

McPartland stood up and stretched. "Where's Marian?" he
said. "They must be moving that piano around the block."
He sat down and picked up his horn and released three heavy
"*pew*"s. "Everybody worked for the mob in Chicago. Al Ca-
pone used to come into one place where I was, and he always
asked for 'My Gal Sal.' Then he'd send one of his torpedoes
over with a fifty or a hundred. One night, one of 'em shot a
hole in Jim Lanigan's bass and then asked me how much a
new one would cost. I knew Lanigan had paid two hundred,
so I said eight hundred and fifty. He gave it to me on the
spot, and I passed Lanigan three hundred and fifty and kept
the rest. I left the Wolverines before they broke up, and went
with Art Kassel and then with Ben Pollack, who got a gig at
the Little Club, in New York. Bix was in town with Paul
Whiteman, and we lived together for a while at the Forty-
fourth Street Hotel. Bix had reached the point where he had
to take a slug of Gordon's gin before he answered the phone
in the morning. Later, when the Little Club job blew up, I

didn't eat for three days. I ran into Bix at a Park Avenue
party where they had plenty to drink but no food, and asked
him for a loan. All I needed was ten or twenty dollars, but
he gave me five fifties. 'Take it, kid'—which is what he always called me, never my name—'and pay me back when
you're working.' Pollack landed a job at the Park Central Hotel, where Arnold Rothstein was killed, and we doubled for a
while in Lew Fields's 'Hello Daddy,' and made records every
other day. Benny Goodman and Jack Teagarden and Glenn
Miller were in the band, and after work we went uptown and
sat in with Fletcher Henderson and Duke Ellington and
Willie the Lion. But we took care of ourselves, or at least
Benny and I did. Benny was very athletic, and he and I
sometimes played handball before work, which was fine until Pollack got tired of me coming to the bandstand with dirty
shoes and fired me. When that happened, Goodman told Pollack he'd quit, too, and he did. About this time, I married
Dorothy Williams, of the Williams sisters, and Roger Wolfe
Kahn, who had a fine band, married Hannah, her sister.
Neither marriage lasted very long, but Dorothy and I had
a daughter, and on nice afternoons Jimmy Dorsey and I
wheeled our babies down through Central Park to Plunketts,
a speak at Fifty-third and Seventh where musicians hung
out. Plunketts was the last place I saw Bix. It was the summer of 1931, and he had a terrible cold. I had long since paid
him back, and he asked me if I could help him out. I gave
him what I had—about a hundred and fifty dollars. He died
three days later, of pneumonia, out in Queens, and everybody
at Plunketts cried. I was with Russ Columbo and Smith
Ballew and Horace Heidt after Pollack, and I spent most of
the thirties in Chicago with my brother's group and with my
own bands. In 1939, I worked at Nick's with Pee Wee Russell and Georg Brunis, and then I joined Jack Teagarden's big
band and stayed until the war."

The phone rang, and Marian told McPartland to come

down in ten minutes. He leaned his chair against the wall
and fired off half a dozen well-spaced "*pew*"s, each delivered
as if he were pushing a pig across a pen. "Some musicians
tried to duck the war, but I was a patriotic drunk and enlisted
in the Army, and ended up in automatic weapons. I had my
cornet, and on the troopship to Scotland I formed a band. But
I was still a corporal down in the hold. Then the third mate,
who'd heard me at Nick's, wangled it so that I could move
into his cabin for the rest of the trip. That cabin was full of
whiskey, and I stayed drunk until we went over the side and
into the tender in the harbor at Greenock. I was standing on
the deck, and suddenly I remembered 'The Blue Bell of Scotland,' so I took out my horn and played it. It was early morning and as still as church and you could hear for miles. The
townspeople and the bagpipers were lined up on the dock,
and I played it real pretty, jazzed it up in the middle, and
went back to the melody. When we got ashore, the mayor ran
around shouting 'Where is the mon that played the trompet?
Where is the mon that played the trompet?' and when he
found out there was a lot of hugging and celebrating. We
practiced for the invasion off the coast of Wales, and I went
in on D Day-plus-4. I was in a Jeep fitted out with a fifty-
calibre machine gun. I was scared. Very scared. All I could
do, seeing everybody getting hit around me, was apply for
help Upstairs, and I got the word: Go ahead, you're trained,
you're strong. I relaxed and was all right. I went through
Saint-Lô and the Bulge and got five battle stars and was
never hit, and I've never been scared of death since. But,
man, I got tired of thinking about it, and finally they transferred me to Special Services. I met Marian playing in a tent
in the Ardennes. She rushed the tempo, this English girl
playing jazz piano, but her harmonies killed me. She tried
to talk and act G.I., but I knew she was a lady. I courted
her for weeks, and we got married in February of 1945 in
Aachen. We played at our own wedding."

McPartland put his horn in its case, hunched into his blazer, and took the elevator down to the Carlyle lobby. When he got to the door of the Café, which is glass, he peered through into the darkness, hesitated a second, and opened the door. "Happy Birthday," played by Marian, Bob Wilber, and Vic Dickenson, hit him, his face went blank, then regrouped, and he charged over to the piano and gave Marian a kiss. McPartland made a short speech; greeted his guests (Willis Conover, Bob and Jean Bach, Gene Shalit, George Shearing, John Lewis, Teddi King, Mabel Mercer); read some telegrams, one of them from Benny Goodman, which prompted him to recall that he had taken Goodman to Marshall Field in Chicago when they were kids to help him buy some knickers, and to suggest that Goodman was probably still wearing them; and played several numbers with Lewis, Wilber, and Dickenson. Then he sat down at a table in a corner and ordered some tea. "My mother taught me 'The Blue Bell of Scotland,' " he said. "Her name was Jeannie Munn, and she came from Paisley, near Glasgow. She had sharp features and was very pretty. She always wanted me to be a little gentleman. She had been a schoolteacher, and had seven sisters, one of whom, Aunt Bell, is still alive and is a peach. Her father's name was Dugald, which accounts for my name—James Dugald McPartland. Old Dugald was a tool-and-die maker and an inventor. I remember a patent-infringement case he won. He also was a thirty-second-degree Mason. Every Sunday, he would read the Bible to me, and his burr was so thick I couldn't understand a word. But he paid me fifteen cents, and afterward I'd shoot craps under the 'L' at Lake and Paulina, which was a tough neighborhood. My father was born in Burlington, Iowa, and he met my mother in Chicago, where they were married. He was big and husky and looked like me. He could do anything, including drink, which he didn't start doing until he was twenty-one and didn't stop doing until he was dead. He was a boxer and a baseball player and a musician. He played third base with Anson's Colts, who became the Chicago Cubs. He started me on violin when I was six and boxing a year or so later—by the time I was twelve or thirteen, I was in the club fights, which were like the Golden Gloves now, and I never lost. But when I was seven, my mother and father separated, and my brother Rich and I were put in an orphanage—the Maywood Baptist Orphanage. Ruth and Ethel, my two sisters, and both older, went with an aunt. Rich got sick and went to stay with my mother, and I got in an argument with Roy McGilvey's son and knocked him through a glass door. It was snowing, but they gave me my little bundle and three cents carfare and told me to get the hell out. My mother and father were back together, so I lived with them and went to the William H. Brown grammar school, on Warren and Hermitage. It wasn't long before Rich and I were in the Hermitage gang, which had pulled a half-million-dollar train robbery. I was the leader of the younger kids. We'd draw chalk circles in the street and stand in 'em and challenge anybody and everybody to knock us out. I knew how to hit and move, and the only fight I didn't win was a draw. Then we took a forty-five automatic from the side pocket of a touring car parked outside Jimmy Murphy's Bucket of Blood, and started stealing chickens. We'd go out to isolated houses around Cicero, a lot of them with their own chicken coops, and twist the chickens' necks enough to keep them quiet, then sell them to restaurants, no questions asked. Pretty soon, I had ninety-one dollars in the bank. But one night somebody fired a shotgun at us and we fired back, and there was a headline in the local paper 'CHICKEN THIEVES ARMED.' Then Baldy, who was in the gang, got caught in a coop, and the police found the gun, and Rich and I were up for reform school. All that kept us out was my mother. She used to make extra money translating in court, mainly for immigrants, so she knew the judge we came up before. He told my mother he wouldn't send us away if she moved to a decent neighborhood. He put us on probation for a year, and we moved to Austin, and after that things began to straighten out. My Uncle Fred Harris was a big help. He was married to one of my father's sisters, and was a well-to-do lawyer. During the summers, he took Rich and me fishing in Indiana and Michigan, and even to Rifle, Colorado. He taught us how to swim, and he taught us just about everything about fishing and fish—about habitats, where fish spawn, when they are at the bottom, how they feed along the shore in the evening. He made us learn the Latin names—*Esox masquinongy* for the muskie, *Oncorhynchus kisutch* for the coho salmon, *Esox niger* for the chain pickerel. I even got good enough to work one summer as a guide at Ed Gabe's Lost Lake Resort, in Sayner, Wisconsin. Uncle Fred was a fine gent."

March 25th

Dave McKenna does not consider himself a jazz pianist. He is, he says, a pianist who loves melody and loves to play for dancing. He is tall, secret, stooped, and big-boned. His eyes are deep-set and close together, and his wide face has eagle lines. His long arms end in banana fingers. His keyboard concentration is impenetrable. He acknowledges applause by looking off to one side, and sometimes he becomes so caught up that he plays songs consecutively. He rarely leaves Cape Cod, where he has lived for ten years. His style has deepened and loosened since his first solo recording, twenty years ago. Each McKenna improvisation has a hand-printed quality. His runs are apposite, his tempos *juste*, and his harmonies never swallow the melody. His first album should have made more of a stir than it did, for it returned to the two-handed playing of Hines and the stride pianists. The bop pianists had turned the rhythmic responsibilities of the left hand over to their bassists and drummers, and allowed their left hands to wither. Mc-

Kenna ignored this fashion and championed his left hand. He uses marching tenths and clusters, jabbing offbeat single notes, ostinato basses that resemble boogie-woogie, and single-note melodic lines that rise to middle C and fall away. McKenna's left hand generates such momentum that he needs no bass or drums. He strikes his notes a fraction behind the beat in his right hand, and he emphasizes unexpected notes within each phrase. These ingeniously chosen accents set up an irresistible rhythm—a rock-pause, rock-pause, rock-pause rhythm that continually threatens to capsize the ship but never does. He breaks up these single-note phrases with strong chords and with high-strung Tatum arpeggios. McKenna swings ecstatically hard.

He certainly swung tonight at Bradley's. He got his legs under him around the fifth tune of the first set (which lasted well over an hour), and he didn't stop until he had played close to thirty numbers. He often forgot to pause between numbers, and at one point he passed through, as he often does, a sequence of songs with a common denominator— "When Day Is Done," "What a Diff'rence a Day Makes," "Day by Day," and "Day In, Day Out." Some of the other songs in the set were "Am I Blue?," "At the Jazz Band Ball," "It Might As Well Be Spring," "Masquerade," "If I Had You," "Hello, Young Lovers," "Stars Fell on Alabama," "Runnin' Wild," "Thanks a Million," "It's Wonderful," and " 'S Wonderful."

McKenna does not like recording studios. But a group of admirers prevailed on him to sit down not long ago at a grand piano in Jordan Hall at the New England Conservatory, and the results are on "By Myself" (Shiah). The echoing sound suggests that a single hanging microphone was used and that the hall was largely empty. He plays three very slow ballads ("The Shadow of Your Smile," "All My Tomorrows," "Daydream") in which his ad-lib openings, which swing, shade into quiet four-four time. There are two

fine blues—"No More Ouzo for Puzo," medium tempo, with
no fewer than four stop-time choruses, and "Take the 'A'
Train." A medium-tempo "It All Depends on You" is remarkable for the legato way McKenna states the melody in
the first chorus. And he tips his hat to Tatum on "Kerry
Dances" with a streaming stride passage and a couple of fifty-
foot arpeggios.

April 17th

The Hines tradition, in the person of Mary Lou Williams,
and the avant-garde, in the person of Cecil Taylor, collided
in Carnegie Hall tonight, and it was no contest. That the two
pianists agreed to play together at all was startling. It was
Wyeth versus Picasso, James Gould Cozzens versus Nathalie
Sarraute, John Henry Belter versus Charles Eames. Mary
Lou Williams explained in a program note how this came to
pass:

> I was booked to England . . . in 1969. During
> that time I went to Ronny Scott's in London and
> heard Cecil Taylor play. I asked Andrew Cyrille,
> Cecil's drummer . . . to introduce me to Cecil.
> This, of course, he did. I felt great warmth from
> him. . . . Later when I was working in the Cookery
> in New York, Cecil came to hear me practically
> every night. To my surprise he mentioned the in-
> spiration I gave him to create. One night I said to
> him "let's do a concert together" and he agreed.
> And he gave me the beautiful title "Embraced."

The reports during the weeks before the concert declared
that the two were rehearsing together and that all was har-
monious. Mary Lou Williams is sixty-six and has been playing professionally for fifty years. She has displayed a hard,
modern single-note attack since the forties, when she had
considerable mother-hen influence on the young beboppers.

She has not changed, except that she can, when she's of a mind, play rather far out, demonstrating advanced harmonies and almost atonal single-note lines. Cecil Taylor is forty-four, and his career is twenty years old. But he is an omnipotent, unwavering one-man avant-garde, whose style engulfs. His arpeggios are made not of single notes but of chords played consecutively in both hands. He plays at staggering speeds and with an opaque intensity. His selections may last more than an hour, yet he never falters. He is more overweening than Tatum. I do not know whether Taylor can still play as he did when he started out. He grew up in an Ellington-oriented household and reportedly once resembled Erroll Garner and Thelonious Monk; occasionally one catches glimpses of them in his playing. If he were to look back and Mary Lou Williams were to look forward they might meet.

Here is the concert: The two pianists come onstage at the same time. She is in an elegant navy-blue gown, and he is in white—a white watch cap, a white shirt, and white pants. He also wears dark glasses. They sit down facing one another at grand pianos whose snouts dovetail at center stage. He plays a low left-hand figure at once, and works his way quietly up the keyboard. She follows him with her left hand. He fashions light, sharp chords in the right hand, she returns to the bass, and the two voices back and fill nicely. Anticipation sharpens. He indulges in some mock stride in the left hand. A passage of offbeat chords follows from both. She offers blues figures in her right hand while he clumps up and down the keyboard. The volume rises, and he bends lower and lower. They keep glancing up at one another. Suddenly he explodes, loosing one of his descending chordal arpeggios—his hands blurred humps. She looks startled and drops her hands, and he fires another arpeggio, and pauses. She plays a tentative, lyrical single-note passage in her right hand. He grows more strident. She again takes her hands from the keyboard, then unreels a batch of tremolos, a gentle riff that lasts for a chorus, some flatted notes, and four bars of stride. She falls quiet and he erupts. The bassist Bob Cranshaw and the drummer Mickey Roker unexpectedly appear, looking as if they had the wrong address. They move between free time and a regular beat, but they seem to have come to her aid, and, emboldened, she throws more blues figures at the feet of some ascending Taylor chords, and the two arrive at a coda, which he plays. The intermission lasts almost half an hour. The first twenty minutes after their return are civilized. Taylor softly states an eight-note theme, Mary Lou Williams plays soft counterfigures, and a spell circles down. He moves through pools of Debussy and Ravel, and she adds quiet, affirming chords. But it does not last. Taylor's chords thicken and his arpeggios quicken. She seems to lose heart and looks as if she were sitting by the wayside watching a noisy parade. Taylor dominates the next forty minutes. He lays out just once, but when he returns Cranshaw and Roker do, too, and the music comes to a circus climax. Taylor leaves the stage immediately—not to return—and Mary Lou Williams plays a couple of numbers with the rhythm section. Her playing is certain and inventive, and the house digs in ravenously.

April 24th

Albert Murray—novelist, sociologist, polemicist—is a subtle and original thinker on black matters who, as he demonstrated in "South to a Very Old Place," abhors black cant as much as, or possibly more than, white cant. He has a good ear for black dialects, and he is a skilled writer. But his new book, *Stomping the Blues* (McGraw-Hill), is almost unreadable. It is several books: an appreciation, strenuously inflated to a celebration, of jazz (particularly of the blues and of music played for dancing, or what Murray calls the "Saturday Night Function"); an arch apologia for the music which would have had heft thirty years ago; and an argument that the blues and jazz belong wholly to the black man. Murray's language betrays him: "But blues performances are based on a mastery of a very specific technology of stylization by one means or another nonetheless. And besides, effective make-believe is the whole point of all the aesthetic technique and all the rehearsals from the outset. Nor does the authenticity of any performance of blues music depend upon the musician being true to his own private feelings. It depends upon his idiomatic ease and consistency." If a musician is not true to his own feelings, that is immediately apparent. If he does not feel what he is playing, he is pretending, and what he is playing is not authentic. Performing the blues with "idiomatic ease and consistency" produces imitation blues. Jazz has stood easily on its own for a couple of decades. It has become the American classical music and needs no apologists. Nor can it be regarded any longer as a black music. Listen to the guitarist Jim Hall: "I've always felt that the music started out as black but that it's as much mine now as anyone else's. I haven't stolen the music from anybody—I just bring something different to it." And consider the admissions in recent years by such black musicians as Lester Young and Rex Stewart and Duke Ellington and Anthony Braxton of the effect that white musicians have had on their work. The opening section of the book is a facetious disquisition on the blues: what they are and how they can be at least temporarily forestalled by listening to blues music. But when blues music—especially the Kansas City variety that Murray reveres—performs this inestimable service, what *are* the emotions it releases? What *are* those mysterious, bittersweet wellings-up that no other music evokes? Murray doesn't say.

May 9th

Adam Makowicz (pronounced Ma*k*ovitch), the highly touted thirty-six-year-old Polish pianist, opened at the Cookery tonight. He is a slight, good-looking man, with a small beard, a wide smile, and self-hypnotic pianistic concentration. Barney Josephson, the owner of the Cookery, introduced Makowicz, saying that this was the first time in all his years as an impresario that he had announced an act but that he could not help himself, since he found the pianist so moving. John Hammond, who helped bring Makowicz over, reacted with such ecstasy that each note appeared to be a personal gift. The applause brimmed and spilled over time and again, and one was reminded of the Parisian ladies who used to secrete Liszt's discarded cigar butts in their bodices. Makowicz has a dazzling technique and an unembarrassed passion for Art Tatum. His passion, though, is very nearly parodic, for he has mastered all Tatum's mannerisms—the encircling arpeggios, the bursts of stride, the plethora of notes—and he uses them fulsomely. Each number swirls and races and plunges, and each is a baroque performance that sounds much like the preceding selection. But he lacks Tatum's touch and shocking harmonic sense. Instead of improvising on his materials (a mixture of old-fashioned standards and his own quirky compositions), he endlessly philosophizes on Tatum. Perhaps the reaction to Makowicz at the Cookery was caused by the sudden realization by those present of just how much they miss Tatum.

May 18th

The Association for the Advancement of Creative Musicians, a black musical self-help group, was organized in Chicago in 1965 by a thirty-four-year-old pianist and composer named Muhal Richard Abrams. Before long, it included the reedmen

Joseph Jarman, Roscoe Mitchell, Kalaparusha, and Anthony
Braxton, the trumpeters Lester Bowie and Leo Smith, the
drummer Steve McCall, and the violinist Leroy Jenkins. It
has continued to grow, and now numbers around a hundred
and fifty. It is at once a music school, a finishing school, and
a singular avant-garde movement. It came into being because
of racial dissatisfactions, because its founding members were
tired of the gray musical landscape of the early sixties, and
because they had no place to play or be heard in Chicago. If
no one else would listen, they would listen to each other, and
grow from mutual esteem. In due course, various groups issued from under the wing of the A.A.C.M., among them the
Art Ensemble of Chicago, the Creative Construction Company, Air, the Revolutionary Ensemble, and the countless
Anthony Braxton combinations. But the A.A.C.M., like its
spiritual ancestors of fifty years ago, has been slow to leave
Chicago, and it did not venture to New York until 1970,
when the Creative Construction Company gave a concert in
a Greenwich Village church. Its provincialism is weakening.
The Art Ensemble has spent a couple of years in Europe, and
even appeared at the Newport Jazz Festival in 1973. The
Revolutionary Ensemble is based in New York and turns up
with reasonable frequency, as does Anthony Braxton, who
has become well known in the past couple of years and was
the first A.A.C.M. member to sign with a commercial label.
But the first real invasion of New York by the A.A.C.M. began four days ago, when WKCR, Columbia's ingenious student radio station, initiated a week-long festival of A.A.C.M.
music, which is being delivered in two parts: a ninety-hour
non-stop broadcast of over a hundred A.A.C.M. recordings,
unreleased tapes, and interviews; and four concerts, which
start tomorrow night and will continue through May 22nd,
at Wollman Auditorium, on the Columbia campus. The
broadcast, which ended today, was intelligent, thorough, and
persuasive. Every principal recording by A.A.C.M. members

was played (alphabetically and chronologically), and the music was beautiful, infuriating, savage, surrealistic, boring, and often highly original. It is primarily a "free" music, and there is a great dependence on instrumental variety. Most A.A.C.M. members play several instruments. Pocket trumpets, regular trumpets, and flugelhorns are common, as are bassoons, various tubas, and soprano saxophones, and there are percussion instruments from everywhere in the world. The recordings in the broadcast were spelled here and there by extensive interviews with A.A.C.M. figures, and here is a sampling, in paraphrase:

> The A.A.C.M. has expanded the science of options for the music.

> Keeping "the shout" in the music is what it's all about.

> The A.A.C.M. sound? If you take all the sounds of all the A.A.C.M. musicians and put them together, that's the A.A.C.M. sound, but I don't think anyone's heard that yet.

> Composition is as important as improvisation.

> We are opposed to the word jazz. Jazz means nigger music.

> In our meetings, we argue, fuss, get things straightened out orally.

> Sometimes I take eight hundred pounds of instruments with me on a gig.

> The A.A.C.M. introduces the musician to his complete self, and he joins for life.

> The A.A.C.M. doesn't consider a creative musician an entertainer; his purpose is to enlighten— himself first and then the audience.

You take new musical steps and you refresh the
public.

The broadcast revealed a determination to bring into being
a new and durable music—a hard-nosed utopian music, without racial stigmata, without clichés, and without commer-
cialism.

May 19th

The origins of the A.A.C.M.'s music are reasonably clear.
Paramount is the revolution set in motion in New York in
the sixties by Ornette Coleman, John Coltrane, Eric Dolphy,
Archie Shepp, and Cecil Taylor, and by the Jazz Composer's
Guild, which was formed a year before the A.A.C.M. (The
Guild, as far as I know, was never mentioned during the
WKCR interviews, which is odd, but perhaps it was because
of sheer Chicago hubris or because the Guild eventually became dominated by whites.) One also hears the methods and
voices of Sun Ra and bebop and hard-bop, which many of the
older A.A.C.M. members grew up with, and the receding
sounds of Ben Webster, Coleman Hawkins, Fats Waller,
James P. Johnson, Cootie Williams, and King Oliver. There
are classical influences, too—Stockhausen, Boulez, Schoen-
berg, Berg, and John Cage. Revolutions aren't hatched in
vacuums.

The first concert at Wollman began tonight with the
Ajaramu Ensemble, which consisted of two trap drummers (Thurman Barker and Ajaramu), a reedman who doubled on percussion (Wallace McMillan), a conga drummer
(Kahil-El-Zabar), a bassist (Felix Blackman), and a singing
pianist (Amina Claudine Myers, an important presence in
the A.A.C.M. firmament). Ajaramu started by himself and in
time was joined by McMillan, and then by Amina Claudine
Myers, who did some vocalise. Zabar, Barker, and Blackman
appeared, and there was a lot of reed doubling. After a half

hour—the conga drummer sailing, the trap drummers circling, Myers wailing and pounding, the reedman doubling—a sizable tumult was going. The volume fluctuated, and, just as a listener sensed the finale, someone had an afterthought and they were off again. The next group was a duo, made up of the trombonist and tubist George Lewis and the tenor and sopranino saxophonist, clarinettist, flutist, piccolo player, and bass clarinettist Douglas Ewart. Their music never stopped evolving, and frequently it sparkled. Ewart acted chiefly as a backstop off which Lewis, a tall, champing, cherub-faced twenty-two-year-old dressed in giant overalls, bounced an endless array of growls, glisses, slurs, harrumphs, cries, tremolos, roars, and whispers. Although the two musicians appeared to be reading, they played with a freshness and spontaneity that seemed improvised. The closing group was an all-star trio—a Charlie Parker/Dizzy Gillespie/Bud Powell group—that included Anthony Braxton, Leroy Jenkins, and Leo Smith, and it, too, appeared to read everything. The last of its three numbers had soft lyrical passages in which the voices talked away a summer's afternoon; agitato passages full of staccato alto saxophone and trumpet bursts; and a couple of Braxton clarinet statements, wherein he demonstrated a flawless tone and technique. But there was not enough of Jenkins's violin. The trio had a contrapuntal clarity that opened all sorts of musical rooms, some of them familiar and some only glimpsed before.

May 20th

The Third Wave Sextet (odd echoes of the Third Stream and the *nouvelle vague*) included Barker, Blackman, and Zabar as well as Ewart, the reedman Edward Wilkerson, and the pianist Adegoke Steve Colson. All are in their twenties or early thirties. Incense burned, and in the last number Zabar spent a good deal of time chanting, "Cree-a-tore, help us," pitching the first word somewhere around middle C and the next two a couple of tones lower. Aside from what appeared to be an attempt in the second number to get two complex rhythms going at once, the music was fairly safe. The last number had a regular beat, and there was a good deal of improvisation. Ewart showed again that he is a first-rate musician and a good and intense improviser, especially on tenor saxophone and bass clarinet. Kalaparusha came next. Born Maurice McIntyre, he appears to be in his forties, and he admires Charles Parker, Dexter Gordon, Sonny Rollins, and such marble-toned players as J. R. Monterose and Johnny Griffin. His first four numbers were done a cappella on alto and tenor saxophones and included a couple of standards and the bebop blues "Disorder at the Border"; then he was joined by bass and drums. Kalaparusha is a fox. His saxophone solos, which were vibratoless and bold and straightforward, were framed by interludes in which he read verses about creativity and music and life and played some purposely inept acoustic guitar. His nonsense was a relief; the A.A.C.M. music has been largely humorless. Air, the final group, had Fred Hopkins on bass, Steve McCall on drums, and Henry Threadgill on reeds and hubcaps. Hopkins was thunderously amplified, McCall's bearded face passed through hypnotic contortions, and Threadgill produced pleasing steel-drum sounds on his hubcaps. It was the freest group we have heard. There were long solos, and everything was improvised. It suggested the feckless, churning ensembles of Ornette Coleman at the Five Spot in 1960.

May 21st

The A.A.C.M. has a galactic sense of time. Its concerts begin forty to fifty minutes late, and intermissions last half an hour. The musicians wander on and off the stage in slow motion. Their solos are often Coltranean in length, and their

numbers—in order not to mistakenly lock out a soloist before
he is done—sometimes last a couple of hours. Consider the
final group tonight, a septet led by Muhal Richard Abrams.
It included Barker and McMillan and some newcomers—the
bassists Leonard Jones and Brian Smith, the baritone saxophonist Mwata Bowden, and the trumpeter Frank Gordon. It
played just one number: After a marching-band ensemble,
the horns and bassists went offstage, leaving Abrams and
Barker. Abrams played an immense solo, full of knotted
chords and florid Luckey Roberts right-hand passages. The
bassists and horns returned for an impassioned passage,
backed by Abrams banging the keys with the palms of his
hands. Abrams and the horns exited, and the drummer and
bassists went through a long seesawing conversation. Gordon
appeared, stuck a mute in his bell, and played some Miles
Davis, accompanied only by the bassists. He switched to
flugelhorn and played a blues. Then McMillan charged on,
playing his tenor at top volume, and was eventually driven
off by Bowden. The bassists and drummer appeared and reappeared, but along the way the bassists soloed and so did
the drummer, who kept leading up to and backing off from a
steady four-four barrage. Everyone assembled for an ostinato
unison figure, and the music subsided with a string of tinkles
and hums and pings. An hour and fifty minutes had elapsed.
Most A.A.C.M. members belong to the first L.P. generation,
and they think in twenty- or thirty- or forty-minute blocks.
The 78-r.p.m. generations were conditioned to three- and
five-minute limits, which forced them into improvisational
compactness.

George Lewis had preceded Abrams's septet with a champion solo performance. He hereby assumes the avant-garde-
trombone crown long worn by Roswell Rudd and the virtuoso-
trombone crowns at Albert Mangelsdorff and Bill Watrous.
Lewis gives the impression that there are two or three of him
onstage at once. He moves a lot: his right arm, or slide arm,

flaps up and down, like a duck taking off; winds of emotion shake him; he tick-tocks his head. And his attack is constantly changing. No sooner has he completed one virtuoso bit of business than he is off on the next. These included four con-secutive—almost overlapping—ascending arpeggios played in sixty-fourth notes and in different keys; a muted passage in which he seemed to play two melodic lines at once; an open-horn passage in which, after having sprayed water into his mouthpiece, he sounded like an echo chamber; another muted passage (this time using a plunger mute), in which he mum-bled gibberish through his instrument, all the while using his slide and seeming to blow out the words; and his runs and glisses and roars, done with relish and enormous humor. Lewis could easily have made the Ed Sullivan show or ap-peared with the fat lady at Ringling Brothers. But, for all his cavorting, he is a serious musician. Several times during the heaviest chuckling he sneaked in legato melodic passages and whispering blues figures that were startling and beautiful.

The opening group, led by Amina Claudine Myers, was the A.A.C.M. at its weakest. The ensemble included two dou-bling reedmen (Ewart and McMillan), two percussionists (Ajaramu and Kahil-El-Zabar), and a bassist (Leonard Jones). Their one number lasted an hour and ten minutes, and had long percussion passages, long reed solos, and some Myers singing (gospel-like) and piano playing (gospel, with bop petticoats).

May 22nd

What has come to be the A.A.C.M. repertory company (Thurman Barker, Brian Smith, Kahil-El-Zabar, Wallace McMillan, Adegoke Steve Colson) started the concert tonight as the Colson-McMillan Ensemble. It played with the earnest, youthful long-windedness that it had manifested in its earlier appearances. The numbers clocked twenty, twenty-five, and thirty-five minutes, and proved, despite the group's avant-garde patina, to be the same old hard-bop of the fifties and early sixties. It is the predecessor of the popular electronic salads of Herbie Hancock and Chick Corea and Freddie Hubbard. The A.A.C.M. brand could be equally popular, with its vocals, unison flutes, larruping timbres, and myriad percussion sections.

The festival was closed by the A.A.C.M. Orchestra, which has grown out of the experimental big band that Muhal Richard Abrams first assembled in Chicago in the early sixties. Tonight, it included eight reeds, two trumpets, two trombones, four percussionists, three bassists, three pianists, and three singers. The single number lasted an hour and a half. Everybody has been trying to figure out how to replace the old six-brass, five-reed, four-rhythm big band that wore out sometimes in the forties. Mingus has put forward contrapuntal ensembles, and this has worked with ten or twelve pieces, but he has never shown us where to go from there. Gil Evans envisions the big band as a radiant sunset, and he pins down its colors with French horns and tubas and woodwinds. The Jazz Composer's Orchestra makes large granitic sounds. Sam Rivers offers sliding sections that sometimes overlap and sometimes collide, and he uses multiple soloists. All these inventors have one thing in common: the *group* takes precedence over the materials. The A.A.C.M. big band does it the other way around. Abrams presents his band with a series of ideas—rhythmic, melodic, harmonic, humorous— which suggests the kaleidoscopic images in "Yellow Submarine": sounds keep evolving and changing shape and color. The band may resemble a small group or a giant rhythm section or an old swing band or John Philip Sousa. Some of the chameleon images we heard tonight were Amina Claudine Myers's singing backed only by Martin Alexander's trombone, and Bernard Mixon's by bassoon, clarinet, and alto saxophone; John Jackson's bursting Dizzy Gillespie trumpet improvisation spelled out over a tightly muted Frank Gordon counter-trumpet line; a dense, almost turgid reed figure played against rolling drums; George Lewis's tuba accompanied by Brian Smith on pizzicato bass and Kahil-El-Zabar on gourd. Then, after half an hour or so, the band abruptly fell silent and everyone leaned back and started talking, as if they had been told to take five. It was massed vocal counterpoint. This lasted a minute, and ended as sharply as it had begun, with an abrasive ensemble figure that melted into a conga solo. An oboist and a soprano saxophonist joined Lewis's tuba while the band rested, and a baritone saxophone, an alto saxophone, and a bassoon began an angry discourse that dissolved into two voices and two flutes in unison. The second hour was announced by a splintering ensemble figure sandwiched between piercing trumpet sounds and a galloping rhythm section. This changed into a marching-band section with goose-stepping rhythms. An Ellington dream passage—all reeds, with an alto saxophone improvising on top—filled the air, and the marching band resumed. George Lewis got his chance, accompanied by a hefty ensemble figure, and he made the best of it. He played at an outrageous volume, and he used a thousand notes, his slide arm flailing. Then the band did some reverse showing off. To prove to all the squares and doubters out there that it, too, could play that old-fashioned jazz music, it switched into a medium-tempo blues, complete with a Mixon blues vocal and straightforward solos by George Lewis, Amina Claudine Myers, and Kalaparusha, who delivered a fine, pushing tenor-saxophone solo. The band swung and rocked, and, school being out, so did the audience. Then Abrams, who was conducting, decided that the point had been made. He leaned far into his reed section and made a rapid faucet-turning motion with his right hand. The band shifted into a chaotic collective roar, and crashed into silence.

Fortunately, the four A.A.C.M. concerts were underwritten by grants: the total attendance was probably about four hundred. But such events are carried by the wind, and in due course take hold.

June 24th

A perfect G above high C, a flawless arpeggio, a fusillade of one-hundred-and-twenty-eighth-note drumbeats, a trumpet-like tuba solo—all are virtuoso achievements whose flash and wizardry we rank with tall buildings and long bridges. Consider Sarah Vaughan, who opened the sixth Newport Jazz Festival-New York at Carnegie Hall tonight with her trio (Carl Schroeder on piano, Walter Booker on bass, and Jimmy Cobb on drums). It was her fourth straight appearance at the festival, but the wonders and eccentricities of her style remain wondrous and eccentric. Like Art Tatum, she falls between jazz and formal music. Her voice, which has four octaves and equals that of many operatic sopranos, comes in unequal parts: a rich middle section, a little-girl high register, and a sometimes vulgar, echoing bottom range. She uses her voice like a horn, and is a first-rate improviser, whose long, turning phrases rival those of Milt Jackson and Ruby Braff and Lucky Thompson. When she began, thirty years ago, she was a daring singer; now she is a virtuoso player, whose songs are merely catapults. Her arabesques engulf her lyrics, which become merely suggestive, no more intelligible than moos. Her ending tonight to a fast "The Man I Love" went like this: "I'm dreaming of the maaaaaaaaaaa Iiii loooooooooowhooooooh." The keystone of her performance was an ad-lib a cappella "Summertime," which she summed up in a thousand notes; Gershwin's lullaby was in there somewhere among the eight-bar phrases, the ruined lyrics, and the dense grace notes. She also did a lot of scat singing, by herself and with Clark Terry and Dizzy Gillespie, the latter of whom arrived onstage, unannounced. At one point, when

Terry and Gillespie and Vaughan were all going at once, you could scarcely see the trees for the rococonuts.

June 25th

The singer Betty Carter, who opened the midnight concert at Carnegie Hall tonight, makes Sarah Vaughan sound like Kate Smith. She first sang with Lionel Hampton's big band in the late forties, and, proclaiming Billie Holiday her major influence, she has been a fanatic jazz singer ever since. Lithe and smiling, she pours around the stage, freezing here and there in Martha Graham positions, as if she were attempting to make her melodic lines three-dimensional. These melodic lines are surrealistic. She starts many of her phrases with the dying notes that Billie Holiday locked herself into in the early forties, and then she works tortuously through purposely off-pitch improvisations, full of jolting intervals and sour harmony. She is hard going, not because she is different and surprising but because she invariably seems to take the perverse melodic turn. She pulverizes her lyrics, and when a "skylark" or a "spring can really hang you up" comes through clearly, it is a road sign glimpsed in the fog. Betty Carter is a better scat singer than Sarah Vaughan. She uses rests and sudden, rhythmic starts and stops, and she gives her consonants and vowels coloration. She must have studied Leo Watson when he was still about.

June 26th

More singing, this time of a classic nature. Mel Tormé has grown into a superb big-voiced singer with a way of flawlessly shading and adjusting his attack for each song. He also writes some of his songs and all of his arrangements, conducts his accompanying band, and plays drums and piano. He is a generalissimo onstage, and during his performance at

Carnegie Hall tonight (among other songs, he did "Send In the Clowns," "Carioca," "Lulu's Back in Town," "Gloomy Sunday," "Mountain Greenery," "Misty," "Blues in the Night," "Lady Be Good," and "When the World Was Young") he conducted Herb Pomeroy's band (which accompanied him) with one hand and his back; summoned Gerry Mulligan onstage by first smothering him with superlatives (superegos handle superegos best); supplied a piano accompaniment to Mulligan's baritone-saxophone solo in "Misty" (Mulligan played better during his several numbers with Tormé than he did earlier with his own group); and dared to make a fast swinger of "Send In the Clowns."

June 27th

Double Image and the Revolutionary Ensemble were on hand tonight at Alice Tully Hall. Double Image is made up of two vibraphonists—David Friedman and David Samuels—the bassist Harvie Swartz, and the drummer Mike DiPasqua. All six numbers were originals, and all were short and full of double improvisation, instrument switching, and sudden starts and stops. Because of the group's collective treble tone, it resembled the Modern Jazz Quartet. More often, though, it had a floating, aluminum quality, and one expected it to take off—supported by vibraphone wings and driven by bass and drums—and fly easily and swiftly through the high-ceilinged hall. The Revolutionary Ensemble was less elusive. The Ensemble's subtlety, humor, and audacity make it one of the most inventive of the avant-garde groups, and tonight it raised another bold banner by playing without amplification. This gave it a pure, huddled sound that forced the audience to lean mentally forward. The rewards were plentiful: Sirone's long open-horn trombone solo, played against Cooper's one-two mallet beats on his tomtoms; an Oriental piece played by Jenkins on a small xylophone, backed by

Cooper's sticks on gourds and Sirone's arco bass; all three on recorders and tin whistles and piccolos (birds during false dawn); Jenkins's violin against more of Cooper's softly thundering mallets; and the fine collective turmoil of their last number.

A flood of proficient, inventive alto saxophonists came along after Charlie Parker and Lester Young in the early fifties, and chief among them were Lee Konitz, Phil Woods, Sonny Criss, Sonny Stitt, Jackie McLean, Lennie Niehaus, Bud Shank, Herb Geller, Art Pepper, and the late Paul Desmond. Pepper worked for Stan Kenton in the forties and fifties, and then put in a couple of long stints in prison for drug violations. These vicissitudes have made him something of a legend, and he was added to the program at Tully tonight not because he fitted in stylistically but because he was making his first visit to New York in a very long time and there was no other spot for him. Despite his obvious nervousness, he played with conviction and passion. He was perhaps best in his own ballad, "My Laurie," done at a variety of tempos, and in a very fast "Caravan." Pepper began as a Parker admirer but has added John Coltrane, so that his playing now has a split-level effect. His solos first rise and fall through Parker patterns and then shift into Coltrane shrieks and yells. He was ably accompanied by Gene Perla on bass, Joe LaBarbera on drums, and Onaje Allan Gumbs on piano. Gumbs took several spacious solos; he has heavy hands and a tumultuous, swinging attack.

June 28th

George Wein appeared before the early event at Carnegie Hall tonight to announce that the idea for what we were about to hear—a string of great jazz soloists unencumbered by accompaniment—had been stolen from a concert given not long ago in Berlin. But Wein need only have looked to the New York jazz lofts, where unaccompanied soloists are common. And anyway, all the instruments at tonight's concert, with the exception of the violin, were percussion and rhythm instruments, which have long been accustomed to standing on their own. John Lewis led the parade with three of his own tunes and Thelonious Monk's " 'Round Midnight." Lewis does not have a notable left hand and is incapable of driving anywhere without bass and drums. He wandered in Debussy circles, and when he moved into a regular beat it was in a tentative way. Gary Burton has been building abstract solos for years, but he did even better when he brought out his friend Steve Swallow, on Fender bass, for duets. They developed some excellent counterpoint, and Swallow, using his instrument with discretion, demonstrated again that he is one of the founders of present-day bass playing. Indeed, he easily edged his forebear Charles Mingus, who appeared with the pianist Robert Neloms for two brief numbers: a slow arco Ellington hymn, in which Mingus played flat, and a pizzicato "I Can't Get Started," in which he got a bamboo sound—probably the fault of his amplifier. Art Blakey delivered two drum solos; Buddy Rich or Max Roach would have been better. Joe Pass is the preternatural guitar soloist, and his four ballads shone with Tatum figures and rich harmonic imagining. Joe Venuti closed the procession, and it didn't sound easy for him; his style has leaned on rhythm sections for fifty years. But he got by with a pinch of this and a pinch of that. Then the soloists formed what amounted to a rhythm section plus vibraphone and violin and played "C Jam Blues." Lewis, borne by Mingus and Blakey, played eight rocking choruses, outclassing everyone and making the old complaints about his unswinging stiffness even more incomprehensible.

June 29th

Toshiko Akiyoshi, the Manchurian-born Japanese pianist, and
Lew Tabackin, the American reedman, formed the T.A.-L.T.
big band four years ago in Los Angeles, and it appeared tonight at Avery Fisher Hall. (Sixteen strong, it is made up
largely of young West Coast studio musicians.) Tabackin is
the principal soloist, and Toshiko, his wife, leads and does
the handsome arrangements, which incorporate *nō* songs,
fancy section writing (the section as a soloist, in the Benny
Carter manner), unusual voicings (flutes pitted against a
bass trombone), and, more often than not, a rhythmic attack
that suggests the early Woody Herman Herds. Tabackin first
appeared in New York ten or twelve years ago, and it was
soon clear that he was out of the ordinary. He had the com-
plaining tone of the hard-bop saxophonists, but he also revealed an affection for Ben Webster and Paul Gonsalves, and
for Sonny Rollins. Tonight he played at length at a variety
of tempos, and each statement was exceptional. His respect
for Webster and Gonsalves and Rollins is undiminished, and
his tone has softened and widened.

It was a surprise to arrive at Carnegie after the Toshiko-
Tabackin and find that the concert of four solo pianists already in progress was unamplified. There sat two concert
grands on an otherwise empty stage. Teddy Wilson and
Adam Makowicz, the Polish Tatum pianist, had finished, but
George Shearing had just settled down for what appeared to
be his patented all-purpose night-club-and-concert program—
"Dream Dancing" and "Greensleeves," done in a variety of
styles; "Happy Days Are Here Again," done as a lament;
"Lullaby of Birdland," done as Tatum and Bach; "Misty,"
done as a rhapsody and as Garner would have played it; and
"Let It Snow," possibly done as a comment on the backstage
air-conditioning. Shearing's playing was mischievous and
perfect. Every note rolled easily through the hall, and the

same was true of Earl Hines's sound, which followed. The Master did "I Cover the Waterfront," a long "My Monday Date," "I Feel Pretty," and "Jitterbug Waltz," and he showed off all the devices he invented fifty years ago—the little vibratolike tremolos, the arrhythmic escapades, the glittering treble figures, the elevator left hand. As is his wont now, he enclosed them in clouds of Jamesian pianistic syntax, entirely appropriate to the most august of American jazz pianists.

June 30th

Eighteen years have passed since Ornette Coleman set off the most recent revolution in jazz. Louis Armstrong fired the first revolution, in the mid-twenties, and it is instructive to compare what had happened to him a couple of decades later. His playing had grown somewhat lackluster, and he had been forced temporarily out of favor by bebop, which had been brought into being, in part, by Dizzy Gillespie, one of his stylistic grandchildren. Armstrong, bewildered and diminished-looking in photographs taken at the time, had been the king of jazz only ten years before, and he must often have wondered what had happened. Coleman has suffered vicissitudes, but they have been largely self-imposed. He is a poor businessman and, like Sonny Rollins, he has hidden himself away for long periods. The improvisational, structural, and thematic freedoms he introduced are still being experimented with—by the A.A.C.M. in Chicago and here, by American expatriate musicians, by Europeans and Japanese, by the downtown loft musicians, and, most important, by Coleman himself. Despite, or perhaps because of, his various voluntary exiles, he is more famous than ever before, and he is playing with greater invention and discipline. Nonetheless, he must have been surprised by the full house at Avery Fisher tonight, for it wasn't long ago that he had difficulty filling half of Town Hall. He must have been surprised, too, that perhaps a third of those present were about five years old in 1960; they had come to hear a legend. What they did hear was brilliant and very real—or at least the first half was. Coleman surrounded himself with seven musicians (Don Cherry on trumpet, Dewey Redman on tenor saxophone, James Blood Ulmer on guitar, David Izenzon and Buster Williams on bass, and Edward Blackwell and Billy Higgins on drums), three of them (Cherry, Blackwell, and Higgins) carryovers from the old Five Spot days. They played five Coleman numbers, and each was a surging display of what he has wrought. "Name Brain" was short, and had brief jammed ensembles and solos by Cherry on pocket trumpet and by Coleman. Eighteen years ago, Cherry was a beanpole whose pants were a foot too short, and his playing had a flailing, uphill quality. Tonight, wearing a gold-threaded blue pantaloon suit, his bony face aged and secret, he played with emotion and fluidity. His solo in "Sound Amoeba," full of bent notes and long pauses, was of the highest lyrical order. Coleman was once a torrential player who believed in drowning his listeners. But his solo in "Name Brain" was played in a legato half-time. He moved through Benny Carter ascending-and-descending steps, and he stayed in the middle register. He used easy repetitive figures, and loose blue notes. His playing was the same in a long, harrowing lament called "The Black House," in the fast "Raceface," and in "Sound Amoeba," in which a long written ensemble was followed by eight to-the-point a cappella solos. Nearly as effective was "Mr. and Mrs. Dream." This consisted almost wholly of ensemble, whose gradually increasing intensity became almost unbearable, provoking Coleman, who was clearly seized by what they had just played, to say to the audience, "We'll take a little breather so that the dream doesn't wake up." In the second half of the concert, Coleman brought together two highly amplified guitarists, an electric bassist, and two drummers, one of them his son. They played loud modified rock,

and Coleman just about disappeared from hearing. It is un-
imaginable that Coleman, who has been working on this electronic group two years, considers it his highest achievement.

July 1st

Count Basie, recovered from his heart attack and looking
fresh and fit, appeared tonight at Carnegie Hall with his
band, and in under two hours played a dozen or so instrumentals (among them vehicles for the tenor saxophonists
Eric Dixon, Jimmy Forrest, and Eddie Lockjaw Davis, the
trombonist Al Grey, and himself), and then provided accompaniment for Joe Williams (who sang "Every Day," "Goin'
to Chicago," "Blues in My Heart," Jon Hendricks's "Evolu-
tion of the Blues," "In the Evenin'," and "Rocks in My
Bed"), all the while piloting his ship from the keyboard with
an occasional raised finger, an almost imperceptible nod, a
sudden widely opened eye, a left-hand chord, a lifted chin, a
smile, and playing background and solo piano that is the
quintessence of swinging and taste and good cheer, even
when almost nothing happens around it, as was the case
tonight.

July 2nd

The New York Jazz Repertory Company swung into action
tonight at Carnegie with brief retrospectives of Roy Eldridge
and Earl Hines. Eldridge declined to be present at his portion
of the evening, and one reason certainly must have been a
reluctance to hear others re-create solos that he himself can
no longer play. And what majestic, scarifying solos they are!
Joe Newman, Jon Faddis, and Jimmy Maxwell played the
transcriptions together with precision and great rhythmic
drive, and they included "Wabash Stomp" and "Heckler's
Hop" (1937), his celebrated rampage on Gene Krupa's 1941

"Let Me Off Uptown," and his sedate "Little Jazz," made in 1945 with Artie Shaw.

Hines presided at the piano during his half of the concert, and he was accompanied by a band that included, in addition to Maxwell, Newman, and Faddis, Bernie Privin and Doc Cheatham, trumpets; Eddie Bert, Janice Robinson, and Eph Resnick, trombones; Budd Johnson, Bob Wilber, Norris Turney, Frank Foster, and Cecil Payne, reeds; Carmen Mastren, guitar; George Duvivier, bass; and Bobby Rosengarden, drums. We heard "West End Blues" and "Weather Bird" from his Armstrong Chicago days and "My Monday Date" and "Apex Blues" from his Jimmy Noone Chicago days, and we heard big-band re-creations from the thirties and forties of such numbers as "G.T. Stomp," "Deep Forest," "Number 19," and "Father Steps In." But best of all were two piano solos with rhythm—"Rosetta" and "Blues in Thirds." In the last, Hines played three quick, irregularly spaced ascending chordal explosions and, a chorus later, four bell-struck single notes, placed just behind the beat and scattered around middle C. He received a standing ovation, which caused one observer to say, "While they were standing and clapping, I was down on my knees praising God."

September 12th

Though it is a deliquescent music, jazz has long behaved as if it were immortal, flinging its improvised beauties to the unattending air and prematurely consuming some of its most gifted adherents. Only the recording machine prevented it from remaining a provincial Southern music that in due course would probably have returned to its native silence. But recordings have never been perfect. The early, acoustic ones made jazz piping and toylike—music for a Teddy bear's party. And current recordings are of such microscopic intensity that the mechanics of music-making—the clank of valves, the scrape of bows, the intake of breath—often overshadow the music. Other shortcomings are the Arctic properties of recording studios; the habit that recording companies have of rarely keeping their goods in print long enough for people to find out they exist; the unbelievably decrepit record-distribution system (frontier women had an easier time ordering Paris gowns); and the Reissue Problem, which is aggravated by greed, whim, and a lack of foresight and taste.

Jazz began to be widely recorded in the twenties, and the first reissues appeared in the mid-thirties. They were doubly welcome, for they restored Bessie Smiths and Louis Armstrongs that had become rare and expensive, and they were generally reprinted with full discographical information, correcting the heedless taciturnity of the original labels, which offered only the names of the featured performer and the composer of the song. (Bessie Smith's original Columbia recording of "The St. Louis Blues" lists the composer, W. C. Handy, and "Organ and Cornet Accomp."—the cornet accomp. being by Louis Armstrong.) Reissues came out on single 78 r.p.m.s or in stout pasteboard albums that held from four to six ten-inch records and eventually included photographs and pioneer liner notes. In the early fifties, reissues were transferred to ten-inch and then twelve-inch L.P.s, and now transfers are being effected to tape. But it is only in recent years that recording companies have begun to reissue valuable jazz material properly: chronologically; in complete recording sessions; and with one or more alternate takes, which allow the listener to follow the musicians' thinking and inspiration (or lack of it). RCA, which used to start and abandon new reissue programs every other year (the Camden label, label "X," the Collectors Issue series, the Vintage Series), has reactivated its Bluebird label and is bringing out, complete, its Benny Goodman, Glenn Miller, Tommy Dorsey, Fletcher Henderson, and Fats Waller. And it has reissued for the first time all the small-band sides that Lionel

Hampton made for Victor between 1937 and 1941, thus eras-
ing more than twenty years of mistreatment it had subjected
Hampton collectors to. This privation began in 1954, when
the company put out a twelve-inch L.P. called "Hot Mallets."
Nothing was right about it. It had twelve three-minute numbers instead of the sixteen that L.P.s could hold, the selections
were erratic, and no more than two numbers from any one
session were used (generally four were made). Two years
later, Jazztone, a mail-order record club, leased twelve equally
scatter-shot titles from RCA and sent them out as "Lionel
Hampton's All-Star Groups." The following year, Camden
reissued twelve Hamptons on "Jivin' the Vibes." One had
been previously reissued, and there were no complete sessions. In 1959, another Camden, "Open House," appeared
with twelve numbers, five of them repeats, and in 1961
Hampton was restored to the RCA Victor label with twelve
titles on an album called "Swing Classics." Six of these titles
were repeats, but the clebrated "Sunny Side of the Street"
with Johnny Hodges and the classic "Haven't Named It Yet"
with Red Allen, J. C. Higginbotham, Charlie Christian, and
Sid Catlett were reissued for the first time. A decade passed.
The silence was finally broken by the Vintage Series' "Lionel
Hampton, Volume I," which had the first four Hampton sessions complete and in order. But Volume II never materialized, and silence fell again until the release of Hampton's
collected works. (Between 1954 and 1971, six Hampton albums were issued, but they included only fifty-four of the
ninety-one Hampton sides.)

Herewith some Arista and RCA reissues, with the Hampton set first:

"THE COMPLETE LIONEL HAMPTON" (Bluebird)
Hampton was both a curiosity and a strong musical force in
the late thirties. He was born in Louisville, in 1913, and

raised in Chicago, where, as a neophyte drummer, he (along with Sidney Catlett) fell under the influence of the Chicago band instructor Major N. Clark Smith and of such drummers as Zutty Singleton, Jimmy Bertrand, and Jimmy McHendricks. In 1927, he went to California and worked with Les Hite, Louis Armstrong, Buck Clayton, and Herschel Evans. He stumbled onto the vibraphone in 1930 and recorded on it with Hite and Armstrong, although he was still a drummer. (He had also picked up enough piano to be a good Earl Hines emulator.) In 1936, he took a band into the Paradise Club in Los Angeles. One night, Benny Goodman sat in, and he invited Hampton to record with the Goodman trio on vibraphone, and soon after to join the band, where he stayed until 1940. Hampton captured the public fancy immediately. He was the second black that Goodman had hired, and he was ambidextrous and a showman. He hummed and grunted, he threw his drumsticks in the air and danced on his drums, and he played lightning two-finger piano. (The regular pianist took care of the left-hand part.) Hampton's vibraphone style was loose and swinging, and had come in part from Hines and Armstrong and Coleman Hawkins. Hampton used a lot of loud pedal, he played on or near the beat, and he made his solos and those around him *go*. His drumming, in the fashion of the times, was frantic. He soloed mainly on fast tempos and crowded his beats tightly together. His speed was deceptive, and it made him sound like a virtuoso and hid his gifted, hard-pressing amateurism. His piano playing, though, has never received due consideration. He borrowed his two-finger attack from the vibraphone, and used it with passion and clarity. He carried off tremolos and staccato passages that no ordinary pianist could manage, and it is entirely possible that Charlie Parker and Dizzy Gillespie studied Hampton's pouring figures. Hampton played with joy: he knocked himself out and he mesmerized his musicians and his audiences.

Hampton was enough of a sensation to be asked by Victor
in 1937 to lead a series of small-band recordings designed to
compete with the Teddy Wilson-Billie Holiday series under
way at Brunswick and to be an extension of Benny Goodman's Victor trio and quartet recordings. He took his first
group (nine Goodman sidemen) into a New York studio in
February of 1937, and his last one (eight sidemen from his
fledgling big band) into a Chicago studio in April of 1941.
He drew his personnel mainly from available big bands (he
recorded in New York, Chicago, and Hollywood), and he
often mixed styles and schools. He blended an Ellington horn
section (Cootie Williams, Lawrence Brown, Johnny Hodges)
with a rhythm section (Allan Reuss, John Kirby, Cozy Cole)
drawn from Goodman, the Mills Blue Rhythm Band, and
Stuff Smith's group. He combined musicians from Goodman,
Basie, and the John Kirby band, and musicians from Louis
Armstrong, Goodman, and Roy Eldridge. On one date, he assembled the whole spectrum of 1939 jazz, with Benny Carter,
Edmond Hall, Coleman Hawkins, Joe Sullivan, Freddie
Green, Artie Bernstein, and Zutty Singleton. On another,
he played all-star, by inviting Carter, Ben Webster, Hawkins, and Chu Berry, who were accompanied by a Benny
Goodman-Cab Calloway rhythm section. One of his most successful sessions was drawn entirely from the Earl Hines band
of 1938. The records were not haphazard. Most have head arrangements, some have almost sumptuous scores (Benny
Carter as arranger), and even those that are largely jammed
have their own order and logic. Not surprisingly, the records
are built around Hampton as vibraphonist, pianist, drummer,
and vocalist, but ample solo space is reserved for his guests.
As a result, many of the Hampton records are among the
longest of their time—several in the album run close to three
and a half minutes. The delights in the album include all the
accompanying and all the solo work of Jess Stacy and Clyde

Hart, who were Hampton's principal pianists during his first two years of recording (the records are uncommonly well made, and Hart's accompaniment to Hampton's vocal on "I'm Confessin' " is brilliantly clear); the ease and irresistible swing of the Hart/Charlie Christian/Artie Bernstein/Catlett rhythm section on "Haven't Named It Yet" and "I'm on My Way from You," which has one of Red Allen's most lyrical trumpet solos; Coleman Hawkins's pressing solo on "Singin' the Blues"; Cootie Williams's tearing crescendo growl solo and Sonny Greer's fine snicketing four-bar drum break on "Ring Dem Bells"; the duet by Lawrence Brown and Harry Carney on "Memories of You"; "Rock Hill Special," with its oblivious, plunging Hampton piano; the stampeding "Gin for Christmas," a reworking of "Bugle Call Rag" in which Hampton's drumming and Ziggy Elman's bar-mitzvah trumpet produce go-man-go shouts during the last chorus; and Nat Cole's lovely piano solo on "Blue (Because of You)."

The best of the recordings were done between 1937 and 1939. After that, Hampton was busy getting his own big band going, and the novelty had worn off. The best are also surprisingly and resolutely old-fashioned. If Teddy Wilson and Billie Holiday (abetted by Lester Young and Jo Jones and Buck Clayton) were pointing in new directions on their Brunswick dates, Hampton was working strictly within the New Orleans-dominated tradition of Zutty Singleton and Louis Armstrong. There is a hot, heavy atmosphere on a lot of the recordings, and the rhythm sections are almost always foursquare and relentless. (Compare any of the 1938 Hamptons with the Young/Clayton/Walter Page/Jo Jones Kansas City Six sides from the same year: the Hamptons barge, and the Kansas City Sixes fly.) But Hampton's Victor recordings provided a brilliant climax for a form of jazz that would soon be set aside by Young and Charlie Parker.

"THE RED NORVO TRIO WITH TAL FARLOW
AND CHARLES MINGUS" (Savoy)

A pointillistic distinction: It was apparently Red Norvo, and
not Lionel Hampton, as the histories have long claimed, who
first played the vibraphone in jazz. Norvo played it in 1928,
soon after the Deagan company invented its Vibra-Harp, but
he did not switch to it full time until the forties, preferring
the small, neat sound of the xylophone. Even if Norvo had
chosen to stay with the vibraphone, it is doubtful whether he
would have eclipsed Hampton's omnipresence. Norvo was too
subtle and too light on his feet to be a founding father. Instead, he was an ingenious musical designer who invented a
succession of streamlined groups, each far enough ahead of
its time to be copied and then obscured by its imitators. In the
mid-thirties, he put together the first working non-Dixieland
small band. It was a soft, swinging octet that used the honeyed
arrangements of Eddie Sauter. It was the first working group
to have a full-time jazz singer: Mildred Bailey. Norvo led
various quicksilver groups in the forties, and was in one of
Benny Goodman's best small bands. He starred with Woody
Herman's First Herd in 1946, from which he extracted a
chamber group for some recordings that were harmonically
advanced versions of his group of ten years before. Then, in
1949, he organized a daring trio that certainly must have
passed within the hearing of John Lewis and Milt Jackson
when they were toying with the notion of the Modern Jazz
Quartet.

Its best edition had Tal Farlow on guitar and Charles Mingus on bass. Like all innovators, Norvo preferred malleable
unknowns to stars. He found Farlow in a small New York
club, and Mingus in Los Angeles, through the pianist Jimmy
Rowles, who remembered Mingus's work on a Billie Holiday
gig. Norvo stepped off into space with the trio. What, he
wondered, should a vibraphonist do behind a guitar solo, and

what should a guitarist do behind a vibraphone solo, and
how should either or both accompany bass solos—what, in
short, should be done to keep the trio from simply unravel-
ling? Keep soft and busy, he discovered. When Farlow soloed,
Norvo supplied little islands of chords or suggestive runs,
and when Norvo soloed, Farlow either kept time or played
dreaming, behind-the-beat accents. Norvo and Farlow took
turns shimmering behind Mingus's solos, and Mingus provided constant mushrooming support. The ensembles were
generally set variations on the melody played in counterpoint or unison and were boppish in nature. Unlike most of
the bebop groups, the Norvo trio did not dress other people's
chords up with its own titles but used undisguised standards
("Night and Day," "Cheek to Cheek," "This Can't Be Love")
and such fashionable creations of the time as "Swedish Pastry"
and "Godchild." The Savoy reissue is taken from material
recorded in 1950 and 1951, and it makes several things clear.
The Norvo trio preferred lightning tempos. It was self-
charging: Farlow seems to activate Norvo, who plays some
admirable solos ("Night and Day" and the three takes of
"Godchild"), and Mingus stirs both and, in turn, produces
some of his best recorded solos. The trio had a hot delicacy, and
it seemed to spin its music out of the air around it.

"THE COMPLETE FLETCHER HENDERSON, 1927–1936"
(Bluebird)
All thirty-four of the numbers, good and bad, that Fletcher
Henderson recorded for Victor. The bad ones, presumably
made to mollify nervous A. & R. men during the early part
of the Depression, have titles like "My Sweet Tooth Says I
Wanna (But My Wisdom Tooth Says No)," "Malinda's
Wedding Day," and "I Wanna Count Sheep (Till the Cows
Come Home)" and whiny vocals by Ikey Robinson, George
Bias, Dick Robertson, John Dickens, and Harlan Lattimore.

The good ones, done between 1934 and 1936 by the last creditable Henderson band, are a crowd of solos by Roy Eldridge, Coleman Hawkins, Red Allen, and Chu Berry, many of them exceptional and all of them cushioned by Henderson's easygoing arrangements. Hawkins, not yet a chordal locomotive, was continually experimenting with time, delaying the beat, playing wild double-time passages, and in general searching for the limits of four-four time. He was also trying on different-sized tones. He displayed a hard tone, a heavy tone, a rolling tone. He was the most closely attended musician in jazz, and each innovation seemed to spawn a new style. Here, on "Hocus Pocus," are the origins of Herschel Evans; on "Strangers" one hears the mold for Chu Berry. Henderson's bands, so unsuccessful commercially, were equipment-supply houses for the rest of jazz. Eldridge's work sent Dizzy Gillespie on his way, and Berry's (having tipped its hat to Hawkins) helped form Don Byas. Sidney Catlett's drumming on the 1936 "Riffin' " must have been the model for Alvin Burroughs in the 1938 "Down Home Jump" and "Rock Hill Special" on the Hampton album. And, of course, Henderson's arrangements had a good deal to do with Benny Goodman's ascension in 1935. Playing with Henderson was the sine qua non of the big-band world. The scattering of photographs in the album reflects this: everyone looks easy, elegant, refined. Henderson sits at the wheel of a beautiful roadster, a snappy fedora pulled down over his right eye, his expression bemused. Another picture shows his 1927 brass team in tuxedos and patent-leather shoes, and still another has John Kirby and Walter Johnson in linen suits. There are a lot of white shoes, and the poses are cool. It has been said repeatedly that the Henderson band was never properly caught on records, and this must be true. Its recordings tend to imply more than they state. But Eldridge, at least, is still at large, and his power and snapping excitement are what the band was about.

"DON BYAS: SAVOY JAM PARTY" (Savoy)

Coleman Hawkins's influence didn't cease in the thirties. His offshoots had offshoots, so that his genealogy, reaching down to the present, looks roughly like this:

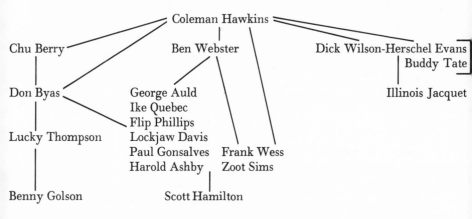

One of the most powerful of Hawkins's admirers was Don Byas, who died in 1972 in Holland. Byas was born in 1912 in Muskogee, Oklahoma, and in the thirties he became part of the same California scene as Lionel Hampton and Buck Clayton. He arrived in New York in the late thirties, and landed a job with Count Basie in 1941. He stayed with Basie three years and then gigged around Fifty-second Street until 1946, when he moved to Europe for good. Byas set down some momentous solos during his New York years. He announced his presence by taking two choruses on Basie's record of "Harvard Blues" which remain among the great blues statements. His tone outswells Hawkins's, and the solo has a unique and insinuating legato quality. The following year, he just about matched himself on Basie's small-band recordings of "Sugar Blues" and "St. Louis Blues." Then, in 1945, he recorded a furioso work of art. He and the bassist Slam Stewart played an impromptu breakneck "I Got Rhythm" to open

a Town Hall concert, and Byas took nine choruses that—
volcanic, vortical, almost vicious—held the place of honor in
Baroque Hall until the arrival of Sonny Rollins, fifteen years
later. (Byas's feat can be heard in the "Smithsonian Collection of Classic Jazz.")

Byas's style was voluptuous. He put bones in Chu Berry's
attack, and he taught himself to think faster than any jazz
improviser had before. His tone was big enough to house all
the notes he played, and he was a master of dynamics. He
had a broad vibrato and liked big intervals and high, almost
split notes that resembled adolescent voice breaks. His New
York flowering coincided with the emergence of bebop, and
he fitted in very well. In 1944, he was a member, with Dizzy
Gillespie, George Wallington, Oscar Pettiford, and Max
Roach, of the first bebop band on Fifty-second Street. He was
a master of the jet tempos the boppers liked, he understood
their harmonic stratagems sometimes better than they did,
and he liked to completely alter the materials he improvised
on. But Byas never mastered the irregular, suspended rhythms
of bebop. He was locked in Coleman Hawkins's four-four box,
and perhaps, being a man of ego, that helped send him off to
Europe, where Hawkins's style was revered. Byas recorded
around a hundred titles in New York, and thirty-two are on
the Savoy reissue. The best of his colleagues are Charlie
Shavers, another encyclopedist; Clyde Hart, Byas's buddy,
whose death in 1945 may have been another reason for his
departure; Slam Stewart; and Emmett Berry. "Riffin' and
Jivin'," "Don's Idea" (two takes), "Bass C Jam" (two takes),
"How High the Moon," and "Cherokee" are superior up-
tempo Byas. About half the numbers are ballads of various
speeds: here is Byas the voluptuary, the heart-render, the
worshipper of softness. Byas came back to this country just
once—in 1970, when he appeared at the Newport Jazz Festival. He played well, but the response was lukewarm. His
beautiful, unabashed romanticism had gone out of fashion.

October 30th

John Hammond's autobiography, *John Hammond on Record*
(Ridge Press/Summit Books), is the reverse of what one expected. It is frank and buoyant about his family and background, and low-voiced and defensive about his place in jazz
music and civil liberties. Moreover, the book, written in col-
laboration with Irving Townsend, is delivered in a styleless,
store-bought monotone that is the direct opposite of Hammond's ebullient, superlative-spattered self.

Hammond was born in 1910 in a Vanderbilt mansion on
East Ninety-first Street, which still looks down on Andrew
Carnegie's Georgian house across the way. The mansion had,
Hammond tells us, six stories and two cellars, a ballroom
seating two hundred and fifty, two elevators, and a staff of
sixteen. It also had gleaming parquet floors, eighteen-foot
ceilings, and immense marble fireplaces. Hammond took
pains when he was at St. Bernard's, a nearby boys' private
school, to enter the house by a circuitous back route, so that
no one would know where he lived. His father came from the
Midwest and was the son of a Union general. He became a
wealthy banker, railroad man, and lawyer, but the boss was
Hammond's mother, Emily Vanderbilt Sloane, a great-
granddaughter of Commodore Cornelius Vanderbilt, and an
enormously wealthy woman. She still engages Hammond. He
says of her:

> She was both fascinated and repelled by the high
> society which was her natural station, and she soon
> fashioned her own way of living with it. It was not
> possible for her to rebel politically as a young girl,
> and she knew little of politics anyway. But through
> religion she could rebel socially. She would not
> flaunt wealth as her mother did. Instead she would
> impose, first upon herself and later upon her family,
> a code of moral behavior and responsibility which

would serve as an example to her small world of the
duties of the blessed. She was a beautiful woman,
tall for her time, and with the erect bearing the
nineteenth century required of elegant ladies. There
was no arrogance in it, simply evidence of good
breeding. Vanity was lavished only on her hair and
ankles. She had her hair—a woman's "crowning
glory"—cared for regularly by the only Jewish
woman she knew, Mrs. Block, whom she described
as a Hebrew. She cared little for clothes, never wore
a dab of powder in her life, and would not allow lip-
stick to be brought into her house. Her only formal
education was private tutoring by Miss Spence; her
parents did not approve her mixing with even the
uncommon herd in private schools. Like all Vanderbilt women, with the exception of my sister Adele,
she did not go to college.

She never drank or smoked. She did not approve of Demo-
crats, and her knowledge of racial minorities was limited to
fantasies. "I want you to know that everybody is born alike,"
she told Hammond. "But with Negroes their skulls harden
when they are twelve. There *is* a difference." She played the
piano, recited poetry and the Bible, and believed in an after-
life. She did not dance or swim, and was physically in-
hibited—unlike her mother, Emily Thorne Vanderbilt, who
was "extremely proud of her bosom and very daring for her
day about revealing it." Hammond's mother was a soft touch
and a philanthropist, who toward the end of her life (she
lived to be ninety-six) became so involved with Moral Re-
Armament that he and his sisters feared for the family for-
tunes and were forced to intercede.

Hammond switched to Browning from St. Bernard's, and
until he went away to Hotchkiss he "lived the life of a coddled little rich boy, tolerant like my mother of weaknesses
and sins in others, intolerant of any fall from grace in my-

self, ignorant as Mother was of the world beyond our island
of social and financial equals, except to realize that there
were people out there who were not like us. I shared her religious fervor, her prejudices, and her saintly resolve to set an
example for others, then to forgive them when they failed to
measure up to it. Like her, I was already the reformer, fired
with her energy, certain in the right, oblivious to physical
infirmities [his mother had become a Christian Scientist]
which all right-minded flesh could overcome, an inheritor of
the guilt and therefore the obligations of wealth." Hotchkiss,
in the persons of its headmaster and a senior English teacher,
both the sort of provincial Puritan liberals who have aerated
New England prep schools for seventy years, turned Hammond around. He entered Yale in the fall of 1929 but within
two years had dropped out, because of two attacks of hepatitis
and an already consuming interest in jazz and black people.
(He recovered from his second bout of hepatitis at the Mil-
lionaires' Club in Georgia, where he would bring the Chicago
Defender, the Baltimore *Afro-American*, and the Pittsburgh
Courier into the dining room, to the astonishment of the
black waiters.) In September of 1931, he produced his first
recording, for Columbia, with the pianist Garland Wilson,
and shortly afterward he moved from Ninety-first Street to
an apartment on Sullivan Street.

By this time, Hammond was well grounded musically. He
had taken up the violin at eight (he later switched to viola),
and had been exposed to improvised music at twelve, when
he heard Paul Specht's Georgians in London. He had already started reading *Variety* and collecting records, and
soon he was sneaking out to shows. Hotchkiss let him come
to New York to pursue his violin lessons, after which he got
into the habit of dropping in at the Alhambra Theatre or the
Club Saratoga or Smalls Paradise in Harlem to hear the likes
of Bessie Smith, Duke Ellington, Sidney De Paris, Red Allen,
J. C. Higginbotham, and Bill Coleman, and he continued

these adventures while he was at Yale. Before long, he had
become an impresario out of sheer pluck, and as the thirties
went on his accomplishments grew dazzling. He "discov-
ered," helped discover, or furthered the careers of Count
Basie, Billie Holiday, Charlie Christian, Teddy Wilson, Meade
Lux Lewis, Pete Johnson, Albert Ammons, Chu Berry, Benny
Carter, Benny Goodman (who married Hammond's sister
Alice), Red Allen, Jo Jones, Lionel Hampton, Helen Humes,
Lena Horne, Fletcher Henderson, Gene Krupa, Israel Crosby,
and more. He made bellwether recordings, for Columbia and
its affiliated labels, with Henderson, Holiday, Goodman, Bessie
Smith (her last and in many ways her greatest recordings),
Wilson, Mildred Bailey, and Basie. He broke the color line
repeatedly by putting together mixed bands for in-person appearances, radio broadcasts, and recordings. (Hammond covered the Scottsboro trials in the early thirties for *The Nation*,
and he joined the board of directors of the N.A.A.C.P. in
1935. He was never entirely happy with the organization,
feeling that it was too conservative, and he resigned in 1967.)
He also put on the two invaluable "Spirituals to Swing" concerts at Carnegie Hall in 1938 and 1939, and had recordings
of them released on the Vanguard label in 1959. Hammond
had a quiet time in the forties, but in the fifties he engineered
a superb series of recordings for Vanguard and Columbia
around Buck Clayton, Vic Dickenson, Ellis Larkins, Ruby
Braff, Jimmy Rushing, Mel Powell, and Jo Jones. And he has
not been idle since, for he has also shepherded Mahalia Jackson, Bob Dylan, Aretha Franklin, Leonard Cohen, and Bruce
Springsteen. Hammond's various emprises have sometimes
obscured his larger accomplishments. He helped clear the
way for desegregation. He showed Americans that they had
for their delectation an amazing new music that was largely
the invention and the glory of American blacks. He changed
the course of Western music by championing Basie and Holiday and Goodman, to say nothing of enabling them to have

solid careers when they might not have had any. He got America swinging.

Hammond seems somewhat dazed by all this himself, for he puts little energy into recounting his exploits. He mentions hearing Lester Young when Young was with a faltering King Oliver in 1933, but he doesn't say where or how or what. He mentions making Bessie Smith's last records, but again gives us almost no details. He does reveal, slowly and unwittingly, that he does not understand (or sometimes even like) those musicians who have not needed his help or have rejected it. He favors Fletcher Henderson's Joe Smith over Louis Armstrong, which is like rating Utrillo over Picasso. He doesn't like Frank Sinatra, and he has mixed feelings about Duke Ellington, who kept him at arm's length. His attitudes toward Mildred Bailey and Red Norvo, who were sometimes his guidons, are oddly ambivalent. (He accuses Mildred Bailey of being jealous of Billie Holiday!) Some of his musical opinions are refractory, too. He declares that Coleman Hawkins reached his peak in 1933, when Hawkins, dispensing styles right and left, had just slipped into gear. He dismisses the admirable violinist Claude Williams, and he puffs the lachrymose, romantic Chu Berry. And, in a queer passage, he refuses to accept the new and seemingly watertight version of Bessie Smith's death advanced by Chris Albertson in "Bessie."

Hammond the enthusiast sums himself up: "It will always be difficult for me so sit still, to wait for a moment or a day before setting out to discover the world all over again. I am an early riser, among the first to buy each day's *Times*, and my daily armful of new magazines is as much my trademark as my crewcut. Since I first discovered Mr. Epstein's newsstand at 91st Street and Madison Avenue I have never missed an issue of any periodical with something to say. This compulsion to see, to read, to hear everything as soon as possible, is as strong now as it ever was, and to be the first to know—or, certainly, never the last—is vitally important to me."

December 9th

The pianist and composer Herbie Nichols died in 1963 at the age of forty-four. He was gifted, elusive, bedevilled. He made his living in Dixieland bands when, in truth, he compared favorably with Thelonious Monk and Bud Powell. Almost his entire mature recorded output was done between May of 1955 and November of 1957, when he set down thirty-two titles for the Blue Note and Bethlehem labels. The critics made much of the recordings, and for a time Nichols was petted and admired, but this didn't change the shape of his career. Perhaps it was too late. Bebop already sounded conventional, even old-fashioned, and hard-bop was full of pianists who at first hearing played rings around him. Then Ornette Coleman arrived and slammed the door on the forties and fifties. Nichols died in obscurity, but he has recently begun to flourish in memoirs and reissues. Bethlehem has brought out its 1957 L.P. as "Herbie Nichols," and Blue Note has put together its four Nichols sessions as "Herbie Nichols: The Third World." The Blue Note reissue has a fine memoir by the trombonist Roswell Rudd, who studied with Nichols in 1960. And the short chapter on Nichols in A. B. Spellman's *Four Lives in the Bebop Business*—that wayward, fascinating, critical-political set of biographical studies (Cecil Taylor, Ornette Coleman, and Jackie McLean are the other subjects)—is available again in a Schocken paperback, which has been inexplicably retitled *Black Music: Four Lives*. Nichols was born in New York of West Indian parents, and he was a kind, proud, bemused, very tall man with intellectual leanings. He had roamed widely in the literature of classical piano, and he knew every jazz style. It is not clear from reading Rudd and Spellman why his career was such a botch. He frequently exchanged ideas with Monk, he worked for Lucky Thompson and Sonny Stitt and Archie Shepp, he showed his songs to Mary Lou Williams, who used some of them. But nothing happened, and he kept finding himself on the bandstand with Wilbur De Paris and Big Nick Nicholas.

Whether they admit it or not, most jazz improvisers are caught within the space created by the composer of the tune they are playing. Nichols, though, created his own space. All but four of the numbers on the reissues are his, and he doesn't burrow into them, as improvisers are wont to do, but constantly enlarges them. He likes his melodies, and he keeps returning to them, so that by the end of the performance they seem twice as imposing. His style owes its squiggly runs to Ellington and Monk, its broken phrase-endings to Bud Powell, and most of its harmonic content to Monk. And Monk governs many of his songs. When Nichols plays, there are no rests or bare places or patches of blue sky. His music is dense and vertical. The right hand moves through stop-and-go single-note melodic lines that fall on the beat or run ahead into arpeggios or glisses, or into chords that quickly dissolve into fresh single-note lines. All the while, the left hand clucks and fusses. It plays offbeat chords and single notes, stridelike rhythms, and echoes of the right hand. At first, it is difficult to tell whether Nichols's technique was faulty or he purposely played in such a haphazard, fluctuating way. He misses notes, lets the final notes of phrases die, and allows runs to come out faded and almost inaudible while the succeeding phrase trumpets and blares. But Nichols knew exactly what he was doing. Indeed, his self-knowledge and pianistic abilities were so acute that his playing has a calculated, almost cold cast to it. It asserts and proclaims, and maybe this quality put off some of Nichols's colleagues, most of whom took their talents for granted.

Nichols was a pianist of considerable originality who fash-

ioned attractive umbrellas of sound, and it is easy to dip into
the reissues anywhere. His minor-key songs, often arranged
in descending chords ("The Spinning Song," "House Party
Starting"), are almost catchy, and so are some of his fast
numbers ("Terpsichore," "Brass Rings"). Nichols's best solos
dance, and to such an extent that they would work well for
many modern choreographers. He uses three alternating bassists (Al McKibbon, Teddy Kotick, George Duvivier) and three
drummers (Art Blakey, Max Roach, Dannie Richmond), and
it is interesting that none of the six have ever played better
on records. Nichols said that he would have loved to be a
drummer (the tonal effects of drums fascinated him, and he
felt that they formed a central part of any performance), and
there is an enfolding percussiveness about his playing which
clearly surprised and challenged his accompanists. Red Norvo
once pointed out that many musicians end up playing the
wrong instrument. Perhaps Nichols was one.

December 28th

A new and highly original history of recorded jazz is nearing
completion. It is part of the "Recorded Anthology of American Music," a Rockefeller Foundation-supported project to
preserve on a hundred L.P.'s some of the rarest and choicest
American music. The L.P.s—half are reissues and half are
new—are being produced by experts, academic and otherwise, and are on the special New World label. In addition to
jazz, the anthology includes premier recordings of Gertrude
Stein and Virgil Thomson's opera "The Mother of Us All"
and of nineteenth-century organ music by Dudley Buck,
Horatio Parker, John Knowles Paine, and W. Eugene Thayer,
along with reissues of John Philip Sousa, Alan Lomax's gospel recordings, and Gershwin, Porter, and other composers
performing their own songs. The reissue albums are not for
sale to the public, but they can be borrowed from libraries

here and abroad. The jazz releases are made up mostly of re-
issues taken from various labels, and nine of thirteen albums
are out. They are, in rough chronological order: "Steppin'
on the Gas: Rags to Jazz, 1913–1927"; "Sweet and Low
Blues: Big Bands and Territory Bands of the 20s"; "Jammin'
for the Jackpot: Big Bands and Territory Bands of the 30s";
"Little Club Jazz: Small Groups in the 30s"; "Jive at Five:
The Style-Makers of Jazz, 1920s–1930s"; "Bebop"; "Jazz in
Revolution: The Big Bands in the 1940s"; "Nica's Dream:
Small Jazz Groups of the 50s and Early 60s"; and "Mirage:
Avant-Garde and Third-Stream Jazz." The album notes have
been written by Larry Gushee, Frank Driggs, Nat Hentoff,
Gunther Schuller, Burt Korall, Dan Morgenstern, J. R. Taylor, and Richard Seidel, which, give or take a few souls, is
the old *Jazz Review* crowd—jazz's New Critics. Two consid-
erations have governed the selection: the anthology's the-
rarer-the-better philosophy and the availability of materials.
Many record companies have been gracious about lending
their jazz recordings and apparently many have not. So the
jazz history turns out to be a repository of the second-rate,
the freakish, the also-rans, and the forgotten. (This rightly
and refreshingly suggests that the surest way to teach the
arts is to expose students to the best *and* the second or third
best. Mix Blake with Felicia Hemans, Louis Armstrong with
Taft Jordan, Max Beerbohm with Spy.) Benny Goodman is
represented by a sextet number and Ellington by four of his
small bands. There is one Bennie Moten, just two Basies, and
no Luncefords. Louis Armstrong has one middling big-band
selection from the thirties. King Oliver is absent, and so is
Jelly Roll Morton. There is little Fats Waller and no Billie
Holiday or Art Tatum or Roy Eldridge. What we are given
includes two selections by Jim Europe's 1914 orchestra which
verge on jazz and have the extraordinary drummer Buddy
Gilmore; the dreadful Brown Brothers, a sextet of saxophonists from 1915; two 1927 numbers by the swinging contra-

puntal Sam Morgan band from New Orleans; "Dunn's Cornet Blues," made in 1924 by the New York cornettist Johnny
Dunn, whose blue notes refused to bend; three 1929 sides by
the elastic, racing trumpeter Jabbo Smith, who sometimes
outclassed Louis Armstrong and foreshadowed Dizzy Gillespie; the obscure, by-night territory bands of the thirties—
Hunter's Serenaders, Grant Moore and His New Orleans
Black Devils, J. Neal Montgomery and His Orchestra, Zach
Whyte's Chocolate Beau Brummels—which were largely reflections of their urban betters (they produced such players
as Sy Oliver, Herman Chittison, and Elmer Crumbley); a couple of Stan Kenton's three-hundred-men-in-a-boat excursions;
and an awful "Knock, Knock" number by Stuff Smith's
harum-scarum 1936 band. Some of the selections are needlessly second-rate. The great bass saxophonist Adrian Rollini
made far better recordings than "Bugle Call Rag," and if Joe
Marsala's Hickory House band was to be included, what
about "Jim Jam Stomp" complete with a rampaging, very
young Buddy Rich? John Kirby's creamy "Bugler's Dilemma" is hardly fair to the listener when the headlong
"Royal Garden Blues" was available, and neither is Sidney
Bechet's "What Is This Thing Called Love?" when "Lady Be
Good" has never been reissued. But the history unavoidably
contains marvels, among them Bobby Hackett's subtle and
ingenious solo on "Jungle Love," which is an odd Teddy
Wilson small-band date from 1938 that also includes Johnny
Hodges (Hackett's solo explains the excitement that greeted
his arrival in New York that year); Cootie Williams's "Blues
in My Condition," done in 1941 with a bunch of Benny
Goodman's boys not long after Williams had defected from
the Ellington band; "I Wish I Could Shimmy Like My Sister
Kate," one of the gracious lyrical small-band dates that Red
Allen and Coleman Hawkins did in the early thirties; Charlie
Parker's twin monuments "Embraceable You" and "Parker's
Mood" (hardly rare, though); Red Norvo's "Congo Blues,"

with Parker and Dizzy Gillespie; two cool, serene numbers by the Joe Mooney Quartet; Claude Thornhill's 1947 band, with its mauve Gil Evans sonorities; and Duke Ellington's startling "Clothed Woman," a part-stride-piano, part-atonal construction made in the same year.

1978

January 3rd

The brilliant explosion known as Benny Goodman went off in 1935, and it hasn't gone out yet. Born to parents of Russian-Jewish extraction in Chicago in 1909, the eighth of eleven children, Goodman became a proficient clarinettist in his early teens. When he was sixteen, he was hired by Ben Pollack, who brought him to New York in 1928. He quit Pollack a year later, and for the next four years he was a busy New York radio, pit-band, and recording musician, who appeared with Andre Kostelanetz, Bessie Smith, Paul Whiteman, Enric Madriguera, Sam Lanin, Red Nichols, Ruth Etting, Hoagy Carmichael, Ted Lewis, and Bix Beiderbecke. He put together his first band in 1932 (for Russ Columbo, at the Woodmansten Inn, on the Pelham Parkway), and another in 1934, which became a weekly fixture on the three-hour Saturday-night "Let's Dance" radio show. ("If anyone were to ask what was the biggest thing that has ever happened to me," Goodman said recently, "landing a place on that show was it.") In the middle of 1935, Goodman and the band set out on a cross-country tour, and for a long time it was disastrous. The band bombed in Michigan and then in Denver, where it competed with and lost to Kay Kyser (who later travelled as Kay Kyser and His Kollege of Musical Knowledge). Jess Stacy had just joined the band, and he describes Goodman's reaction: "Goodman began saying he was going to quit this nonsense and go back into radio in New York. I said, 'Benny, get over the mountains first and see what happens.' I didn't tell him 'I told you so,' but when we got to Sweet's Ballroom in Oakland they were standing in lines a block long, and when we got down to the Palomar Ballroom in Los Angeles everybody went crazy. And on our way back it was that way in Chicago, at the Congress Hotel, and then in New York, at the Pennsylvania Hotel and the Paramount Theatre." Goodman was on radio almost nightly after his success on the Coast, and the near-riot that attended the band's Paramount Theatre appearance was the first instance in this country of the frightening power of electronics. He kept a band together for ten years, finally disbanding after graduating from his Swing Academy the likes of Bunny Berigan, Bud Freeman, Harry James, Ziggy Elman, Gene Krupa, Jess Stacy, Charlie Christian, Teddy Wilson, Lionel Hampton, Mel Powell, Billy Butterfield, Lou McGarity, Stan Getz, Zoot Sims, and Jimmy Rowles. Since then, a man of means, he has worked as he has seen fit, with jazz and classical groups of all sizes and in every imaginable place. He is not a sentimental man, but on January 17th he will celebrate the fortieth anniversary of his famous 1938 Carnegie Hall concert with another Carnegie Hall concert. There has been no need to advertise, for the old Goodman power prevails. The day tickets went on sale, the concert sold out.

Most eccentrics are private people, and Goodman is no exception. As a result, he has long been surrounded by legends, some true and some not. One is the legend of the Jack Benny skinflint who delights in paying his musicians low wages and then cadges their cigarettes. Zoot Sims, who first played with Goodman in 1943, once brought an apple with him to a re-

cording session and put it on his music stand. When Sims
took his first solo, Goodman picked up the apple and started
eating it. After Sims's first chorus, Goodman had him take
another and then another. Sims was only seventeen and never
said a word, but it is the longest solo Goodman has ever given
him. Another legendary Goodman is a Simon Legree at rehearsals and on the stand. Goodman is a perfectionist about
his own playing, and he expects no less than perfection of his
musicians. When he is displeased by a sideman, he fixes him
with a stony look that has come to be known as "the ray."
Still another legendary Goodman is the befuddled, inarticu-
late maestro. Instances abound of elaborate anecdotes left
hanging, of sentences delivered in low gargles. When he was
questioned not long ago about having fired the great drummer Sidney Catlett in 1941, he replied, "It's always been one
of my enigmas—drummers." But there has never been any
confusion about Goodman the musician. He was one of the
first jazz virtuosos, and the first jazz musician to cross the
barrier between jazz and classical music and become an adept
and respected classical soloist. (It is not a move he is settled
about yet; he feels his jazz playing may have suffered because of his adventurousness, and he knows he is not the best
of all classical clarinettists.) Though it was once a pervasive
jazz instrument, the clarinet has had little influence outside
its own intense and difficult discipline. So it is not clear how
much effect Goodman's playing has had on jazz improvisers.
He helped iron out the rhythmic chunkiness that had afflicted
jazz phrasing since the twenties. He made jazz musicians
more conscious of tone, which had been wholly intuitive. He
was the first serious improviser to champion melodic playing.
Entire solos followed the melody closely or were ingenious
and subtle paraphrases. And when he broke loose, his improvisations, no matter what their speed, were a flow of new
melodies that continually intimated their originals: the flick-
er's sharp undulations constantly suggesting the arc of pure

flight. Goodman was also a *hot* player, of which there have
been surprisingly few. (Ben Webster, Wild Bill Davison, and
Dave McKenna come to mind.) He used a "dirty" tone and
intense on-the-beat and staccato phrasing, and he frequently
sank into the chalumeau register, which endows the clarinet
with great intimacy and lyricism. He favored fast tempos—
the high winds of jazz playing, which invariably give the
effect, even when the musicians are being blown galley-west,
that everyone is swinging like crazy. But, above all, there was
a rare ease about his playing. Bix Beiderbecke and Frankie
Trumbauer had it, and both Goodman and Lester Young
learned from them.

By 1938, Goodman was almost as famous as Franklin Roose-
velt, and when it was announced that he was going to give
the first jazz concert ever held in Carnegie Hall, the tickets
went so fast he had difficulty getting his family in. The concert consisted of twelve numbers by the big band (chief soloists: Goodman, Harry James, Jess Stacy, Vernon Brown,
Gene Krupa), two numbers by the trio (Goodman, Teddy
Wilson, Krupa), five numbers by the quartet (the trio plus
Lionel Hampton), re-creations of the Original Dixieland Jazz
Band, Ted Lewis, and Louis Armstrong, and three numbers
by a group of ringers (Bobby Hackett, Count Basie, Freddie
Green, Walter Page, Buck Clayton, Lester Young, Cootie
Williams, Johnny Hodges, Harry Carney). Irving Kolodin
had suggested that the evening include a brief history of the
previous twenty years in jazz, and John Hammond had suggested that some Basie and Ellington sidemen might add texture and color to the proceedings. Hackett played a Beiderbecke solo, and the Ellington musicians did "Blue Reverie."
The Ellingtons and Basies, together with Goodman, Krupa,
James, and Brown, played a long "Honeysuckle Rose" that
was designed as a jam session. The recording of the concert
brought out twelve years later by Columbia—it is one of the

biggest-selling jazz albums of all time—reveals a curious evening. The band sounds aggressive, and Krupa, who was inadvertently overrecorded on the single microphone, is loud and uneven. The trio and quartet numbers are too long, and three are taken at dismaying killer-diller tempos. The jam session is stiff (Basie, Young, and Clayton were used to Jo Jones's bicycling drumming, not Krupa's piston attack), and so is "Sing, Sing, Sing," the band's pièce de résistance—except, of course, for what has come to be recognized as the single classic stroke of the concert: Jess Stacy's unscheduled two-minute solo, an airy, calm, circular improvisation that rises heedless into the noisy air. Bob Bach, a television producer and a longtime jazz fan, was there. "I went with a friend and his mother," he said recently. "She was an elegant Park Avenue lady who attended the opera and the Philharmonic. Her presence created a certain amount of tension, because everybody knew how much the older people looked down on the concert. Of course, we had our own nervousness, too. The atmosphere was like having someone in your family bar mitzvahed or doing the valedictory at commencement. We were deeply immersed in the Goodman band. We hung out in the Madhattan Room at the Pennsylvania Hotel, and we knew Gene Krupa and Harry James. We'd been to Central Park to the softball games between the Goodman band and the Basie band. Harry James pitched for the Goodmans, and Gene Krupa and Harry Goodman and Babe Russin and Chris Griffin were the infield. Lester Young pitched for the Basies, and Herschel Evans played first and Earle Warren caught. Basie and Jimmy Rushing would come out in their fedoras, and so would the song pluggers and the flotsam and jetsam of the music business, but you never caught Benny there. We knew what we'd hear at Carnegie—the trumpet riffs in 'Sing, Sing, Sing' and the rideouts in the last chorus of the hot numbers and Gene Krupa wrapping everything up with a solo, but we didn't know what would get the biggest applause, what would blow the roof off. Truthfully, nothing really did. The jam session didn't catch fire, and Martha Tilton's singing was pretty dull. But there was a real jam-session moment—a moment of unexpected greatness—and that was when Jess Stacy suddenly took off near the end of 'Sing, Sing, Sing.' It made all the excitement we'd suffered for weeks worthwhile." Another longtime jazz enthusiast, W. W. Nash, remembers the concert somewhat differently: "Two things have stayed in my mind about the evening. The first was 'Don't Be That Way,' which the band started off with. The atmosphere was very highly charged in the hall. In fact, I can't remember any other musical event quite like it, unless it was a particular Toscanini concert or Oistrakh's first appearance here. So when 'Don't Be That Way' came rolling out, it was as if a hundred-piece band were blasting at you. It was even brassier and louder and more hard-driving than we had dreamed. The other thing that has stayed with me was Jess Stacy's solo. For some reason, I was standing in the back of the hall when it started, and a magical stillness came down immediately over the audience. I recall thinking, This is certainly the finest thing that has happened tonight. One has to remember that Goodman's band was simply a *dance* band. Wherever it played, people danced to it. Jazz concerts hadn't begun yet—or, rather, they began that night—and the sitting-and-listening places, like the clubs on Fifty-second Street, were just getting started. Hearing the Goodman band in Carnegie Hall wasn't just startling. It somehow gave jazz an aesthetic stature it hadn't had before."

The concert was held on a cold Sunday night. The *Times* sent its first-string music critic, Olin Downes, who wrote at considerable length for the Monday editions. It took him several paragraphs to warm up, after which he announced:

Jazz has given way to "swing." "Swing" is that subtle creative something, the je ne sais quoi in

popular music, which has superseded the older prod-
uct and gained a greater power of popular appeal
. . . than jazz ever exerted.

Having unwittingly put his thumb in jazz's terminological
soup, Downes continued:

It may therefore be imagined with what a thump-
ing of the heart the present scribe got into his seat,
in good time before the concert began, to hear the
very first notes of Goodman's orchestra. It may be
said immediately that he was enormously impressed, though not in the precise way he expected.
When Mr. Goodman entered he received a real
Toscanini send-off from the excited throng. It took
some minutes to establish quiet. There was quiver-
ing excitement in the air, an almost electrical effect,
and much laughter. The audience broke out before
the music stopped, in crashing applause and special
salvos as one or another of the heroes of the orchestra rose in his place to give his special and ornate
contribution to the occasion.

He then bore down on the music:

This form of sound is a curious reduction, almost
disintegration of music into its component elements.
There is hardly an attempt at beauty of tone, and
certainly none at construction of melody. A few
fragments of well-known popular tunes suffice for a
sort of rough material, subject to variation by the
players. They do such feats of rhythm and dexterity
as occur to them on the tune's basis. The tone of the
brass instruments, almost continually overblown, is
hard, shrill and noisy. The other instruments add
what they can to swell the racket. . . . The playing last night, if noise, speed and syncopation, all
old devices, are heat, was "hot" as it could be, but

nothing came of it all, and in the long run it was decidedly monotonous.

Goodman, Wilson, Hampton, and Stacy played up to and over their heads at the concert, and so did the Ellingtons and Basies in their brief stints, but Downes, as Lester Young used to say, had no ears for what he was hearing. He boomed on:

> Nor is Mr. Goodman, when he plays his clarinet, anything like as original as other players of the same instrument and the same sort of thing that we have heard. Nor did we hear a single player, in the course of a solid hour of music, invent one original or interesting musical phrase, over the persistent basic rhythm. Not that they lacked technical accomplishment and amazing mastery of their medium. Musically, they let us down.

Near the close of his review, Downes looked into the future. " 'Swing' of this kind," he predicted, "will quickly be a thing of the past."

The *Herald Tribune* sent its second-string music critic, Francis D. Perkins, and he was a lot lighter on his feet than Downes. He even managed, after vivid pictures of Krupa and Goodman, some pioneering and quite accurate jazz criticism:

> The foremost contributor to [the visual aspect of the concert] was Mr. Gene Krupa, the group's super-expert percussionist, whose gestures and facial expressions proved unusually engrossing for those near enough to note them in detail, and suggested that he has talents as an actor as well as an instrumentalist. In the usual symphony concert the conductor has the major share of the gesturing, but here Mr. Goodman was the calmest in mien, even when he did incredible work on his clarinet, and he presided over the sessions of the trio and the quartet with an air of paternal benevolence.
>
> To an incompletely initiated listener, last night's

swing had not altogether departed from certain fundamental features of the jazz set forth by Mr. Whiteman fourteen years ago [the Aeolian Hall concert, at which Whiteman introduced George Gershwin's "Rhapsody in Blue" but played just two jazzlike numbers], except that it suggested a turning away from the trend toward politer music and more sophisticated forms represented in more recent programs of Messrs. Whiteman and Grofé. The fundamental rhythmic one-two beat pervaded the program throughout, as in the jazz of yore, although the variations of rhythm over this basic beat have become freer, more changing and higher-flying before returning home; the individual soli are more elaborate, more venturesome and considerably more brilliant and effective. As before, there is a notable range of instrumental sonorities and colors, from proclamative, ear-filling plangence and rousing brilliance to mellow smoothness, and another prominent feature was the expert dynamic control of the orchestra, especially in long gradual crescendi which aroused the audience to roars of applause.

Goodman himself is of about the same heft he was forty years ago. His face is bigger, and whereas he once had a grocery-clerk look, his expression is now owlish and quizzical. His patent-leather hair has become tousled and somewhat thinner, and his rimless spectacles have given way to horn-rimmed ones. His once tight-lipped mouth bears permanent clarinet scars; that is, it slopes toward his right, forming a kind of sluice, out of which his words come. Goodman talks in clumps, which may last two or three minutes before ending suddenly in reverberating silences. His speech resembles his playing. He often starts in a hoarse, dog-eared voice, which suggests his chalumeau tones. His voice slowly ascends until it reaches the clearer, lighter middle register, and as he gathers momentum he occasionally lets loose a falsetto phrase before abruptly falling back to the chalumeau. His words follow each other closely, and sometimes they pile up; then he clears his throat vigorously, and the flow resumes. He laughs a lot, but it is not the kind of laugh you laugh along with, because it demands a great deal of breath. It goes on and on metronomically on the same note, and it calls to mind a stone skipping across the water about twenty times. A few days ago, Goodman talked about the fortieth-anniversary concert, in the living room of his East Side apartment, where he carries on his business (planning some seventy appearances a year, collecting art, jamming with musicians like Jimmy Rowles, listening to records).

"It's remarkable after forty years that I'm still here," he said. "Particularly when you think of all the musicians at the 1938 concert who are gone—Carney and Hodges and Lester Young and Hackett and Gene Krupa. But I think we should have this little celebration. You can't go back forty years musically any more than you can put together the New York Yankees of Joe DiMaggio and Lou Gehrig. But we can do a show with a good air about it. Lionel Hampton and Jess Stacy are set, and I *think* Teddy Wilson will work out. Vernon Brown called, but I don't know whether he'll make it. Harry James can't do it, because he'll be in Hawaii. I suppose the original concert changed the nature of the business. It wasn't very long afterward that everybody was playing concerts. I wish I could say that the whole thing was my idea, but it wasn't. In fact, a press agent named Wynn Nathanson came to me and asked, 'You want to play Carnegie Hall?' I remember saying, 'Are you out of your mind? What the hell would we do there?' I acquiesced, but there was a certain reluctance, an apprehensiveness. I went to see Bea Lillie after I'd accepted, to talk her into doing a skit. I was a great fan of hers, and I thought it would relieve the monotony, and anyway the stage shows we played in theatres always included comics. She was smart enough to say no. Sol

Hurok's name was on the evening, but he had nothing to do with it outside of sending me a wire reminding me to tell the musicians they would be playing in Carnegie Hall and to be on their best behavior. That was an interesting band. It didn't get uptight about anything. It had its good and bad nights, but that particular night it was on. The only reason the concert was recorded was because of Albert Marx, a booking agent, who was married to Helen Ward, who'd been my vocalist. In those days, I had air checks of the band made all the time—just to hear how new things sounded—and my hotel room was flooded with them. So I thought I'd skip having the concert recorded. But when Marx told me he was going to record it and would I like a copy, I said sure. I think he sent the acetates in two tin boxes. I had them in my office for a while, and then I took them to my apartment on Park Avenue and put them away and forgot them. When I moved, my sister-in-law Rachel took over the apartment, be- cause it was rent-controlled, and she found the acetates in a closet. She told me I'd better take them before her son did. I had them played at the Reeves sound studios, because I didn't know what shape they were in, and felt a tape should be made. It was quite something hearing the concert again. We'd rehearsed for it a couple of days in Carnegie to get used to the acoustics, which is what you might call bringing the musicians in to hear the hall. We'd been playing in the Madhattan Room, where the sound was stuffy and dense, and to go into a place where it was so lively was very upsetting at first. Big bands were always difficult to handle acoustically anyway, because of their unorthodox instrumentation."

Then Goodman talked about clarinet playing. "Jimmie Noone was one of my favorite players, and Leon Rappolo was another," he said. "Noone had a clarinet clarinet sound, but Buster Bailey had an academic sound. Bailey and I shared the same teacher in Chicago, and we used to do duets to- gether. Frank Teschemacher was talented, and I liked Volley

De Faut, whose name was Voltaire De Faut, and Larry
Shields, who was with the Original Dixieland Jazz Band. I
think Pee Wee Russell was kind of an anachronism. I first
heard him in St. Louis. I don't think he knew much about
the clarinet. In fact, I think his clarinet was leaking air half
the time. Artie Shaw was a hell of a clarinet player. My
time was always more legato than his, but his sound was
more open. It carried a lot farther. And, of course, Bob Wilber is a superb clarinettist.

"Hindemith wrote a clarinet concerto for me in 1947, and
I played it with the Philadelphia. I listened to it recently—
the version by Louis Cahuzac, the great French clarinettist.
It takes some doing, that piece. You always have to have
chops if you play classical music. I studied with Reginald
Kell, and he was the sort of teacher who analyzed every inch
of what you were playing. He was terrific in that sense. He
wanted to know what you were *doing*. The pressures are
quite violent in classical music. You reach your art on the far
side of technical matters, yet every once in a while you have
to go back to the basics. People have often said to me, 'You're
so relaxed when you play.' Relaxed, my elbow. It's practice.
You do the same thing over and over so many times that it
comes to sound relaxed and easy. But, to turn it around, I've
never been able to play one of my own transcribed jazz solos.
Louis Armstrong and Lester Young and Bix Beiderbecke and
Earl Hines didn't learn to improvise out of a book. They
learned the tradition of it first. When Mel Powell joined me
on piano, Dixieland was about finished, but he knew all the
old pieces, like 'That's a Plenty' and 'Riverboat Shuffle.' It
was the same with Charlie Parker. His blues were older than
time. When you improvise, you're thinking partly about the
chords and partly about the melody. You think about a scale
you might have been working on, or a motif that's been in
your head. Improvisation also depends on the tune you're
playing. Fletcher Henderson tried to arrange songs that swung

to begin with. Good improvising has to be done with complete authority, and with taste and grace. And I always have to know the lyrics first. I sing them to myself, and that helps to get the tempo right. The quality of a lyric—the way the words fit the melody—can affect the way you play. You don't always put the greatest things down. You have moods about music, just the way you have about sunshine or darkness. Jazz is very romantic. I've frequently thought of Brahms as one of the great jazz composers. The last movement of his first clarinet sonata sounds like Bix Beiderbecke." Goodman hummed a melody rapidly, in falsetto. "The *sound* of instruments doesn't seem to matter the way it used to. Bix and Louis and Chu Berry all got big, fat sounds. Sometimes I think about the jam sessions we used to have. The whole damned thing was quite beautiful. You were sent—to use an old expression. I've occasionally thought about my position in music, then discarded the thought. It's terribly hard for one who has made history to talk about it, to be objective. As a musician, I see myself in others' reactions, and that stretches all the way from Glenn Miller to Dennis Brain. I don't think I'll ever stop playing. The clarinet is difficult to play as you get older—just as difficult as a brass instrument. There's a good deal of physical wear, I've noticed, and you have to pace yourself. I'd miss all the problems if I quit. But I'm very lucky. I can pick and choose the problems I want."

January 18th

The forthieth anniversary concert last night was a shambles. Goodman had three pianists shuffling on and off stage (John Bunch, Mary Lou Williams, Jimmy Rowles), and he used a girl singer he had only just heard. The big band he assembled was unfocused and unswinging. So was he. At one point, he sat on a stool and put his feet up on Lionel Hampton's vibraphone and played.

March 6th

Duke Ellington's Boswell turns out to be Stanley Dance, a sixty-seven-year-old English jazz chronicler and aide-de-camp, who by dint of sempiternal doggedness has put together what amounts to a three-volume biography. With the publication of *Duke Ellington in Person* (Houghton Mifflin), written with Ellington's son Mercer, it is now complete. The first volume, *The World of Duke Ellington* (Scribners), was brought out in 1970. It consists of a couple of interviews with Ellington, a transcription of an Ellington press conference, interviews with twenty-six sidemen and three alter egos (Tom Whaley, Ellington's copyist; Mercer Ellington; and Billy Strayhorn), and Dance's own accounts of a Latin-American tour, Ellington's seventieth-birthday party at the White House, the first two Sacred Concerts, and Ellington preparing for a Monterey Jazz Festival. The second volume, Ellington's limpid and funny autobiography, *Music Is My Mistress* (Doubleday), was published in 1973, a year before he died. Except for an extended final chapter of questions and answers compiled by Dance, the book was written by Ellington himself. Mercer describes the process: "Stanley had expected that it would be done with a tape recorder, following the same method they had used for articles, so he was surprised to find that Pop intended to write it himself. The manuscript that eventually materialized was . . . written on hotel stationery, table napkins, and menus from all over the world. Stanley became so familiar with the handwriting that he could often decipher it when Pop could not." In *Duke Ellington in Person*, Dance taped Mercer, and edited the results. All three books, like Ellington himself in his last twenty years, are somewhat helter-skelter. They are sometimes inconclusive, patchy, and—considering their subject—unaccountably flat. There are countless photographs in the three volumes, but little sense of Ellington in the flesh—of his umbrous, polished voice; his gracious laugh; his accent, which was universal and aristocratic; his long, handsome, beautifully lived-in face; his careful, philosopher's gait; his locked concentration when he worked; his quick searching of the middle distance before zeroing in with a mot: "Selfishness can be a virtue. Selfishness is essential to survival, and without survival we cannot protect those whom we love more than ourselves." But the three books help. With his wit and elegance and cool and originality, Ellington was one of the most oblique and elusive of all twentieth-century masters. Toby Hardwick, who was in Ellington's first band, got a glimpse before Ellington slammed the door: "The amazing thing about him is that the language, the slant, everything . . . didn't rub off from someone else, and it wasn't a legacy either. He went inside himself to find it. He's an *only*, that's for sure."

Ellington was a combination of romantic and realist—or perhaps he was a realist who learned early that it is easier to pass as the opposite. His prose reflects this. Others might write in black and white, but Ellington wrote in color. Yet underneath was a sharp vision of life. An excursion on night life in *Music Is My Mistress* begins with typical Ellington sumptuousness, but soon it narrows: "Night Life is cut out of a very luxurious, royal-blue bolt of velvet. It sparkles with jewels, and it sparkles in tingling and tinkling tones. . . . Night Life seems to have been born with all of its people in it, the people who had never been babies, but were born *grown*. . . . Some of them were wonderful people, and some were just hangers-on of a sort. . . . There were a few hustlers, who depended upon finding suckers for survival. And there were some who were too wise to hustle, who only wanted to have enough money to be able to afford to be a sucker."

He expands on the celebrated announcement he made when he was informed that he had almost won a citation from the Pulitzer Prize committee, and ends with a genial, begloved sarcasm. The entry has its own page, and he calls it "Acclaim":

> The Pulitzer Prize music committee recommended me for a special award in 1965. When the full Pulitzer committee turned down their recommendation, Winthrop Sargeant and Ronald Eyer resigned.
>
> Since I am not too chronically masochistic, I found no pleasure in all the suffering that was being endured. I realized that it could have been most distressing and distracting as I tried to qualify my first reaction: "Fate is being very kind to me; Fate doesn't want me to be too famous too young."
>
> Let's say it had happened. I would have been famous, then rich, then fat and stagnant. And then? What do you do with your beautiful, young, freckled mind? How, when, and where do you get your music supplement, the deadline that drives you to complete that composition, the necessity to hear the music instead of sitting around polishing your laurels, counting your money, and waiting for the brainwashers to decide what rinse or tint is the thing this season in your tonal climate?

When he has nothing but good tidings to impart, he relaxes, and becomes almost spare and supple: "To me, the people of London are the most civilized in the world. Their civilization is based on the recognition that all people are imperfect, and due allowances should be and are made for their imperfections. I have never experienced quite such a sense of *balance* elsewhere." The opening paragraph of his autobiography is a fairy tale, a put-on, and probably the truth: "Once upon a time a beautiful young lady and a very handsome young man fell in love and got married. They were a

wonderful, compatible couple, and God blessed their marriage with a fine baby boy (eight pounds, eight ounces).
They loved their little boy very much. They raised him, nur-
tured him, coddled him, and spoiled him. They raised him in
the palm of the hand and gave him everything they thought
he wanted. Finally, when he was about seven or eight, they
let his feet touch the ground."

Like all working romantics, Ellington was highly supersti-
tious. He believed, Mercer tells us, that windows had to be
shut in thunderstorms lest a draft bring the lightning in; that
giving people shoes meant they might walk away from him;
that it was bad luck to bring peanuts or newspapers backstage or to arrive there whistling; that thirteen was a lucky
number; and that the color brown was bad luck, because he
had on a brown suit the day his mother died. (The dust
jacket of his autobiography was originally brown but was
changed to blue at his horrified insistence.)

Mercer's book is unsparing but fair. He says that Ellington
had a sadomasochistic streak that caused him to hurt others
when he most needed them. He also affirms Toby Hardwick's
early judgment: *"He likes to manipulate.* It's a little quirk
all his own. He thinks no one has the slightest idea about
this. He likes to manipuláte people around him, and gets the
biggest kick when he wins. It's not like using someone, it's
more like a game." Another game that Mercer discovered
was Ellington's inviting him to his motel room on the pretext
of looking at a new arrangement or checking a faulty ledger
when all he wanted was company. This fear of showing
weakness eventually hardened into a genuine toughness.

Ellington's reputation as a composer has lately been under
revision, and *Duke Ellington in Person* will hasten the process. He was more of a primitive than most people knew.
Mercer writes:

So far as learning to read music was concerned, he was never exactly avid. . . . There were many people in those days, of course, who went to schools . . . so that they would be recognized as being "able to do it"—being able to read—and they would have considered it cheating to play a record and copy what was on it—and do it just by ear. Ellington sat down and did that time and again. He'd gradually figure out what somebody had done, listen to the beat, and analyze the whole thing. How he ever learned the value and time you'd give a note so that you could represent it on paper, I don't know, but he was able to do this without tutors or formal training. He finally wound up knowing how to write music.

Most primitives are trapped in their only invention—their style. But this was never true of Ellington. Mercer says, "Formal training, to him, implied adhering to the rules and a lack of creativity. He didn't like the rules in anything. To discard a rule was a source of inspiration . . . because he immediately saw the way to make it work in reverse. One whole composition was dedicated to making the seventh chord rise instead of resolve downward. It was a number that never gained much recognition, but I remember his telling me how he had gotten away with it and how nobody had ever thought it sounded bad." Feeling his way early in his career, Ellington got in the habit of listening closely to what was played around him and of asking his musicians for suggestions. This attentiveness became a collective method of composing, which never completely left him, and which in his later, prize-ridden years he perhaps would not have readily acknowledged. Ellington's sidemen repeatedly mention this method in *The World of Duke Ellington:*

> SONNY GREER: "We'd just talk things over and make suggestions on the interpretation."

> HARRY CARNEY: "He was always a great compiler, and one of the guys' ideas would suggest something else to him."
> BARNEY BIGARD: "When I played a solo, or Johnny Hodges played a solo, he'd be listening, and if you made a passage that he liked, he'd write it down and build a tune on it."

Mercer Ellington says that this method sometimes caused grief. "In the past, [Johnny Hodges] had sold his rights to songs for $100 or $200, just as Fats Waller and Ellington had done when they were young and gullible. When Pop turned some of these songs into hits, Rab [Hodges] wanted the deal changed, and when he was refused he became unhappy. That explains why he would sometimes turn toward the piano on-stage and mime counting money."

Ellington was more than a composer. Like a great film director, he was a catalyst, a synthesizer. He had the divine gift of impelling his musicians to offer him their best, which he would put toward the musical vision he had in mind. Hodges or Bigard or Ben Webster would give him eight or twelve beautiful bars and those would pass through his head and come out as "Mood Indigo" or "Sophisticated Lady." (Mercer Ellington says little about Billy Strayhorn, who, a kind of second son, remains a mystery. It is conceivable that without Ellington pushing him Strayhorn would have been a minor, if greatly gifted, composer. But those songs directly credited to him certainly equal Ellington's, and in some instances come close to surpassing them.) The Ellington afflatus was dangerous. It drained his musicians, and at the same time, because so many of his tunes were written specifically for them, it spoiled them. When longtime sidemen left, they either dropped into obscurity or, thirsting for the Master's attention, returned to the fold.

An Ellington tune played in an Ellington arrangement by the Ellington band was unique. Mercer describes this eloquently: "[Ellington] sought a sensuality in the way his music was expressed; there was always an emotion attached to the sound. Or I might say that he was always very conscious of the need to make the listener *feel* experiences with the sound, almost as though he were creating apparitions within the music."

April 12th

Two pianists from the pianistic river that flows through New York:

Joanne Brackeen is tall and shy and bespectacled, and she has four teenage children. Her hair is fuzzy, and she wears long, thin flowered dresses. She was born in Ventura, California, which is between Oxnard and Santa Barbara, and the principal pianist she heard around home was Frankie Carle. Then she discovered Art Tatum and Bud Powell, and not long after that in Los Angeles she discovered Ornette Coleman, still unknown here in New York. John Coltrane, whose influence is yet to be reckoned, came next. She took lessons from a famous local pianist named Sam Saxe, who also got his best students good jobs. She worked for Dexter Gordon and Charles Lloyd on the Coast, and since then she has been with Stan Getz and Art Blakey and Joe Henderson as well as on her own. She has lately joined the elect at Bradley's, where she now is playing. She is a brilliant, close-textured pianist. Her solos have the insistence and intensity of Coltrane, who before becoming long-winded and extra-musical played as if he wished to inhabit not only each tune but each listener. Brackeen's intensity takes her into every number in the same Coltrane way. (Her repertory is humdrum, but it doesn't matter. Her choice of songs provides sufficient inspiration, form, and melodic support.) Her attack is basically single-noted. She likes arpeggios that run along just this side of full slides, and she gives their notes slightly more value than they would ordinarily have, which makes each tooth flash as the smile goes by. She breaks her single-note figures in odd places, like Powell and Coleman, and she will resume with double-time patterns or an open cluster that dissolves into one of her highly detailed arpeggios. Her chordal passages are somewhat forbidding: they tend to be cold and without resolve. (Every pianist should study Jimmy Rowles's wooded, graceful harmonic progressions.) Her left hand is strong and variously arranged, and she is not overly romantic. In a slow ballad ("Days of Wine and Roses," "These Foolish Things"), she will move to the edge of the swamp where Keith Jarrett and McCoy Tyner and Chick Corea disport in slow motion, but she stops there to watch.

Jazz musicians often worked behind vaudeville performers in the twenties and thirties, and sometimes they joined in. Drummers danced and threw their sticks into the air, clarinettists and trumpeters made silly noises, and pianists wore gloves and played standing up. These antics lasted into the forties, when jazz musicians, suddenly self-conscious about being called artists and/or about the possibility of being taken as Uncle Toms, pulled down a scrim between themselves and their listeners. But a few of the vaudeville musicians survive, and one is Dorothy Donegan, who is at Jimmy Weston's with the bassist Arvell Shaw and the drummer Ray Mosca. She is a medium-sized Rubens, with a court jester's face, and everything she plays is translated into action. She rocks back and forth and from side to side. She forms her feet into a giant wedge and stomps it. Her head rolls wildly, and her face is possessed by fearful middle-distance stares, a whorl-like mouth, and bowsprit lips. She bangs her eyes shut and hums demonically. This frenzy—a balletic music—obscures her playing, and that's too bad, for Donegan is a first-rate Tatum pianist. She has a rich, flying left hand and a right hand whose roller-coaster lines and ten-pound chords summon up Tatum's. She constructs mountains of sound on such foundations as "Tea for Two" and "The Man I Love," interlarding the layers with bits of "Rhapsody in Blue," boogie-woogie, stride basses, key changes, and loud-pedal chords, all the while playing at the speed of light. She has been showing off so long she probably doesn't remember what you are really supposed to do when you sit down at a keyboard.

June 1st

For a time, the line of descent from the brilliant trumpeter Fats Navarro, who died in 1950, at twenty-six, kept breaking down. Navarro's banner was picked up almost immediately by Clifford Brown, another dazzling player, but Brown was killed in an automobile accident in 1956, also at twenty-six. Two years later, Booker Little appeared, but he died suddenly in 1961, when he was twenty-three. By the mid-sixties, Navarro seemed forgotten. But now his legacy, streamlined and brought up to date, has reappeared in Woody Shaw, who is thirty-four.

Navarro, who was of Cuban, Chinese, and black extraction, worked his way up through the bands of Snookum Russell, Andy Kirk, Billy Eckstine, and Lionel Hampton. Here is how Charles Mingus introduces him in his autobiography, *Beneath the Underdog:* "There was a man named Fats Navarro who was born in Key West, Florida, in 1923. He was a jazz trumpet player, one of the best in the world. He and my boy [Mingus, that is] met for the first time on a cold winter night in 1947 in Grand Central Station in New York City. Lionel Hampton's band had just got off the train from Chicago and [the trumpeter] Benny Bailey gaily said good-bye and split: he was leaving for Paris, France. The guys all stood around in their overcoats by the clock, waiting for the new man joining the band. A big, fat fellow walked up carrying a trumpet case and asked in the oddest high squeaky

voice 'This the Hampton crew?' and [the trombonist] Britt
Woodman introduced Fats Navarro." Mingus adored Navarro,
and he makes him into a self-destroying angel (Navarro
died of tuberculosis and heroin addiction) as well as a Mingus
mouthpiece who detests white men, bookers, managers, club
owners, audiences, and all the impedimenta that weigh down
black jazz musicians. Navarro is given several Mingus dia-
tribes. One goes:

> Mingus, I still ain't as scared to die as I am to go
> home to see my mother and family in Florida. You
> should see all the churches we got out in Key West.
> The white man's got 'em too. I heard 'em praying
> once when I was little in some kind of weird tongue.
> I later found out it was Latin. Imagine! Nigger-
> hating Southern white man that can't hardly read
> or write English sitting up in a church looking holy
> with his big red turkey neck, speaking in Latin!

Navarro was a gentle, becoming man who apparently
brought out the perverse in his celebrators, most of whom
imbued him with evil spirits. Ross Russell, the Charlie
Parker hagiographer and bebop critic, converts Navarro into
a combination of Sydney Greenstreet and a well-known a. and
r. man of the time in his novel *The Sound*. The hero of the
book, based closely on Parker, is a benighted, drug-ridden
trumpet player named Red Travers, and Navarro, who is
given his real nickname, Fat Girl, is an unnervingly omni-
scient record collector who also happens to be a pusher:

> Red was accompanied by a great butterball of a
> man with drooping mustaches and a Charlie Chan
> face called Fat Girl . . . Fat Girl had large, liquid
> eyes that swam under beautifully modeled lids and
> lashes. They reminded Bernie of the eyes in an east-
> ern idol . . . His dress, manners and speech were
> the quintessence of hip, up-to-the-minute Harlem.

"Gassed!" Fat Girl said. "Big eyes to hear you blow, man!"

The origins of Navarro's trumpet playing are not altogether clear. He is said to have idolized Charlie Shavers (who was a cousin), and perhaps this accounts for his fondness for eighth notes, delivered in non-stop up-and-down patterns. If he listened to Shavers, he must have heard Buster Bailey and Billy Kyle, who were in John Kirby's band with Shavers and were equally rococo and multi-noted. And Charlie Parker and Dizzy Gillespie surely turned Navarro from improvising on standard chords to improvising on augmented ones. But after wandering among these masters Navarro sought his own way. Bebop had a harum-scarum quality, a fondness for odd notes, broken rhythms, and jet speeds. Its soloists started and stopped in strange places; rushes of notes would be followed by silence or half-speed phrases; blasts would subside into whispers, and whispers would suddenly become shouts; solos would last far longer than their players' invention warranted; tempos would be so fast they'd freeze the soloist or make him gibber. None of this perturbed Navarro. He understood that the frenetic quality of much bebop derived partly from the ineptness of some of its players and partly from the exuberance its superior players felt at having new chords and freer rhythms to ride around in. So in his solos he clothed the genuine departures from swing inherent in bebop with logic and beauty. Set against the background of his often dishevelled peer, a Navarro solo was like an immaculate fairway flanked by ankle-deep rough. His solos compare extremely well with Dizzy Gillespie's most famous effusions of the time, but they got less attention from the public, because they lacked the italics and bold face that Gillespie always set himself up in. Gillespie liked to clown and blare and do the fandango up and down his registers. He liked to blow the grass flat and divide the waters. But the truth is that Navarro was the better trumpet player. He concentrated on his tone, which was full and even; on his chops, which were almost perfect (he rarely split or dropped notes, the way most bebop trumpeters did, Gillespie included); and on his sense of order, which gave his solos a Churchillian ring and flow. He stayed largely in the middle register, but his occasional ascensions were masterly. The notes, though high, were big and smooth, and there was none of Gillespie's occasional pinched quality. Sometimes Navarro's phrases lasted ten or twelve bars: they crossed meadows and stiles and copses before landing. But every so often he would insert a clump of whole notes that would have the effect of briefly throwing his solo into slow motion. He would punctuate these serene juxtapositions with silence, and shift back into his handsome parade of eighth notes.

Navarro can be profitably studied on "Fats Navarro: Fat Girl" (Savoy). There are twenty-eight tracks, made in 1946 and 1947, and the best are those with the pianist Tadd Dameron, a gifted and largely unsung bebop arranger and composer who brought order and inspiration to the recording sessions he participated in. Of interest as well is "Charlie Parker: One Night in Birdland" (Columbia)—a radio broadcast Navarro did at Birdland with Parker and others, supposedly a week before his death. But this seems hard to believe, for he is in sparkling, driving condition.

Clifford Brown, who was seven years younger than Navarro, rose quickly after Navarro's death. (In the year before he died, Navarro dwindled to about a hundred pounds. Dan Morgenstern tells, in his liner notes for the Savoy album, of running into him in the subway in the summer of 1950 and finding him so depleted as to be almost unrecognizable.) By 1955, Brown, who was from Wilmington, Delaware, had become the most applauded young player in jazz. He had color and fire and great forward motion. His solos in outline resembled Navarro's, but they were delivered with greater intensity and they were more prolix. Brown raced and swam around his horn, as if he had intimations of his limited time and had to get as much said as possible. When he was killed, there was an uncommon rush of sentiment in the jazz world. (The tenor saxophonist and composer Benny Golson wrote a resonant dirge-ballad called "I Remember Clifford," which was widely recorded and continues to be played today.) Then Booker Little, out of Memphis and barely twenty, began to move to the fore, and Navarro and Brown were with us again. Little belonged somewhere between Navarro and Brown. He was a thoughtful player who seemed to release his notes unwillingly, as if he feared he would never find their like again, and he had a certain moroseness of tone and attack which suggested he had also studied Miles Davis. But Little had clarity and warmth and invention, and a distinct flair for composing and arranging.

Woody Shaw appeared in the mid-sixties. He worked with Eric Dolphy (as had Little), Horace Silver, Art Blakey, Mc-Coy Tyner, Gil Evans, and the drummer Louis Hayes, and lately he has led his own group. He lists as influences Gillespie, Navarro, Brown, and Little, together with Freddie Hubbard, Lee Morgan, and Donald Byrd. Also audible are Ornette Coleman and Don Cherry. Shaw was a fancy player at first. But, with the help of the unique Dolphy, he began to realize that ceaselessly running the chords of a tune was a form of imprisonment, that chords were commands as well as signposts. He also realized that Dizzy Gillespie runs had become clichés, and another form of bondage. He expanded his sense of invention. He began using sizable intervals (all trumpeters should study Ruby Braff's, which resemble air pockets) and nests of legato notes where one could pause and rest. He shied away from the chord structure, throwing in bursts of notes that had little to do with their environment but fitted anyway. And he mixed everything up cleverly. He would open a chorus with a turning, half-time phrase, its notes played in an almost impressionistic way, pause, leap into his high register for two quick, jabbing notes, the second broken off purposely, sail into a fine, hilly Navarro-Brown passage, which ended in an old-fashioned, waving vibrato reminiscent of Frankie Newton's in the mid-thirties, and close out the solo with a couple of blistering, descending arpeggios and a final group of calm, legato notes. (Shaw has also made his first album for Columbia, a sturdy effort called "Rosewood." "Rahsaan's Run" and "Theme for Maxine" are done by Shaw's current group, which includes Carter Jefferson on reeds, Onaje Allan Gumbs on piano, Clint Houston on bass, and Victor Lewis on drums. The four other titles are with an augmented and not necessarily superior band.)

For all his originality and energy, Shaw suffers two shortcomings that have afflicted almost every trumpeter since Fats Navarro and Clifford Brown. One is a sharp, shallow tone (compare the rich brassiness of Thad Jones, the velvet musings of Braff, and the impeccable, almost octagonal sound of Joe Wilder), and the other is a tendency to make everything he plays seem difficult to execute. When audiences are reminded of the effort it takes to please them, they grow restive. Audiences are interested in being entertained, a state of euphoria that should appear as effortlessly given as it is received.

June 21st

Calvin Coolidge and Herbert Hoover didn't invite Louis Armstrong to the White House, nor did F.D.R. ask Fletcher Henderson or Count Basie or Duke Ellington. Harry Truman had a classical singer in the family, and Dwight Eisenhower was not musical. Neither were the Kennedys, but they did swing, and in the spring of 1962 the Music Committee of the

President's People-to-People Program sponsored an International Jazz Festival in Washington. It was given everywhere in the city but at the White House. Seven years and two Administrations later, the White House officially opened its gates to jazz by giving Duke Ellington the Presidential Medal of Freedom and a seventieth-birthday party. It was a joyous time. Richard Nixon, his Uriah Heep mask set aside, was almost buoyant, Ellington was serene and gracious, and the tributary music (by the likes of Jim Hall, Urbie Green, Paul Desmond, Hank Jones, Gerry Mulligan, Earl Hines, and Willie the Lion Smith) was excellent. Then, three days ago, the President and Mrs. Carter gave a "jazz concert" on the South Lawn of the White House.

The music began at five o'clock and ended just after dark. A buffet supper of jambalaya was accompanied by the Young Tuxedo Brass Band, from New Orleans. Just after six-thirty, President Carter jumped up on a bandstand that had been erected at the northwest corner of the lawn, and gave a capsule history of the music. He refreshingly pointed out that racism had slowed its acceptance, admired its freedom and self-discipline, told of first listening to it in the early forties, and closed by saying that "over the period of years the quality of jazz could not be constrained," which had a fine Faulknerian surge. The President spent most of the concert seated on the grass about fifteen feet from the front of the bandstand, and he listened closely. When he was particularly moved by a musician, he got quickly to his feet and congratulated him. He told the pianist McCoy Tyner that what he had just played was "beautiful," and after Cecil Taylor was finished he pursued him (Taylor's stage exits are phenomenally swift) across a corner of the bandstand and under a low-lying magnolia tree. He spoke with Lionel Hampton and Phyllis Condon, and with Charles Mingus, who was confined to a wheelchair. The musicians were clearly impressed by Carter's appreciation, and after a time it seemed to affect the music itself.

Eubie Blake started the main part of the concert. Now ninety-five, he played two of his own numbers, "Boogie Woogie Beguine" and the famous "Memories of You." One has come to relish Blake for his unflagging turn-of-the-century spirit and for his two-foot hands, whose fingers stroke up and down the keyboard like trireme oars. With Dick Hyman, Doc Cheatham, and Milt Hinton accompanying her, Katharine Handy Lewis, the daughter of W. C. Handy, sang her father's "St. Louis Blues," and her sweet, faraway voice was cushioned by Cheatham's elegiac obbligatos. Mary Lou Williams did an eight-minute a cappella history of jazz piano playing which went somewhat awry—the little sea of sound she created was filled with waves of ragtime and boogie-woogie and blues and ballads and bebop, and they tended to break every which way. The first group to appear on the bandstand was made up of Clark Terry, Roy Eldridge, Benny Carter, Illinois Jacquet, Teddy Wilson, Hinton, and Jo Jones, and it played "In a Mellotone" and "Lady Be Good." Not much happened. Jones dragged the tempo, Carter was dicty, Terry was calligraphic, and Jacquet decorated the evening with his lustrous Southwestern tone. Bebop and hard bop, in the persons of Sonny Rollins, McCoy Tyner, Ron Carter, and Max Roach, did Rollins' "Sonnymoon for Two," and the concert came alive. Rollins played a brilliant, compressed solo, full of vertical melodies, repetitions, and quotations, and Roach matched him with staccato snare-drum figures—super-double-time figures, executed at teeth-gritting speed. A group of stylistic first cousins, which included Dizzy Gillespie, Dexter Gordon, George Benson, Herbie Hancock, Ron Carter, and Tony Williams, did ebullient versions of "I'll Remember April" and "Caravan." Williams equalled Roach's staccato ruminations, and Gordon refloated Lester Young. Then Ornette Coleman, accompanied only by his son Denardo, on drums, played two of his own compositions back to back, and his tone and boldness and invention were like proclamations. His songs were classic Coleman—long, sorrowing, descending melodic lines, enlivened here and there by double-time passages—and his improvisations would have carried even further without Denardo's heavy drumming. Cecil Taylor came next, and President Carter, his back curved and his arms clasped around his raised knees, was transfixed. Taylor was dazzling and brief. He got off several of his almost staccato arpeggios, a lyrical passage, and some jackhammer chords. The last scheduled group was a mixed grill consisting of Lionel Hampton, Stan Getz, Zoot Sims, George Benson, Chick Corea, Ray Brown, and Louis Bellson. It did "How High the Moon," and Zoot Sims, playing two excellent choruses, brought the evening to a climax. Getz did two choruses of "Lush Life," and it was a case of the song (Billy Strayhorn) and the musician fitting perfectly: "Lush Life" prodded Getz and Getz filled in its sinuous outlines.

Then President Carter returned to the stage and declared that jazz was "just as much a part of the great things of the nation as the White House itself or the Capitol Building down the street," and asked for more music. Hampton set off "Flyin' Home," and Jacquet played his old solo. Pearl Bailey rose out of the audience in response to a request from Mrs. Carter, sang a couple of songs, and sashayed back into the audience. The darkness had about touched ground when Dizzy Gillespie and Max Roach reappeared for a stamping, funny duet, with Roach using only his high-hat cymbals. The President and George Wein were watching side by side next to the bandstand, and Wein looked as if his mother, who was in the audience, had neglected to tell him that there would be no need for him to turn to stone if he ever found himself cheek by jowl with a President of the United States.

Gillespie, dropping several "Your Majesty"s, asked Carter if he would sing the old bop tune "Salt Peanuts." It isn't easy. The singer, at a fast tempo, is obliged to chat a dozen "Salt peanuts." "Salt" is one note; "pea-," also one note, jumps an octave; and "nuts," one note, too, drops back three tones. Carter brought it off. Gillespie then asked him if he would care to go on the road with his group, and the President said, "I might have to after tonight."

The scenery and furnishings for such occasions matter. The South Lawn, with its hummocks and dells, is a beautiful piece of geography. The crowd, numbering around a thousand, sat on the grass or at picnic tables set up diagonally to the bandstand. When the concert began, the sun, coming in over the old State Department Building, was merciless. But it obliged and went down, making way for a pale-blue sky and a lemon moon. Honeysuckle replaced the air, and swallows rocketed between the trees. After the music, the President, surrounded by family and friends, walked back to the White House at roughly the speed of a slow blues.

June 23rd

One is burdened by arithmetic at the outset of this year's Newport Jazz Festival-New York. The words "Silver Anniversary" are emblazoned on the festival's program cover, and on page 3 its producer, George Wein, declares, "For the past twenty-four summers, at the conclusion of each jazz festival, one question was omnipresent: 'What are we going to do next year?' " One had hoped that first off we would tell the truth about how old we are. The Newport Jazz Festival *was* started twenty-five summers ago, in 1954, but there have been only twenty-four festivals (including the one beginning tonight), since none was held in 1961, the year after the Newport Riot, which caused the festival to be shut down on its third day. The rest of the math is easier. This is the sev-

enth year of the Newport Jazz Festival in New York, the
fifth straight year that Sarah Vaughan has sung at the festival, and the second straight year that she has starred at its
opening. She did so in Carnegie Hall tonight, and all four octaves were in order—particularly her quasi-baritone, an area
roomy enough to hold a dance in. Her vibrato was sumptuous, and her intervals, ascending and descending, were
chasmal. She did a fast "I'll Remember April," a slow "I
Fall in Love Too Easily," Tadd Dameron's "If You Could
See Me Now," a Gershwin medley, and Duke Ellington's "I
Got It Bad and That Ain't Good," wherein she sang "I'm not
made of wooooooooooood-ah." Audiences now react to Sarah
Vaughan the way they do to drummers. She is a virtuoso, a
high-wire act, an eighth wonder. Her accompanists of these
many years are Carl Schroeder on piano, Walter Booker on
bass, and Jimmy Cobb on drums.

June 24th

Ella Fitzgerald recorded "A Tisket, a Tasket" with Chick
Webb forty years ago. Some of her lower tones have more
resonance now, and her middle register has thickened, but
her voice is still a teenager's—light, pure, boxy, emotionless.
She and Billie Holiday started in the thirties as born singers.
Both had almost unnervingly natural attacks, but by the mid-
forties Holiday was decorating her singing with mannered
bent notes and a long-gowned solemnity, and Fitzgerald got
increasingly "jazzy" until she was doing little besides scat
singing. This jazzlike attack became fixed in the fifties, and,
despite her recorded voyages into Gershwin and Kern and
Porter, she has never shaken loose from it and moved on. She
still tends to pump up certain phrases with anticipatory syl-
lables, as in Cole Porter's "Dream Dancing," which she sang
tonight at Carnegie Hall as "drehehehumeum dancing." She
inserts falsetto notes, needlessly big intervals, and ski-jump

glisses; she often resembles a lesser Sarah Vaughan. She
seemed edgy tonight. Her intonation was off, she never quite
swung, and some of her songs were poorly chosen or were
sung at odd tempos. She included "Satin Doll," with its silly
lyrics, and "Ain't Misbehavin'." She did "I Cried for You"
at a *very* fast tempo, and "That's My Desire," a song forever
associated with Velma Middleton and Louis Armstrong. In
between, she scatted, a forlorn cement that failed to hold her
performance together.

But there was a surprise at the concert. Fitzgerald's accompanists were Tommy Flanagan on piano, Keter Betts on
bass, and Jimmy Smith on drums, and they were given fifty
minutes to themselves. Flanagan belongs with Jimmy Rowles
and Ellis Larkins and Dave McKenna. He has humor, a
zephyr touch, an oblique and original harmonic sense, and
unwearying invention. His great facility makes what he does
sound too easy—the tricky, quiet, single-note melodic lines
that often abruptly slow to a walk just before they end; the
loose, echoing tenths in his left hand; the nimble parallel
chords; the love of melody; and the multilayered improvisations he builds on a tune like "Body and Soul," which he
played tonight. He also played a medium-tempo blues;
"Good Bait"; a bossa nova; Thelonious Monk's "Friday the
Thirteenth," into which he let a lot of light and air; and "All
the Things You Are."

Is it possible, decade after decade, to appreciate a music
that isn't fully comprehensible, that is boring and exhilarating, overweening and lyrical, ponderous and fleet—the
music, in short, of Cecil Taylor? Yes. One simply relishes
Taylor's stamina and technique, his willful and joyous ob-
scurantism, and the immense bath of sound—the omni-
sound—he engulfs us in. At the late concert at Carnegie
tonight, he brought along Jimmy Lyons on alto saxophone,
Ramsey Amin on violin, Raphé Malik on trumpet, Sirone on
bass, and Steve McCall on drums. They played a single one-

hour number with opening and closing ensembles that
sounded like free dirges, and there were extensive solos for
the violin and horns, punctuated by Taylor solos. He was
flamboyant and triumphant. He played glisses, Niagara arpeggios, chords struck with his fist, impenetrable low-register
figures (not helped by muddy amplification), and a long and
lovely passage of improvised Debussy.

June 26th

Wild Bill Davison, at seventy-two, is the same batch of mannerisms, tics, and poor jokes that he was almost forty years
ago, when he first arrived in New York. He puts his cornet
just to the left of the center of his lips, aims it at third base,
and beetles his brows. At the close of each pivotal phrase, he
removes the horn and shakes it. He wiggles the pinkie of his
right, or fingering, hand with each vibrato. He still wears his
hair flat and parted slightly off center (it lines up perfectly
with his embouchure), his blue eyes still snap, and his face
is as smooth as a honeydew. He is probably the best Chicago-
style lead trumpeter-cornettist who ever lived, and he is a
fiery and lyrical soloist. He uses a hoarse tone, he plays right
on top of the beat or ridiculously far behind it, and he is con-
cise to the point of being aphoristic. He is a consummate melodic improviser, and the delight in following one of his solos
is guessing when he will suddenly fall behind the beat into a
soft legato phrase, when he will insert an upper-register
shout, when he will drop an octave. One can hear where
Ruby Braff and a host of lesser players came from, and one
can hear the parts of Louis Armstrong and Bix Beiderbecke
and King Oliver that Davison came from. He is in the middle of his annual two-week stint at Eddie Condon's. He did
easy versions of "Keepin' Out of Mischief Now" and "I Can't
Believe That You're in Love with Me," a fast "All of Me," a

rolling "You Took Advantage of Me," and a fast "When You're Smiling."

June 27th

Between 1930 and 1945, most jazz improvisers played the songs of George Gershwin, Harold Arlen, Irving Berlin, Richard Rodgers, and their like, and in the forties the Gershwins' "I Got Rhythm," disguised in an immense variety of bebop hats, seemed to be their *only* song. Before that, they had written much of their material, and since the early fifties they have resumed the practice. Every so often, George Wein likes to pay tribute to American song at the festival, as he did tonight at Carnegie. Alberta Hunter, accompanied by Gerald Cook and Al Hall, sang six of her own numbers, and confirmed the suspicion that several hearings are more than enough to admire her pipes, pep, and perseverance. (She is eighty-three now.) Dick Hyman (on the Carnegie Hall electric organ) and Ruby Braff did three Fats Waller songs— "How Can You Face Me?" and "Ain't Misbehavin' " and "Honeysuckle Rose." The contrast between Braff's cello tone and the rainbow shades that Hyman got from his various keyboards was subtle and rich. Braff was full of delicate, glancing notes as well as his familiar basso-profundo excursions. Hyman's touch called up Waller's own playing, so the old fox was doubly celebrated. Irene Kral brought along her Anita O'Day-Carmen McRae patterns and imposed them on three Cole Porters ("Experiment," "Easy To Love," "Ev'ry Time We Say Good-bye"). And Stan Getz, in company with the superior pianist Al Dailey, did three Alec Wilder songs ("I'll Be Around," "Ellen," and "The Winter of My Discontent") and Thad Jones's "A Child Is Born," which has Wilder lyrics. Getz played each song straight before embellishing it, and Dailey worked up a series of harmonic adventures in

178   NIGHT CREATURE

"Ellen." The final set was a celebration of Harry Warren, Arlen, Berlin, Arthur Schwartz, and Eubie Blake, done by Mel Tormé, who doubled on piano; Gerry Mulligan, who also sang; and Jimmy Rowles. They were backed by George Duvivier and Oliver Jackson. The group had rehearsed—to the point where it could easily go out on the road. Tormé sang Arlen's "Get Happy," and Rowles sang Warren's "I Wish I Knew." Tormé sang Arlen's "Let's Take a Walk Around the Block," and Mulligan sang Schwartz's and Larry Hart's very early "And Fall Asleep with a Smile." Mulligan, who has a cheerful, attractive voice, also sang Schwartz's "By Myself," while Tormé sang highly effective obbligatos behind him. Jimmy Rowles played a handsome version of Warren's "You're My Everything," and Tormé did Arlen's "On the Swing Shift" and "Accentuate the Positive." There was an Irving Berlin medley in which Tormé did "How About Me?," Mulligan played "Easter Parade," Rowles played "Remember," and Tormé sang "Alexander's Ragtime Band." Tormé, summoning up Ben Webster, closed with a beautiful version of Blake's "Memories of You."

June 29th

Tormé was back tonight—at Avery Fisher, with its exasperating, furry sound—and again he lifted the proceedings. He was accompanied by Buddy Rich's big band, which went through its customary maneuvers and then fell back for a Rich gallimaufry, complete with a whisper-to-crescendo snare-drum roll, ricky-ticking on the drum rims, elephant tomtoms, and straight-ahead, pavement-pounding Chick Webb snare figures. Dizzy Gillespie came aboard for a long, sensational solo. He sent up flares; fashioned a gentle, careering passage of half-valved notes that were almost subliminal; and loosed plumb runs. Tormé warmed up with Count Basie's "Down for Double" and with "You Are the Sunshine of My Life," and brought Stan Getz on for "Here's That Rainy Day." Getz is the last of the romantic saxophonists, and when he plays ballads one just wishes that he wouldn't keep peering out longingly between the notes. Tormé joined him, and the supper-club Tormé of the other night had been replaced by the Las Vegas Tormé. It was the same singer, but in italics— the daring phrasing and dynamics, the hand-wrought substitute notes, the cantorial voice. He sang Toots Thielemans's "Bluesette," and in "I Can't Get Started" he and Gillespie did obbligatos for one another. He sang Harold Arlen's "Blues in the Night," using a five-story Gothic arrangement by Marty Paich, in which the tempo changed continually. Tormé likes to top himself, so he did a whipping improvisation on Ella Fitzgerald's famous scat version of "Lady Be Good."

Meanwhile, over at Carnegie Hall, the Trapp family of jazz, the Brubecks, were bouncing through "Blue Rondo à la Turk," a ballad called "Tea for Jane," and a peculiar tribute to Fats Waller that began with blues and boogie-woogie, neither of them forms that Waller was particularly at home with. Darius Brubeck played several skillfully turned single-note melodic lines on his electronic keyboards, but his brothers (Chris on bass and Danny on drums) were stolid. Brubeck *père* busied himself at his piano with his old impossible task of trying to re-create the lyrical freight he hears within him.

June 30th

Chick Corea, once a Latin-band pianist and now, at thirty-seven, the operator of a small musical empire, gave two concerts at Avery Fisher Hall tonight, and both were sold out. Corea's music, whether in his compositions or in the way he chooses to play them, is soft and romantic and elusive. It hovers on the edge of jazz, of classical music, of rock. It is melodic and pretty, and it often feigns complexity, so as not

to insult its audiences. Woody Herman's band played Corea's
"Suite for Hot Band," and it had blues effects, brass-band effects, and lots of solos. Corea and Gary Burton played a couple of duets, in which their instruments (vibraharp and
acoustic piano) clipped and twined. Then a thirteen-piece
ensemble with strings, rhythm section, horns, and the singer
Gayle Moran went through five long pieces. There were lots
of flute solos and ostinato passages, and Gayle Moran sang
and vocalized in a lunging soprano. In the last two numbers,
Corea, on acoustic piano, was joined by Herbie Hancock on
the Yamaha electric piano. Corea and Hancock toured for
two months last winter, and their duets, on acoustic piano,
were full of Lisztian rhapsody, flash, and empathy. The atmosphere onstage was like Valentine's Day in the sixth
grade, and it wasn't much different tonight.

Sam Rivers is a forty-seven-year-old New York reed man,
pianist, composer, arranger, and visionary. At a midnight
concert in Carnegie Hall, he offered a quintet, made up of
Ted Dunbar on guitar, Mike Nock on piano and synthesizer,
Dave Holland on bass, and Bobby Battle on drums, and a big
band, made up of four trumpets, two trombones, five saxophones, a tuba, a bass, and drums, and including Ricky Ford,
Hamiet Bluiett, and Chico Freeman on reeds, Jack Walrath
on trumpet, Holland, and Barry Altschul on drums. The
quintet played the conservative half of "The Hong Kong
Suite," which consists of eight ten-minute sections, four of
them traditional jazz and four avant-garde. For nearly an
hour, Rivers and his cohorts issued an uninterrupted series of
melodic reflections on the small-band jazz of the forties and
fifties. The tempos and time signatures changed constantly;
there were quiet, studied solos by Rivers and Dunbar and
Nock; and the music circled and circled but never came to
rest. The big band was another matter.

Rivers arranged his musicians in a loose, three-sided box
centered on the tubist, the bassist, and the drummer, while

he played and conducted at its open end. They did an hour-
long piece called "Evocation." It had a lot of "free" figures
played separately by the sections in long, heavily accented
melodic lines or all at once in thick, cacophonic ensembles.
Soloists, one or two at a time, passed between the sections,
and were rarely more than functional. Rivers is a possessed
musician (after a time, he resembled a puppet, spinning just
above the ground among his musicians, his back now toward
us, now toward them), but for all his efforts "Evocation"
never took off. Nor did it have any of the humor of an avant-
gardist like Archie Shepp, who is aware that parody both
blesses and buries what has come before.

July 1st

Lionel Hampton's fiftieth-anniversary concert at Carnegie
Hall tonight was a surprise, for his appearances at the festival
as a leader have generally been given over to exhibitionistic
displays on the drums, piano, and vibraphone. He had a sev-
tenteen-piece band with him. A third of its members were
alumni (Cat Anderson, Joe Newman, Billy Mackel, Benny
Powell, Arnett Cobb), and the rest included Doc Cheatham,
Jimmy Maxwell, Panama Francis, Chubby Jackson, Ray
Bryant, Pepper Adams, Eddie Bert, and Earle Warren. Almost everyone got a solo turn, but Cobb and Cheatham were
exemplary.

Cobb replaced Illinois Jacquet in Hampton's band in the
early forties, and he is another of the big-toned tenor saxophonists who modelled themselves on Coleman Hawkins and
Ben Webster. But he is from Texas, and his tone has the
ribbed, four-by-four texture of the Southwestern saxophonists. He likes long-held notes and arching slurs and the sort
of legato phrasing in which the player *pushes* his notes. In
general, the Southwesterners have never been formidable improvisers, but Cobb's selections—"On the Sunny Side of the

Street," "I'm Confessin'," and "The Nearness of You"—were
winning melodic re-creations. He moved his notes around
grandly, and he made his sound heavy and working.

Cheatham has been startling for years, and he was tonight
in "Don't Be That Way." His lilting, staccato solos are im-
peccably structured, and they have a moonlike ring and
shine. Hampton himself played with delicacy and beauty,
and it was good to hear Teddy Wilson and Bob Wilber, who
helped form a mock Benny Goodman quintet. Wilson leaned
into his solos for a change, and Wilber was his intelligent,
gleaming self.

July 24th

When the tenor saxophonist Scott Hamilton came down to
New York two years ago from Providence, where he was
born in 1954, it was as if Ben Webster and Flip Phillips had
returned in one. Hamilton's big, surprising tone was that of
Webster, and his attack and phrasing incorporated Flip Phillips. But he was not a copyist; the accidents of his upbringing
had largely given him his style. It was also clear that he was
a good musician, that he was inventive and eloquent, and
that his improvisations would move down his own paths as
soon as he was ready to knock away the molds he had borrowed.

Hamilton is of medium height and shape and, given two
or three more inches, could pass as the young Bix Beiderbecke. The tops of his ears fan out, and he wears a small mustache. His brown eyes turn down at their outer corners and
are set wide apart. His hair is thick and dark and divided
down the middle. He talks about himself easily, and without
pose or apology.

"My father, whose name is Robert, is a painter who teaches
at the Rhode Island School of Design," he said the other day.
"In two years, he'll be sixy-five and can retire, and I don't

know what will happen. Now he paints a thousand pictures
and puts them in closets, and then, to make room for new
paintings, he has a burning, which he did in a field in Maine
a while ago. He's had shows in Boston and some critical success, but he's apprehensive about New York. I think he likes
being a big fish in a small pond. He's short, and he's got a
beard and a sense of humor, and we get along fine. My
mother is younger, and she's an artist, too—mostly in fabrics.
And I have a younger sister who's at R.I.S.D. I don't know
what she does, and when I see her I always forget to ask.

"I took piano lessons when I was five, but that didn't last,
and when I was eight I studied clarinet, which didn't last,
either. I played harmonica professionally with local blues
groups at fourteen, and I didn't take up the tenor until I was
seventeen and in my last year in high school. My clarinet
background helped, and I had listened to jazz records since I
was nine or ten. My father had a lot of 78s, and we split his
collection. Half were in my room and half in his studio.
When I was eleven, I listened to the Beatles, but then I went
back to jazz and listened to Lester Young and Coleman
Hawkins and Ben Webster. Unfortunately, I missed seeing
them all. Hawkins played in Providence once near the end of
his life, when I was thirteen or fourteen, but I didn't get
there, and, of course, Webster went to Europe in the mid-
sixties, and Lester died when I was four. Just to have got a
little piece of any of them would have been enough. I started
playing tenor with a blues band that had a Muddy Waters
singer. I sounded terrible, but I knew the notes, and it was
the best training just to jump in and play. In a while, I
worked with organ trios in black Elks clubs in and around
Providence, and I worked a place in Cambridge where they
packed guns and stayed open until ten in the morning. Then
I formed a group with a guitarist named Fred Bates—the
Hamilton-Bates Blue Flames. We had a bass player and the
drummer Chuck Riggs, who's with me now. We drove an old

Ford van, which wobbled all over the highway, and we went up and down New England—Vermont and New Hampshire in winter, and Nantucket and Martha's Vineyard and Block Island in summer. No one wanted a jazz band then. The people who hired us thought *everybody* was a rock group, and when we started playing they were surprised. But they didn't throw anything at us, and, one way or another, we made a living. Block Island was where I met Arnett Cobb, the great Texas tenor player. He'd driven two thousand miles from Houston because he'd been told that Block Island was the Las Vegas of the East, and he didn't know what to make of it when he got there—no laundromat, so he had to wash his clothes in the sink; not enough electric power to run the organ he'd brought; and an out-of-tune piano. But he got through it, and he let me sit in all the time. Fred Bates married and Chris Flory came in on guitar, and we still work together a lot. I think I decided to move to New York when they raised my rent in Providence to twenty dollars a week. I'd played with Roy Eldridge in Boston, and he encouraged me in every way. In fact, I'd be nowhere without him. The first job I had here was a Tuesday night with the house band at Eddie Condon's. Right after, I went into Michael's Pub for six weeks with Billy Butterfield, and on the basis of that I figured I could make it. I've worked steadily since, and for a guy who just walked in I've been lucky. A lot of gigs have been on the road, but I don't mind. Hotel rooms are beginning to feel more like home than the place I have on West Fifty-fifth Street, which is practically bare.

"As opposed to some musicians, I have poor concentration. When I play, I try to relax and *not* think. My best ideas come out of a blank, out of an abstraction. Roy Eldridge says when he plays he tries to imagine he's inside a bubble, and I like that. Some musicians see chords and colors and all sorts of images in their heads when they improvise, but I have no bent toward such things. I work in terms of chords. I have a

good harmonic ear, but I have to struggle to remember melodies. I learn a new ballad by putting on a Frank Sinatra or
Tony Bennett record. My tone goes on and off, but it's more
automatic now than it was two years ago. I figure that what's
going to happen to my style will happen without me, so I'm
just letting my playing take place. I can feel it changing
from month to month. It's more original than when I first
came to New York. Maybe within five years I'll be able to
tell it's me when I listen to one of my records."

Hamilton's style comes in two parts. At fast tempos, he often
recalls Flip Phillips. Despite his demurrers, he makes the
melody float when he states it. He does this by skimming the
written notes in such a way that the melody seems to create
itself. He plays softly, and he uses a short, gentle vibrato.
When he improvises, he alternates long notes with tight,
turning, Paul Gonsalves runs. He indulges in occasional high
notes and booting honks, but he never falters. At slow tempos,
Ben Webster comes to the fore. His vibrato widens, his tone
thickens, silences appear, and he recaptures Webster's hymn-
like power. His sound surrounds the ear. All this is clear at
Crawdaddy, where Hamilton is appearing with Dick Katz on
piano and Chuck Riggs on drums. He has a good repertory,
and two sets went like this the other night: a medium "The
Very Thought of You," a slightly faster "What Is This Thing
Called Love?," a medium "You're Getting To Be a Habit with
Me." He did a very fast "It Don't Mean a Thing If It Ain't
Got That Swing," a slow "Don't Blame Me," a medium "It's
You or No One," and a fast "The Man I Love." The singer
Barbara Lea sat in with great effect on "The Lady Is a
Tramp" and "Someone To Watch Over Me," and Hamilton
continued with a medium "Broadway," a very slow "Lotus
Blossom," and a sailing "Limehouse Blues." John Bunch was
standing in for Katz that night, and splendidly, and Riggs
stayed largely with his wire brushes, which he uses with pre-

cision. (He should perhaps study Sid Catlett's way of invincibly *padding* along on the snare drum with brushes.)

Hawkins and Webster and Young were gone or moved away or were worn out too soon, and Hamilton is a superior replenishing presence. More important, he is an antidote, a corrective, to the flat, hard, toneless way of playing the tenor saxophone that has been fashionable for almost twenty years.

November 20th

The jazz nascence that took place in Detroit and its environs in the forties and early fifties produced four remarkable pianists—Hank Jones (b. 1918), Barry Harris (b. 1929), Tommy Flanagan (b. 1930), and Roland Hanna (b. 1932). All have leaned on each other and on generally shared idols. Jones and Flanagan admired Fats Waller, Art Tatum, Teddy Wilson, Nat Cole, and Bud Powell. Flanagan also learned from Jones, and Jones in later years probably listened to Flanagan. Harris admired Powell and Flanagan, while Hanna admired Flanagan and Erroll Garner. All four remained more or less hidden from the public until recent years: Jones as an accompanist for Ella Fitzgerald and as a studio musician; Flanagan as an accompanist for Tony Bennett and Fitzgerald; and Hanna and Harris as industrious sidemen. Jones, who is just six years younger than Teddy Wilson, is their doyen. His touch is pearled, and his improvisations are spun out of willowy single-note melodic lines that reflect Wilson's fluidity and Powell's harmonic advances. His single notes are polite and his harmonies cast soft light. Homogeneity itself is his style. Harris must have passed through Jones's benign influence, but when he was a teenager he fell under the spell of Powell and Charlie Parker, for he constantly applauds their wheeling, irregular, slightly acidulous melodic lines. Harris's phrase endings tend to wilt and fall away, as if they were being blown out of hearing, and the rest of his attack, lacking dynamics and silence, often drones. Bebop players equated silence with weakness. Hanna is a buoyant, resplendent pianist. He uses a great many chords and baroque melodic lines, and he likes to keep coming to climaxes. His melodic surges continually ascend and descend, and as each breasts a hill Hanna celebrates with a crescendo. Jones, Harris, and Flanagan are cool players, but Hanna toils at his large, domed structures. Flanagan plays with nicely controlled passion and with considerable wit. He sparkles like his old idol Nat Cole. He shares Wilson's delicacy and logic and Tatum's touch and technique, and he clearly admires Powell's circuitous melodic inventions. He ranks with the other Wilson-Tatum-Cole disciples—Jimmy Rowles and Dave McKenna and Ellis Larkins—but he is more consistent. It is rare to come away from hearing Flanagan without something new and ingenious.

Flanagan looks Edwardian. He is of medium size, and is mostly bald, with a hedge of whitish hair at the back of his head. A luxuriant mustache and glasses balance the hair. He has a quick, diffident smile and a soft voice. He does not like to talk about himself, but when he does he fashions each sentence as if it were part of a solo. He is a shrewd, kind man who speaks well of many of the pianists around him—Herbie Hancock, McCoy Tyner, and Cecil Taylor, the last of whom "plays with beauty." Flanagan talked of his life and his playing. "I was born in Conant Gardens, on the northeast side of Detroit," he said. "I was the youngest of five boys and a girl. They still live in Detroit, some of them in the house where we were born. My father was eighty-six when he died, last year. He came from near Marietta, Georgia, and he moved to Detroit just after the first war. He was a letter carrier for thirty-five years. He had great spirit and humor, and he showed us all the things of how to be a good person. Dad and I looked like each other. He was bald, and I lost my hair early, so we looked alike a long time. My mother passed away in 1959, shortly after I moved to New York for good. She came from Wrens, Georgia, and she was Indian-looking and only about five feet two. During the hard years of the Depression, she sold dresses for a mail-order company, and then made patchwork quilts from the samples of fabric the company sent her. She really encouraged me on the piano. She taught herself to play, and when she heard me imitating my older brother, Jay, who also plays piano, she gave me lessons. Later, I studied with Gladys Dillard, who's still teaching in Detroit. She taught me the correct pianistic attack— how to finger correctly and use the tips of my fingers. My mother was always interested. When I put on an Art Tatum record, she'd listen and say, 'Is that Art Tatum?' That made you feel good. I also listened to Fats Waller and Teddy Wilson, but Hank Jones, a more modern Wilson, made a lot of sense to me, and so did Bud Powell, whom I heard with Cootie Williams in Detroit. Powell was the kind of player who made you say right away, 'What? I never heard that before!' And there was Nat Cole. The meaning and the force and the swing—he had that appeal. The pulse, the driving voice of his piano. He made his notes bounce. My older brother introduced me on the scene, helped me get my feet. I had my first job in a club when I was in high school. I was too young to mingle between sets, so I'd go in the back and do my homework.

"For a long time, mostly when I was accompanying Ella Fitzgerald, I never thought I had enough technique for a soloist. But then I found I liked to put myself out there. I always feel after I solo that maybe I should have worked it out more first. I always hear so much space that I could have filled in. The piano takes care of itself when you play it, so I think in terms of horn lines a lot. Also, if I have my eyes closed I see the keyboard in my head and I see what I might want my hands to do. Improvising gives you a great sense of

freedom. When you find that out—that you're making your
own song—you can go on endlessly. Of course, you learn
something each time you play the same song—particularly
if you play it in a different key. That sharpens your wit,
makes you play better, keeps you away from the clichés."

Many improvisers lead the listener directly to the heart of
their work. "Listen to how this arpeggio falls and to how
these ninth chords enfold the melody," they seem to say. But
Flanagan dissembles and distracts. At first hearing, one gets
an impression of immense busyness, of the air being filled
with fluctuating chords and melodic lines, of someone playing for himself. Flanagan seems to be shielding himself with
his music the way a philosopher shields himself with abstraction. But what he is doing—working outward from
within his materials, rather than the far more common reverse—soon becomes clear. He often states the melody with
dissonant, levering chords played offbeat or staccato. Never
decorative, they are fresh and manipulative, and reveal both
a respect for the melody and an intense desire to alter it. He
breaks the chordal flow with single notes on the bridge of the
first chorus, and fashions variations of his opening chords for
the final eight bars. Then he slides into full improvisation,
with his single-note patterns, which come in non-stop Art Tatum arpeggios, done with a salute and a smile (Flanagan
loves to put patches of other pianists' playing on his solos, so
that one comes upon Teddy Wilson runs and Thelonious
Monk seesawings and George Shearing sotto voce grace
notes); his ascending runs that break off, regroup, break off,
regroup; his interval-filled descending figures that suggest
someone going downstairs three steps at a time; his charging
rhythmic phrases whose accented first notes make the succeeding notes *snap*, double-time phrases that race ahead to
clear the way, and legato phrases that form sauntering rear

guards. First-rate improvisation suggests that if one looked
at the sheet music one would find the notes the soloist has
just played. That's what Flanagan does.

Having at last resigned as Ella Fitzgerald's accompanist,
Flanagan has decided to go out on his own, and this is fine
news, for his work with the singer generally prevented him
from appearing in New York more than once a year. (What
finally drove him to his decision was two days last summer
in which, on tour with Fitzgerald, he went from Provence to
Newcastle upon Tyne to Provence to Wolf Trap, Virginia.)
Unlike many jazz musicians, Flanagan comes through equally
well in person and on records. In recent years, he has made
four recordings on which he is the leader, and all of them
have surprises. The albums are "Eclypso," made with George
Mraz on bass and Elvin Jones on drums (Inner City);
"Tommy Flanagan 3," done with Keter Betts on bass and
Bobby Durham on drums (Pablo); "The Tommy Flanagan
Tokyo Recital," done with Betts and Durham (Pablo); and
"Something Borrowed, Something Blue," made with Betts
and with Jimmie Smith on drums (Galaxy). Flanagan is in
fine form in the first album, but he tends to rein himself in
in favor of his sidemen, who are given generous space. "Something Borrowed, Something Blue" is a peculiar effort. Flanagan plays electric piano on two numbers, and Thelonious
Monk's "Friday the 13th" is spiffed up with a ground bass, a
back beat, and shuffle rhythms. The title song, with its attractive descending melody, is Flanagan's, and it implies that he
should write more music. The "Tokyo Recital" album is exceptional, even though the bass and drums are overrecorded.
It has a seven-minute "Caravan" surrounded by strong dissonant chords; a "Chelsea Bridge" full of ascending arpeggios and Debussy single notes; and a "Take the A Train"
that closes with a series of wild, witty four-bar exchanges
with Durham. (The record is made up largely of Strayhorn
tunes, and also includes "The Intimacy of the Blues," "Some-

thing To Live For," "All Day Long," and "Daydream.")
The "Flanagan 3" record, done at the Montreux Festival, is
also worthwhile, especially for a loose, stretching performance of "Easy Living," which Flanagan likes to play.
When he settles into tempo, he gets off a rising-falling upper-
register run that holds the light like a blue sky.

November 27th

The judgments we make of jazz are based on the infinitesimal
amount of music recorded during the past sixty years and on
our often leaky memories of live music. Having only these
two means of trapping jazz (musical notation captures its
bare outlines) has long made listeners aesthetically nervous.
Like dancing, live improvised music disappears quickly from
the mind, leaving unsteady images ("afterimages," Arlene
Croce calls them) that tend to wither or balloon. Recorded
jazz is no easier for the listener. One of the great pleasures of
hearing improvised music is that it has never been heard before, but this exhilaration occurs only on the first hearing of
a record. After that, the music grows more and more familiar, until it becomes fixed and can be whistled note for
note. Then we are free to explore the emotional levels of a
solo (this is mysterious and highly subjective; some charged
moments in recorded jazz improvisation—in Louis Armstrong's 1933 "Basin Street Blues" and Coleman Hawkins's
1943 "The Man I Love"—remain indestructible, while others eventually fade). Although we depend on the studio
recording, for which most musicians are able to distill themselves, live recordings offer us the workaday musician, complete with clams and clichés. They also offer surprise and
beauty of a kind often forestalled by the celebrated chills of
the recording studio. This is certainly true of the invaluable
"Duke Ellington at Fargo, 1940, Live" (Book-of-the-Month
Records)—a recording that has long been available in pirated

form and now, having been cleared with Ellington's estate, is
issued legally for the first time. It is an almost complete docu-
mentation—taken down on a portable acetate recorder by
two local enthusiasts named Jack Towers and Dick Burris—
of a dance played on November 7, 1940, at the Crystal Ballroom in Fargo, North Dakota, by just about the best of all
Ellington bands. (Thirty-five of the forty numbers recorded
have been preserved in the album. The omitted selections,
with one exception, either are musically negligible or have
irremediable sound problems.)

Countless live recordings have appeared in recent years,
and most are from radio broadcasts or from concerts or night
clubs. Few have been done at dances, which jazz musicians
love, because they can see their music reflected in the bodies
of the dancers: the better the music the better the dancing,
and the better the dancing the better the music. Nor do many
of the recorded dances follow the course of the evening from
the cold-lip, off-pitch beginnings at eight o'clock to the relaxed, often bleary doings at one. Catching the Ellington
band on this particular night was extraordinary luck. It was
a time of upheaval: Cootie Williams, an anchor of the band
since 1929, had left to join Benny Goodman five days before,
and his replacement, Ray Nance, had just reported for duty.
The band had changed very little in the previous decade.
Otto Hardwick had departed and returned, Rex Stewart and
Lawrence Brown had been added, Artie Whetsol had been
replaced by Wallace Jones, and late in 1939 Ben Webster
and Jimmy Blanton had joined. By this time, the Ellington
band members could dream one another's dreams and pre-
dict, within reason, one another's solos. With the exception of
Webster, Brown, Blanton, and Johnny Hodges, the 1940
band was a collection of inspired primitives, who were exactly what Ellington wanted. None were first-rate improvisers (Barney Bigard and Tricky Sam Nanton—Bigard

blessed with an unbelievably liquid Albert-system clarinet tone, and Nanton with an eerie "talking" muted style— played endless variations on the same solo), and all had choice musical tricks and peculiarities that Ellington loved to work with. These included Stewart's half-valve effects on cornet, Williams's and Nanton's plunger-mute sounds, Hodges's and Harry Carney's tones, and Sonny Greer's charging, intuitive drumming. It was a superb house of musical freaks, whom Ellington could only attempt to match as they dispersed over the years.

The dance at the Crystal Ballroom began shortly after eight with a short set played without the leader. This included a brisk version of "It's Glory," a rambling "The Mooche," and a jumping but truncated "The Sheik of Araby." The album begins with "The Mooche" ("Glory" and "Araby" are omitted without much loss), which has statements from Hodges, Tricky Sam, and Stewart. At nine o'clock, the radio station KVOX broadcast nine numbers, among them a "Ko-Ko" which is perhaps even better than the studio version done eight months before ("Ko-Ko" remains the most sophisticated and ingenious large-ensemble blues ever written); a "Pussy Willow" in which Nance takes his first, tremulous, but instantly recognizable solo, and which has an exhilarating moment when, after a humming three-note saxophone figure played four times, the last with Carney sliding under to give it bottom, Ellington yells, Greer lets loose an oceanic roll, and the full band roars in; a "Harlem Air Shaft" wherein Rex Stewart takes over Cootie Williams's three brief rampant passages but fails to give them Williams's urgency and power; and a couple of moony vocals by Herb Jeffries and Ivie Anderson during which one can practically hear the dancers' feet. (One *can* hear Freddy Guy's guitar and Greer's brushes. The sound in the album is, almost without fail, good, and by

the time we reach a steam-heated version of "Rockin' in
Rhythm," which must have been played around eleven-
thirty, it is close to studio quality.) After the broadcast, the
band relaxes and we are given a loose "Bojangles," complete
with two excellent choruses of Ben Webster; a fine "You
Took Advantage of Me," called "On the Air," with leaping
Hodges, who is equally good on "Never No Lament" (eventually "Don't Get Around Much Anymore"); and a leisurely,
five-minute "Sepia Panorama" that has two more startling
Webster choruses. The only disappointment in this part of
the album is the omission of "The Sidewalks of New York,"
which has first-rate Jimmy Blanton and a long, muted,
across-the-bay Rex Stewart solo backed by one of Ellington's
beautiful singing reed figures. The evening was two-thirds
over, and the band had found its groove. Rocking rundowns
of "Cotton Tail" (taken very fast), "Conga Brava," and the
slow "Across the Track Blues" (the title refers to the feelings
that the Ellington band members suffered when, after playing to cheering white audiences, they were forced to sleep in
the black section of town) are followed by a jammed "Honeysuckle Rose," in which Ray Nance takes his first violin solo
with the band, and "Wham," in which he scat-sings in the
manner of Leo Watson. Then we come to the peak of the evening—a slow, four-minute "Star Dust" that is given over to
three choruses by Ben Webster. It was Webster's reply to
Coleman Hawkins's "Body and Soul," set down the year before, and it was a formidable one. (It pleased Webster so
much that he took a copy of it with him wherever he went
for the rest of his life.) A medium-tempo "Rose of the Rio
Grande," with Ivie Anderson singing and Lawrence Brown
in limousine form, follows, and the evening closes with a
whooping "St. Louis Blues" that has an Anderson vocal, good
Tricky Sam, and six champing choruses of Webster. Sonny
Greer was Webster's co-star that night—whacking a cowbell

on annunciatory offbeats, using a great pushing afterbeat, punctuating trombone solos with timpani beats, and sloshing everyone with his cymbals. Greer has long been pushed aside as a drummer, but he was, with Sid Catlett, the best of the big-band drummers.

1979

January 1st

In *The Fred Astaire & Ginger Rogers Book*, Arlene Croce suggests that Astaire is "his own form of theatre." That is, he is—as a dancer, a singer, an actor—wholly original, and so incomparable. His dancing was a blend of balletic outlines, ballroom dancing, and polyglot jazz steps. The tap-dancer Bill Robinson called him an "eccentric" dancer, and another tap-dancer, Cholly Atkins, said, "He used balletic turns but came out of them with a jazz kick and slide." Astaire was something of a surrealist in his movie dancing. He danced on clouds and up the wall and across the ceiling, and his grace was such that, though his feet might be making a clatter, he gave the impression of being soundless, of not touching the ground at all. No one has paid much attention to his singing until recent years, but it balanced his dancing. Singers revere Astaire. Anita Ellis, who worked with him in two films in the early fifties, has said, "He was his work. He was a perfectionist. On the set, every inch of every step was worked out, and when he sang I always felt that he eased up and became calmer, that his singing was a nice place for him to be." Sylvia Syms has said, "What he lacked vocally he made up in immaculateness. He invented lyrical economy. His singing was the shortest distance between two points. He danced words. He carried the grace of his dancing over into his singing. The songwriters appreciated him because he was musically pure and they knew he wouldn't confuse anybody. No matter what he sang, it always had movement. He was never interrupted by having a matinée-idol face, and his own songs—the songs he wrote—always remind me of soft-shoe." The singer Barbara Lea has said of him, "He belonged with the incidental singers, like Johnny Mercer. He wasn't trying to sell anything but the song, which he got across with precision, clarity, and humor. There wasn't any ego trip involved. He had no intention of astounding you. Of course, he had great materials to work with. The composers who wrote for him wrote light rhythm songs, because he was a dancer, and a circular thing took effect. Their songs probably made him even more that way, which made them produce more of the same sort of songs, and so on. Another important element of Astaire's singing was that he always sang as a character in a show or movie—not as himself, like a night-club performer. That gave him protection from himself, from any temptation to whoop himself up." (Astaire worked once in a night club, in the twenties, and disliked it.)

For all the clarity and order of Astaire's singing, its origins are mysterious. (He does not say very much about his singing in his autobiography, *Steps in Time*. Nor, for that matter, does he say much about his dancing.) He came up through vaudeville and the early Broadway and London musicals in the teens and twenties. "Popular" singing was still semi-European, and was in the hands of the light-operatic troubadours and the early crooners. Vibrato lingered in the corners of every singing style, and tenors were much admired. Singers used a crying quality (bent notes, even sob effects) in their torch songs, and all aspired to a polish that was supposed to mirror emotion. The singers of the time, with few exceptions, got in the way of the first-rate songs already being written by Jerome Kern, Irving Berlin, and George Gershwin, and their recordings have aged poorly. But by the late twenties Astaire was already on the side of the angels—the angels being Ethel Waters and Bing Crosby and Louis Armstrong. He must have heard their recordings, and it has been said that he was influenced by the prolific South African singer Al Bowlly. Astaire seems to have put his singing together early, for he is quickly recognizable on the "Lady, Be Good!" recordings that he made in 1926 with George Gershwin on piano. The ease and sense of swinging that he lacked then came to him by the time he went to Hollywood, seven years later.

As Sylvia Syms suggests, the rhythmic intensity and brilliance that governed Astaire's legs and feet certainly controlled his singing. He has a light baritone, and his timbre is smooth. It is an angular, tidy, pure-cotton voice with little vibrato. (It had more in the twenties.) It arose from necessity, and it is tough and adaptable. He can sing anything from "A Fine Romance" to a nonsense dialect song like "I Love Louisa." His long notes may waver and he sometimes lands near his notes instead of on them, but he makes every song fresh and full-faced, as if each were important news. His singing is also self-effacing. There doesn't seem to be anything between the words and the listener: the lyrics pass directly from the sheet music to the ear.

Astaire has not made a great many recordings. The most ambitious were done in 1952, when Norman Granz persuaded him to go into a Los Angeles studio, where he set down thirty-four vocal numbers and three tap dances. He was accompanied by Oscar Peterson on piano, Barney Kessel on guitar, Ray Brown on bass, Alvin Stoller on drums, and, in all but nine numbers, Flip Phillips on tenor saxophone and Charlie Shavers on trumpet. The notion of recording Astaire with jazz musicians was a good one, and it is a pleasure to hear him unfettered by visual images and a large orchestra. He sings his old standards—including "Steppin' Out with My Baby," "A Needle in a Haystack," "They All Laughed," "A Fine Romance," "I Concentrate on You," "I Love Louisa," and his own fine "I'm Building Up to an Awful Let-Down" and "Not My Girl." The three tap dances are done with the rhythm section, at tempos ranging from medium to very fast, and they are good, exciting Astaire tapping—often offbeat, legato, and full of his typical sailing-through-the-air open spaces. The recordings have now been reissued on the DRG label as "The Astaire Story."

January 22nd

Jazz began as a collective music played by spasm bands and marching bands and bands put together for picnics and dances and boat rides. Its early practitioners, untutored and certain only of the melodies they played and the aural space they had to fill, leaned together, and their solos were limited to short breaks and occasional statements of melody. This lovely polyphonic music thrived at least twenty-five years, and then, with the arrival in the mid-twenties of such technically accomplished players as Sidney Bechet and Louis Armstrong and the Harlem stride pianists, was set aside, to be briefly renovated in various shapes and sizes by Charles Mingus and Gerry Mulligan and Archie Shepp. By the nineteen-fifties, jazz had become a solo music. The ensemble had shrunk to a skimpy unison melodic line, and soloists, encouraged by the new L.P. recordings and by the jam-session philosophy abroad at the time, became meandering and long-winded. The soloist as an entity arrived in the sixties with John Coltrane's mammoth excursions and Cecil Taylor's unaccompanied one-hour deluges. Now concerts and recordings and night-club appearances by one-man bands like Leroy Jenkins and Anthony Braxton and George Lewis are com-

monplace. But what a lonely and illusory music! Only the
human voice can stand alone as a musical instrument. (The
piano, of course, is multi-voiced.) All others, ironically, strive
to sound like groups by resorting to enlarging devices such as
double-stops and trick-tonguing and overblowing. Jim Hall,
our paramount guitarist and a consummate improviser, has
reduced his musical environment, but only as far as a duo—
a combination he has practiced with constant success for a
decade. There is little that two instruments cannot do together. They can fashion counterpoint, which hones and
brightens their voices. They can pit their timbres and set up
invigorating cross-rhythms. They can subtly comment on
each other in their accompaniment. And they can play in
unison or in harmony, or play dissonantly and give the impression of many voices. Hall has worked most often with
bassists (Ron Carter, Michael Moore, Jay Leonhart, Jack Six,
Red Mitchell), and recently he was recorded with Mitchell
at Sweet Basil. The results have just been released on the
Artists House label as "Jim Hall/Red Mitchell." There are
two blues ("Big Blues" and "Osaka Express"), both by Hall,
a Mitchell original ("Beautiful"), a Hall original ("Waltz
New," based on "Some Day My Prince Will Come"), a Bart
Howard ("Fly Me to the Moon"), and a Hall-Mitchell arrangement of a Mexican folk song ("Blue Dove"). Exceptional things happen: the slow, almost collapsed "Beautiful,"
which is notable for the gradual way Hall moves into his solo
and for the circular figures he plays following Mitchell's
solo; the legato single notes which Hall delivers after a heavy
chorded passage in "Waltz New"; his John Lewis single
notes on "Big Blues," and the six loose sotto voce choruses
that he and Mitchell fall into just before its final ensemble;
and the swaying "Osaka Express."

Hall likes musical surprises, and has appeared at Hopper's with his old friend and compeer the valve-trombonist
Bob Brookmeyer. Brookmeyer, who was much in evidence

during the fifties and sixties, went West to the studios ten
years ago, and has only recently returned. He is forty-nine
and came out of Kansas City, and he grew up in the shade of
Jack Teagarden, Vic Dickenson, Bill Harris, Brad Gowans,
and J. J. Johnson. His style has not changed. He long ago developed a brass-tongued loquacity that has more in common
with such virtuosos as Bill Watrous and Urbie Green than
with Teagarden and Harris. He affects a smoky tone, Dicky
Wells smears and shouts, a placid vibrato, and brief falsetto
leaps. He plays with lyrical glibness, and his phrasing and
aim are unerring. He is, in Wells's way, often funny. It is
odd to find him and Hall working together, for they are almost wholly dissimilar. Hall is spare, elusive, soft, and reluc-
tant to part with his beauties, while Brookmeyer always
plays as if he were attending a convention. At Hopper's, the
two musicians seemed to be playing in adjacent rooms with
the door open. Their ensembles did not blend into a double-
edged voice but remained a trombone and a guitar playing
simultaneously. Brookmeyer's volume forced Hall to play
louder than usual, and he almost never backed Hall's solos
(organ chords, melody, riffs would all have been proper),
which took on a lorn, voyaging air. And Brookmeyer's and
Hall's rhythmic centers were different. Brookmeyer plays in
a pummelling, sometimes staccato on-the-beat style, and Hall
often favors legato, downstream phrasing. Oil and water, the
two men filled the room with powerful improvisations, and
we heard rich, turning versions of "Begin the Beguine," an
Andy LaVerne original called "Exactly Alike," "Baubles,
Bangles, and Beads," "Embraceable You," John Lewis's
"Skating in Central Park," and a medium-tempo blues, in
which Hall got off a solo full of surprised notes.

February 5th

When Louis Armstrong began his spectacular rise in Chicago in the twenties, the generosity and invention and originality of his playing provided source material for a thousand admirers. One of the most gifted is the seventy-three-year-old trumpeter Adolphus (Doc) Cheatham, who before reaching his present glory led a largely subterranean career as a lead trumpeter and sometime soloist. He was born in Nashville, where he worked behind Bessie Smith and Ma Rainey and Clara Smith, and he moved to Chicago when he was twenty-one. He had a lean time until he joined Sam Wooding in 1928 and went to Europe. A few years later, he was with McKinney's Cotton Pickers, and a year after that he began a seven-year stay with Cab Calloway. Brief jobs with Teddy Wilson's and Benny Carter's big bands followed, and he was hired by Eddie Heywood, whose small band included the trombonist Vic Dickenson. It worked at Café Society Downtown, and was famous for its tight ensembles and spirited solos and for Heywood's Earl Hines piano. Then Cheatham suffered a collapse. "I never was a very strong person," he once told Stanley Dance, "and when I was young I was very thin. Travelling on the road a lot, and just living on sandwiches, was more than I could take." When he recovered, he started teaching. Some of his students were Latins, and that led to a fifteen-year stint of playing in Latin bands (Machito, Perez Prado, Marcelino Guerra, Ricardo Ray). He also doubled with Wilbur de Paris and Benny Goodman.

"I went to Chicago in 1926," he said the other night at Crawdaddy where he is appearing with a trio (Chuck Folds and Jackie Williams). "And I heard all the many marvellous musicians who were there—Louis Armstrong, who was the first to really solo on the trumpet, and Tommy Ladnier, who was next to Armstrong, to my way of thinking. I heard King Oliver, who was a gutbucket player, and Freddie Keppard, who had a military style and was so powerful he blew his mute right out of his trumpet and across the stage one night. He was so full of jazz nobody could hold him. And Jelly Roll Morton was around. I liked him, but I guess nobody else did. He was a braggadocio sort of fellow. He would tell you *he* was the pioneer of jazz, and you couldn't dispute him. He had a hard time in Chicago, and he almost starved when he went to New York, in 1928. Of course, that was fifty years ago. In that time, I've learned some confidence, and that's what my playing is based on—experience, and knowing thoroughly the melody and chords of the tunes I play. Tommy Ladnier taught me to always listen to the bass, and then everything would fall into place. It's also important to have the right men with you. They can lead you up the right path, or they can mislead you and break your heart if they don't know what they're doing. I learned from Louis Armstrong how to treat a chorus—not to overdo anything, not to waste notes, to keep things as trim as possible. When you improvise, you have a kind of picture in your mind. If you play a love song, perhaps you see a pretty girl, and if you play a buck-dance sort of number you put yourself in the character of a buck dancer. Generally, you put yourself in the character of what you are playing, like an actor. Duke Ellington's 'Ring Dem Bells' leaves you in a happy frame, and the blues—the real blues—is such a sad thing it fills you with sorrow."

Cheatham laughed. "Sorrow is what filled my father when I became a musician. His parents were descendants of the Indians who settled in what is now Cheatham County, near Nashville. He was a barber who owned a three-story building that also had a tailor shop and baths, and his trade was white. His brothers were doctors and his sisters teachers. My mother was part Cherokee, and she came from Atlanta, Georgia. She was a schoolteacher way back in the eighteen-hundreds, and she was very beautiful and highly educated.

She became a laboratory assistant at a medical college in
Nashville. I had just one brother, and he was a dentist. My
father didn't want me to be a musician because mostly what
you saw in Nashville were circus musicians, and it seems like
they drank all the time. He finally gave in when he realized
it wouldn't be any use to stand in my way. So I was the sort
of black sheep of the family. But when you take up an instrument you become addicted to it. You get a burning desire
to play and play. Maybe that's why I never drank whiskey.
I already had my addiction."

Cheatham is spare and elegant and ageless. His face is nar-
row, his eyes are heavy-lidded, and his nose is geometric and
patrician. He talks in a confabulatory way, and he punctuates his memories of musicians by frequently saying, "They
come and they go. They come and they go." When he plays,
he points his horn toward the heavens and holds his arms
level, as if he were about to take flight. His attack is lyrical
and jaunty. (Armstrong has not been Cheatham's only influence. He has also admired Johnny Dunn and Louis Panico
and Joe Smith and the late Shorty Baker.) He has a gentle
tone and a discreet vibrato. His solos are a succession of lines,
steps, curves, parabolas, angles, and elevations. They move
with the logic and precision of composition, yet they have
the spark and spontaneity of improvisation. Cheatham's
rhythmic underpinnings have a bony clarity and emphasis: *all* his notes seem to stand out. Most brass players his age
barely have the wind and lip to speak and eat, but he is continually adventurous. He loves big intervals, and he rarely
lands on less than one foot. He successfully tries little ascensions that reach toward high C. His phrasing crosses bar
lines with ease, and he constructs melodic lines that run for
ten or twelve measures. There is little he cannot play. His
ballads are round-limbed and placid, and his blues, though
courteous, are melancholy, and even mean. His up-tempo
numbers leap and jump. He is a wizard with mutes—partic-

ularly the plunger mute, which he handles with force and subtlety and surprise that sometimes surpass Cootie Williams's. And this daring, inexhaustible player never falters. He plays and plays, solo after solo, evening after evening, and each time he is fresh and affecting.

In the course of two languorous sets at Crawdaddy, he played "Gee, Baby, Ain't I Good to You?"; a fast, glancing "Just Friends" that suggested his old friend Bill Coleman; a slow "Jelly Roll Blues" with a muted solo that had an inner-mind intensity; a ruminating "Dear Old Southland," in which he sang in his plaintive, piping way; an ad-lib "Just a Closer Walk with Thee," a hymn that he converted into a lullaby; and two displays of his plunger-mute work in a brooding "St. Louis Blues" and a smoking "Summertime." When he executed a diminuendo-crescendo growl with his plunger mute in "Summertime," the sound exploded.

February 19th

In the mid-fifties, a young English advertising man named Jeff Atterton began a transatlantic correspondence with the clarinettist Pee Wee Russell, which lasted until Atterton moved to New York, in 1959. Most jazz musicians care little for writing letters, but Russell had a singular prod—his rare and highly literate wife, Mary. She would sit Russell down and, equipped with a quart of ale, he would talk; she would simultaneously edit and type, and out would come vintage Russell. He was not an accessible man. He was shy, fearful, self-depreciating, and even furtive, and strangers were lucky to get two half-swallowed sentences. But Russell had a strong ego, and Atterton's attentive letters clearly stirred him—so much that some of his answers offer the best looks we will probably ever have into his precarious, lyrical self. Here are some excerpts. Russell was a born dissembler:

Mary, who knows how to spell cat, explained about Boswell and Johnson to me. You didn't expect me to know, did you? I've been approached several times by guys who want to write my biography but I can't figure out why a publisher would be interested. I haven't done anything except spend my life with a horn stuck in my face. My personal life may have been more stormy than the average office clerk but almost everybody's life is more stormy than that. And why would anybody want to read about it. . . . If I ever want to read about myself I could always find some publication that says—Charles Ellsworth Russell, Jr. b. March 27th in Maplewood, Missouri . . .

Russell knew he was good, but he spent much of his life either being paranoid or perversely denying his worth:

I had a couple of little set backs that made me feel lousy for a while but I got over it. After one or two sleepless nights. I had a record date set. Modern musicians and strings. It fell through at the last minute. The modern kids are beginning to discover me. Mary says she always expected it. She told me that before it happened. She says I'm more modern than any of them because she never understood what . . . I am doing. I wanted that date. . . .

He had a sharp sense of hyperbole, the mainspring of humor:

I'm a weary Indian. Home a week and I'm still beat. Fall River was awful. No hotel, I stayed in a motel. The motel was okay but no place to eat. I wish you could have seen me trudging a mile down the road to a bean wagon. And the joint itself was a prohibition type place. Semi-hoodlums who told me how to play. Bass, piano, drums and saxophone.

I don't want to criticize the musicians but I didn't
know what they were doing and they didn't know
what I was doing. The night one of the inch brow
owners told me not to lean against the piano when
I'm on the stand was too much. I snarled at him and
scared him to death. . . .

I have a record date on the 18th and 19th. I'm
going to use Bud Freeman and Nat Pierce. Ruby
[Russell's close friend the cornettist Ruby Braff]
doesn't work as a side man but he will for me. I
hated . . . to ask him, but I got real strong and did
and all he asked me was what time does he show.
It's for a small company so they'll probably put the
album out before it's made. There isn't any waiting
around like the big companies. . . .

Alcohol nearly killed Russell in 1950, and for the rest of
his life he struggled to keep it at bay. Eating properly was
one way:

I'll tell you how I got fat. I drink at least two
quarts of beer every day. I never got drunk on beer
in my life. I drink an eggnog every day. . . . And
I have a glass of milk with every meal. I eat breakfast and dinner and I have a sandwich or crackers
and cheese late at night when I'm watching TV.
When I'm away from home I lose weight. I don't
eat and forget to take my daily vitamin pill. And
I drink too much whiskey. But when I'm home I'm
a healthy guy. Try my diet. I've gained most of my
weight around my middle. But, what the hell. I'm a
middle aged guy and it's time I got fat. . . .

And on death:

Josh's funeral was a pretty sad deal. [Josh Bill-
ings, a sometime drummer from Chicago, died in
1957.] Not too many guys. Condon said a few words.
In good taste, incidentally. Josh didn't have any

> family. The hearse went off alone with no one to
> follow it. . . . Until then I didn't give a damn what
> happens to me after I'm through but right then and
> there I made Mary promise that I'll have a lot of
> people around when it happens and they're all to
> get drunk and say what a great guy I am. No mat-
> ter what they think of me. . . .

Russell's decennial has been marked by four reissues. Two
are of permanent interest—"Salute to Newport: Featuring
Pee Wee Russell" (ABC Impulse) and "Jazz Reunion: Pee
Wee Russell, Coleman Hawkins" (Barnaby/Candid Jazz).
They reaffirm what many of Russell's admirers knew when
he died—that he was the most original of all jazz clarinettists, a unique improviser. Vicissitude had forced him to earn
much of his living with the Chicago-Eddie Condon school of
jazz, but he didn't belong in it. This was made unalterably
clear in the mid-sixties by a late-blooming series of recordings in which he worked comfortably with non-Condon musicians (one date was with Earl Hines, Elvin Jones, and a
batch of Ellington sidemen) and with materials by Thelonious Monk, John Coltrane, Ornette Coleman, Ellington, Billy
Strayhorn, Willard Robison, and Tadd Dameron. There were
three incomparable things about Russell's attack: his tone,
which was subtle and homemade, and unlike a standard clarinet sound; his rhythmic sense, which enabled him to escape
the four-four prison that most swing musicians were caught
in; and his daring, which drove him to try—and almost always get away with—passages of such wildness and complexity that no clarinettist reading them in transcription
would be able to play them. Russell loved the chalumeau register, and he loved the blues. He played the blues differently
from any other musician, with the possible exception of Jack
Teagarden. Russell's blues were an examination of the prop-
osition that there must be a way to make sadness bearable

and beautiful. He would start a solo with half a dozen low, breathy staccato notes jammed together, repeat them and pause, rise almost an octave to a flickering, half-sounded note, and, before this ascension had registered on the ear, drop back to more staccato breathiness and into a dodging, undulating stretch of notes that had a Giacometti sound. He would for the first time bow in the direction of the beat by constructing a four- or six-bar on-the-beat melody, and then sneak back down to the cellar for some asides, subtones, and almost palpable breaths. The first chorus done, he would grow less and less knotted. He would move slowly up the scale, growing louder, until in the last chorus he would reach C above middle C with a banners-unfurled declarativeness. He managed in these solos to make the listener forget that he was hearing a clarinet. (Benny Goodman's playing was the opposite: This is how you play the *clarinet*, it seemed to say. Russell didn't object; he loved Goodman.) Instead, the listener became wholly caught up by the *sound* of Pee Wee Russell—by a strange, solitary voice that had never been heard in jazz before.

That voice can be heard with remarkable strength and clarity on the reissues. The "Salute to Newport" album has twenty numbers, a dozen of them recorded in 1959 with Vic Dickenson, Bud Freeman, Buck Clayton, and Dick Cary. Russell rarely wrote music, but all the selections are his and, as if out of embarrassment, they have such elliptical titles as "Oh No," "Oh Yes," "But Why," and "This Is It." Only one of the numbers lasts more than four minutes, and five last under three minutes, so Russell has little chance to stretch out, although he is superb on "Dreamin' and Schemin' " and "Are You Here?" The remaining sides on the "Newport" album were done three and a half years later by a George Wein group that included—in addition to Russell and Bud Freeman—Ruby Braff and Marshall Brown. (Brown helped Russell, in 1962 and 1965, to record his meditations on Coltrane and Ornette Coleman and Tadd Dameron.) There is an excellent Russell slow blues, "The Bends Blues," but he is spectacular on a medium-tempo "Keepin' Out of Mischief Now." He solos immediately after Braff, who is at his most baroque—runs within runs; big intervals; juicy, low, tomato notes—and Russell is at his (purposely) sparest. His solo seems to occur in a place of his own invention. It has no tempo, no recognizable melody, no immediately obvious underlying chord structure. It is a surrealist solo that turns and lazes and muses, listening to itself and moving gradually across an open, endless part of Russell's mind.

Much of "Jazz Reunion" is on the same level. The recording has Coleman Hawkins, Emmett Berry, Bob Brookmeyer, Nat Pierce, Milt Hinton, and Jo Jones—what Russell considered fast company. There are six extended numbers, including a Russell blues, two Ellington numbers, a Russell original, and James P. Johnson's "If I Could Be with You One Hour Tonight"—a tune that Russell and Hawkins, in company with Glenn Miller and Gene Krupa, recorded in 1929 as the famous "One Hour." Russell never worked harder than he did on "Jazz Reunion," and the five-chorus edifice of melancholy and triumph that he constructed on the slow blues "Mariooch" has no equal.

February 26th

The singer Dardanelle was born Dardanelle Mullen on a plantation in Avalon, Mississippi. She grew up with music. Her father played Scott Joplin and an aunt was a classical pianist. The blues singer Mississippi John Hurt came from the next plantation. She learned piano when she was tiny, and in high school, in nearby Greenwood, she added the bassoon and the marimba. She got a bassoon scholarship at Louisiana State, and stayed "two seasons." Then she went North, to work as a pianist and vibraphonist in Washington,

D.C., and Baltimore (at Doc's, an Adrian Rollini hangout), and Philadelphia, where she spelled Art Tatum. In 1945, she took a trio (with Tal Farlow on guitar) into the Copacabana, and played opposite Nat Cole's trio, John Kirby, and the Phil Moore Four. (That year, in a musicians' poll run by *Esquire* she was voted the best new pianist by Lionel Hampton and the best new vibraphonist by Art Tatum.) RCA Victor asked her to record eight sides, and she sang on half of them. Her agent, the usually unerring Joe Glaser, told her, "You're a great pianist, but you can't sing." She moved to Chicago in 1949, and played Aunt Dodie on a children's television program. By 1970, she was living in New Jersey, near the guitarist Bucky Pizzarelli. Pizzarelli brought her into Soerabaja as a singer in 1974, and she went on to a small restaurant on East Thirty-third Street called Bar None, and stayed several years. Now, after gigging around for a year or so, she has settled into the Back Porch, which is right up the street. She has become a full-time singer who accompanies herself very well on the piano, even though she still considers herself a pianist who happens to sing.

"I have never thought too much about singing," she has said, "but I'm thinking about it a good deal now, and I'm beginning to analyze it." She is in fact a classic untutored singer. A small, pretty porcelain woman with transparent skin and a discreet Mississippi accent, she has a pure, gifted soprano. Singing is like breathing or sighing or walking to her, and song after perfect song rolls out. Her style is reminiscent of Lee Wiley and Mildred Bailey and Billie Holiday. In Wiley's manner, she likes to crimp some of her phrase endings and move up or down a tone midway through a long note. Despite the simplicity and directness of her voice, it is capable of carrying dark songs and of passing affectingly through the blues. She has an elastic rhythmic sense and her improvisational turns enrich rather than distort her songs. Her repertory is drawn from all sides: Michel Legrand, Fran Landesman and the late Tommy Wolf, Burke and Van Heusen, Nacio Herb Brown, Jobim, Arlen and Mercer, Cole Porter, and Billy Joel. Her first record in almost thirty years—"Songs for New Lovers"—has been released on the Stash label. Bucky Pizzarelli, George Duvivier, and Grady Tate accompany her, and she does nine numbers. Two are instrumentals, and the rest include "That Old Devil Called Love," "It Could Happen to You," "You Stepped Out of a Dream," and "Spring Can Really Hang You Up the Most." The album gives one a chance to study her singing, which in its grace and gentleness often vanishes in the hubbub at the Back Porch.

May 7th

Milt Gabler, the founder of Commodore Records, was born in New York in 1911, the eldest of six children of a New York mother (Susie) and an Austrian father (Julius). He went to Stuyvesant High School, and summered at Silver Beach, in Throg's Neck. His father owned a hardware store on Third Avenue, near Forty-second Street, and a radio shop on Forty-second Street, which was called the Commodore out of respect for the hotel across the street. Gabler started at the hardware store, then switched to the radio shop, where he began stocking phonograph records. In the mid-thirties, the jazz bug having bitten him, he and Marshall Stearns invented the United Hot Clubs of America, which leased rare, out-of-print records from various companies and reissued them on its own U.H.C.A. label. A company that put out nothing but jazz records—albeit old ones—was a novelty, and so was its practice of listing on its labels the personnel, instrumentation, and date and place of recording. Gabler, a man of empyrean standards, was not particularly pleased with the way the big companies were treating jazz—despite their release between 1935 and 1937 of a good many superior recordings, among them Billie Holiday's "What a Little Moonlight Can Do" and "Miss Brown to You"; Red Norvo's "Blues in E Flat"; Red Allen's "Body and Soul"; Louis Armstrong's "Mahogany Hall Stomp"; Roy Eldridge's "Wabash Stomp" and "Florida Stomp"; Duke Ellington's "Diminuendo in Blue"; Lionel Hampton's "On the Sunny Side of the Street"; the Bunny Berigan-Tommy Dorsey-Fats Waller jam session at Victor; and Count Basie's "One O'Clock Jump." So Gabler decided, late in 1937, to form his own recording company. He held his first session on January 17, 1938, the day after Benny Goodman's Carnegie Hall concert. The group— of quasi-Chicago persuasion—was the prototype of what became the backbone of Gabler's catalogue. It was made up of Bobby Hackett, Pee Wee Russell, Georg Brunis, and Eddie Condon, all of whom were working at Nick's in Greenwich Village; Jess Stacy, who was with Goodman; the bass player Artie Shapiro (Joe Marsala), Bud Freeman (Tommy Dorsey), and George Wettling (Red Norvo). Only Freeman and Wettling had been directly connected with the Chicago style of playing, although Stacy and Russell had passed through its fringes. It was a gabby, winging-it hand-me-down of King Oliver's Creole Jazz Band and the white New Orleans Rhythm Kings: loose ensembles, often played in a give-'em-hell diminuendo-crescendo fashion; a string of solos, sometimes launched by a brief ensemble burst or by a break, and often underscored with organ chords played by the horns, which recalled glee-club humming; and an occasional drum solo or closing four-bar drum break. Unlike a surprising number of early white jazz fans, Gabler brought a wide intelligence and a good ear to the music. (There were few black jazz "fans." Jazz, instrumental and vocal, was not an alien, collectible form to black listeners but an everyday part of their lives.) Gilbert Millstein, in a Profile of Gabler published in *The New Yorker*, quotes an anonymous musician on Gabler's skills as an A. & R. man:

"There's a ray comes out of him," the musician
said. "You can't help doing something the way he
wants. Here is this guy can't read a note of music
and he practically tells you what register you're going to play in just by the position of your head."

Gabler's early catalogue is imposing, and includes Billie
Holiday's "Strange Fruit," and her great blues "Fine and
Mellow," and "Yesterdays," and the stately "I Gotta Right
To Sing the Blues"; a good number of Chicago-type sides,
many the best of their kind; twenty or so piano solos and
band sides by Jelly Roll Morton, who was still full of music;
a dozen sides by Buck Clayton and Lester Young and Jo
Jones, and as many by Roy Eldridge and Benny Carter and
Chu Berry and Coleman Hawkins and Sid Catlett, all of
them the avant-garde of jazz; and a session with Fats Waller
that belongs with the cream of his recordings.

In 1941, Gabler began working full time for Decca, and he
eventually became its chief A. & R. man. He has said, "It
didn't matter who I had recorded for Decca during the
week—Louis Armstrong, Peggy Lee—or how far I had flown
to do it. I couldn't wait to go into the studio on Saturday and
make my Commodores. I had to get all those musicians down,
I had to preserve them, and I did nothing but enjoy doing
it. It's as vivid as yesterday. The only regret I have is that I
by-passed Charlie Parker and Dizzy Gillespie when they first
appeared on Fifty-second Street. I'd like to have their music
in my catalogue now." Gabler continued making Commodore
records regularly until around 1948, and he wound everything up in 1951. (His father's radio shop, which became the
famous Commodore Music Shop, moved a few feet east and
then across the street, not far from its namesake, where it
closed in 1958.) What Gabler did was preserve—in the face
of the dreary, devouring big bands—the very heart of jazz:
its small bands. He inspired Blue Note and Keynote Records,
which followed his courageous ways, and the host of fly-by-

night labels that documented the new music of Parker and Gillespie. And he is indirectly responsible for the countless independent labels that support the music now. But Gabler's catalogue hasn't been completely in print since the mid-fifties, when the L.P. arrived and chaos began. Gabler himself reissued some material on L.P., and quit. A record club brought out more, and went out of business. Gabler leased masters to labels here and abroad, which reissued them higgledy-piggledy, often as collections of tenor saxophonists or clarinettists or pianists but rarely chronologically and in complete sessions. The last coherent attempt to reissue the catalogue in this country was undertaken by Atlantic seven years ago, but that fell by the way, too.

Now Gabler has decided to bring out his entire œuvre, session by session and including the alternate takes. There are ten L.P.s in the first batch of reissues, which are being distributed by Columbia, and not all of them are knockouts. Eleven Bud Freeman trio sides (with Jess Stacy and George Wettling) are as monotonous and jouncy as ever—despite Stacy, who repeatedly attempts to aerate the proceedings with his laughing tremolos and swimming way of swinging. The four famous Mel Powell-Benny Goodman sides ("When Did You Leave Heaven?," "Blue Skies," "Mood at Twilight," and "The World Is Waiting for the Sunrise") open an L.P., but the rest is filled out with three undistinguished Mel Powell big-band sides and four frumpy Joe Bushkin-Bill Harris-Zoot Sims selections. Another L.P. is given over to four Jack Teagarden numbers (with Ernie Caceres on clarinet, Max Kaminsky, Norma Teagarden on piano, and George Wettling) and four sweating Max Kaminsky sides (with Rod Cless on clarinet and Frank Orchard on trombone). The rest of the reissues are full of delights. A Jelly Roll Morton L.P. contains twelve piano solos, five of them with his naked, melancholy vocals. There is a Lester Young-Buck Clayton L.P. on which Young plays a lot of his skinny, lissome clarinet, and the rhythm section (Freddie Green, Walter Page, Jo Jones) moves in an area no rhythm section had moved in before. These are classic sides, and as flexible and graceful as they were forty years ago. A Coleman Hawkins L.P. includes the 1940 Chocolate Dandies session, with Roy Eldridge, Benny Carter, and Sid Catlett, and in addition to its familiar beauties there is an alternate take of "I Can't Believe That You're in Love with Me," done at a slower tempo than the one originally released. It rocks and sways, and Eldridge takes a fascinating solo—sure, lyrical, biting. A Wild Bill Davison reissue has all the first-rate sessions he did in November of 1943, and they roar and champ and steam. Davison liked to pick up the melody and hurl it down the ensemble, making his cohorts tumble after. The champion of the ten albums is given over in part to the quartet that Sid Catlett had on Fifty-second Street in 1943 and 1944: Ben Webster, who is the leader of the record date; Marlowe Morris on piano; and John Simmons on bass. There are two takes of everything, excluding "Just a Riff," and they are particularly valuable for Webster and for Catlett's brilliant solos on the two "Sleep"s and his just-like-that two-bar breaks on the two "Linger Awhile"s.

May 28th

Keith Jarrett, the thirty-four-year-old Pennsylvania pianist, composer, and musical phenomenon, has his own pedestal. His admirers, who are legion, have put it up, and they haven't stinted. They have made it possible for him to be paid over ten thousand dollars for a one-and-a-half-hour solo concert, and for his record label (ECM) to issue a ten-L.P. album ("Sun Bear Concerts") that sells for seventy-five dollars. They sit in worshipful silence at the outset of his concerts while he lectures them on comportment, and after he has played they show a fervor that would have pleased Liszt.

Jarrett doesn't look like a matinée idol. He is of medium
height and almost skinny. He affects an Afro hairdo, which
crowns a set of triangles—a small, wedgelike face with a
sharp nose and jack-o'-lantern eyes. But he is a Dionysian
performer. His music possesses him, and he goes through a
continuous dance at the keyboard which forms a hypnotic
visual counterpoint to his music. He rarely sits on the piano
bench. He half crouches, sometimes slipping so low that when
he occasionally throws his arms in the air it appears he is
about to catch the lip of the keyboard to keep from plunging
into the abyss. He rotates his shoulders and rocks back and
forth. He twists his head, jerks it, ducks it, and throws it
back. His face passes through demonic contortions. All the
while, he hums in unison falsetto or issues loud ecstatic
"ohhhhh"s—missiles of emotion that both applaud his efforts
and warn the audience that it is in the presence of important
doings. These doings cannot be classified except by saying
that he plays an improvised piano music that anthologizes
much of the Western (classical and jazz) and Oriental music
of the past couple of centuries. A Jarrett performance may
reflect and refract Bill Evans, Indian ragas, Ray Bryant,
Stephen Foster, Chopin, Dave Brubeck, Cecil Taylor, Beetho-
ven, Art Tatum, Debussy, Bud Powell, Brahms, the blues,
Rachmaninoff, Gospel music, Bach, Horace Silver, Lennie
Tristano, flamenco music, folk songs, the "Warsaw Concerto,"
McCoy Tyner, George Gershwin, the "Bolero," boogie-
woogie, and Liszt. These structures have grown encyclopedic.
One of them may last three-quarters of an hour, and may go
something like this: Jarrett begins with a ground bass and
open Debussy chords. He pedals slowly along in this mode,
then shifts into another ground bass and develops a repeated
single-note figure in the right hand, which becomes flamencan before it rises into the upper registers and evaporates. A
third ground bass materializes (repetition is the backbone of
his playing), and he begins hitting hard, offbeat right-hand

chords. He repeats these maddeningly for a minute or so and, suddenly stopping, switches to a passage of soul soap with a rolling bass and dense Ray Bryant right-hand chords. The Debussy opening passes in review again and is transformed into a Bill Evans ballad, which eventually closes with parallel Bach runs. A waltz rounds the corner (despite Jarrett's varying rhythms, there are no rhythmic surprises in his work), and he plays very softly, just at the threshold of sound. He keeps whispering this waltzing softness until the listener falls under a spell. But Jarrett is a masterly melodramatist, who knows precisely when to shift scenes. The waltz fades away, and he lunges into a crowd of dissonant chords, letting them grind against one another until all that remains is a lullaby left hand, which supports a Rachmaninoff melody in the right hand. This is spun out languorously in widely spaced single notes in the highest register—notes that are struck like chimes in an intense, slow-motion legato. He grows softer and softer, over a period of minutes, and the notes, now in the far distance, stop. There is a long pause— for his audiences have learned that they must not tread on his skirts—and the roar begins.

The "Sun Bear" album consists of ten such edifices, built at five concerts given between November 5 and November 18, 1976, at Kyōto, Ōsaka, Nagoya, Tokyo, and Sapporo. Jarrett will probably never surpass them, even though they surpass the celebrated Köln concert of a year and a half before. Their texture and movement, their dynamics and occasional virtuosity are dazzling, and so are the lyrical patches that turn up, particularly in the second part of the Kyōto concert and the first part of the Nagoya. These patches sound like improvisations on such numbers as "Summertime" and "I Loves You Porgy" or like reworkings of a yearning ascending-descending blues motif that appears again and again in his work. They light up the failings in the musical landscape around them. Despite Jarrett's outward prolixity and his poetic flashes, the emotional content of his work is on a level with that of Thomas Wolfe and Judy Garland and Cecil B. De Mille. The playing is bravura and self-indulgent, like a dandy constantly changing clothes. It shouts and day-dreams. It is an improvised music that feeds on itself.

Jarrett began as a jazz pianist in the early sixties, working with Art Blakey and Tony Scott and Charles Lloyd. He caused a small sensation when he appeared with Lloyd at the Newport Jazz Festival in 1966. Lloyd let Jarrett loose on one number, and he played a long, complex rhapsody that seemed startling and highly original. Only Cecil Taylor and Dave Brubeck played that sort of Wagnerian chordal piano. Jarrett's oceanic solo concerts have carried him a considerable distance from his origins, and, perhaps to redress this, he has begun working again in selected jazz clubs with a quartet. (Jan Garbarek is on tenor saxophone, Jon Christensen on drums, and Palle Danielsson on bass.) In New York, he chose the Village Vanguard, because its owner, Max Gordon, was the only one who would hire his trio in the sixties. He told Gordon that he would charge him just a thousand dollars a night but that Gordon could ask no more than six dollars and fifty cents at the door—presumably to allow the faithful to encamp without undue economic anxiety. Gordon agreed (he also agreed to have the piano tuned twice a night), and Jarrett played at the Vanguard for five days. Gordon can handle something under three hundred people a night, and by opening day he was sold out for the week and had turned away at least a thousand reservations. There weren't many surprises in the music except that it had a distinct jazz flavor. Each number had ensembles, a sounded beat, and solos. Garbarek took a couple of lengthy solos, but the rest of the time he provided chordal backdrops or was silent while Christensen and Danielsson pumped away behind Jarrett. Jarrett shaped solo after solo, each full of the likes of Bach and Monk and Bee-

thoven and Copland and Coleman and Evans and Debussy
and Gershwin. At the same time, he undulated like sea grass,
moved his shoulders as if he were inching across no man's
land, made serpentine motions with his neck and head, and
fired off countless booming "ohhhhh"s. In between piano
solos, he secreted himself behind a pillar at one side of the
bandstand and played the timbales with ferocious abandon.
The room was awash with awe at the end of the long first set,
and the line of waiting acolytes stretched up the steps and
down Seventh Avenue.

June 18th

Charles Mingus spent most of his life at the barricades, but
his chief weapons were words. In time, his life was awash
with words. He wrote an immense autobiography, out of
which Nel King quarried *Beneath the Underdog*. He published long, angry letters in magazines, and dictated smoking
liner notes for his albums in the late fifties and early sixties,
when he was at the top of his combative powers. Sometimes
his verbal fervor elbowed clarity aside, as in this disquisition
on the beat, from a 1963 liner note:

> You don't play the beat where it is. You draw a
> picture away from the beat right up to its core with
> different notes of different sounds of the drum in-
> struments so continuously that the core is always
> there for an open mind. While you make it live now
> and then you go inside the beat, dead center, and
> split the core to the sides and shatter the illusion so
> there is no shakiness ever. If one tries to stay inside
> dead center or directly on top of the beat or on the
> bottom, the beat is too rigid on the outside where it
> is heard. The stiffness should only be felt inside the
> imaginary center of the exact tempo's core.

He was a voluminous talker, and his words came out in light, fast, irregular clumps, like the phrases in his bass playing. Sometimes his words went by so fast there was no time for them to reveal their meaning. He occasionally lectured night-club audiences ten minutes at a stretch, issuing a mixture of invective, musical pedagogy, autobiography, and homemade philosophy. These broadsides had a cathartic effect on Mingus, and they stunned his listeners. But once in a while words failed him. Max Gordon, the inventor and shepherd of the Village Vanguard, has described what happened when they did:

> He'd start a set, then stop. "Try that again," he'd cry. Often, when he was several minutes into a number, his hand would go up. "Hold it," he'd shout. He seldom let a number play [unbroken] to the end. . . .
>
> Mingus knew what he wanted; he had written the piece, and by God he wanted to hear it the way he wrote it.
>
> One night, in the middle of one of his compositions . . . he leaned his bass fiddle against the piano, threw his hands up in despair, walked over to Jimmy Knepper, the trombonist, and hit him a thundering blow in his solar plexus. Jimmy went down, and the set was over.

Mingus's physical explosions were indiscriminate. He went after his audience, his sidemen, and the people who hired him. Gordon recalls another night:

> Jazz musicians have the privilege of a cash draw every night. It says so in the contract, and is sacrosanct even when there is no contract. At closing one night, Mingus came around for the usual draw. Unfortunately, the Vanguard didn't have enough cash on hand. Mingus, raging, walked behind the bar, selected several unopened bottles of Scotch, and

vowed he'd turn them into cash somewhere to take
care of the needs of his men. But it was 4 A.M. and
bars were closed, so he smashed a couple of bottles
on the floor, grabbed a kitchen knife, which he held
threateningly in front of me, and, still unmollified,
stood on a chair and punched his fist through a light
fixture. He knocked the fixture askew but the bulb
inside stayed lit. I have never had the thing fixed.
. . . The "Mingus light" I call it. You can see it if
you ask a waiter.

Mingus's music was a distillation of Duke Ellington, Gospel music, Charlie Parker, the blues, Jimmy Blanton, New
Orleans polyphony, and fast small-band swing music. It was
another weapon, another way of talking. At its best, it was a
concatenation of voices, now solo, now in duet, now in quintet
or octet—all shouting, laughing, exulting, announcing. It
was not always meant to be intelligible; each voice was di-
rected at and dependent on the others. Despite its boisterous-
ness and bulk, it kept turning inward, the better for each
voice to hear the others. Mingus's music (his compositions
and his improvisations, together with the improvisations of
his sidemen, which he rigorously patrolled) had no style in
the conventional sense of such composer-bandleader-perform-
ers as Duke Ellington and John Kirby. Ellington was Mingus's
principal inspiration. He taught Mingus to use multiple
themes and original voicings and "talking" instruments. He
probably also helped shape Mingus's gift for writing lyrical
blues-directed melodies and for finding musicians who were
almost invariably adaptable to his needs. (Mingus's bass
playing, an intense elaboration of Ellington's bassists Jimmy
Blanton and Oscar Pettiford, was more annunciatory than
melodic. It had great vigor and virtuosity, and it was always
recognizable, because of its mixture of eighth notes, silences,
and tremolos, and its "vocal" attack and resonant tone.) Perhaps the reason Mingus's music had no style was that it

never stood still long enough. Mingus was constantly experimenting, and his music, which ranged from long-limbed love songs to raging dissonances, had few boundaries. Jazz rhythms—the accents and multi-noted cascades of bebop notwithstanding—had changed little since the thirties, when jazzmen first learned to swing, and this bothered him. He used accelerando and decelerando. He used breaks and stoptimes. He wrote passages that had no sounded beat, and he superimposed tricky, sliding double-time rhythms on plodding four-four time. He doubled tempos and halved them, tripled them and halved them. So intent was he on rhythmic surprise and perfection that he fashioned a drummer, Dannie Richmond, in his own image. When Mingus found him, Richmond was twenty-one and had played drums only a few months. (He'd been a tenor saxophonist.) Mingus taught him unswerving time, the melodic possibilities of drums, and how to make a drum solo fit its environment. When Richmond came aboard for good, in 1957, Mingus's music changed permanently.

Mingus's fascination with time and the beat came in large part from his instrument, but it is not altogether clear where his love of counterpoint came from. Certainly he learned from Ellington, whose music was a steady vying of voices, and he probably learned from his work with the fleet, thickly plotted trio that Red Norvo had in the early fifties. (Mingus often said that all his discoveries were made in the forties, when he lived on the West Coast.) Mingus liked to float six or seven horns at once. He would sketch their general courses, and as they gathered steam he'd urge them on with shouts and with his locomotive bass. Sometimes he let two or three voices tangle and forced the rest into the comfort of riffs, and sometimes he let them all fall into cacophony—presaging the "free" ensembles of Sam Rivers and the Art Ensemble of Chicago. These experiments brought to the fore the texture and excitement of the old New Orleans ensembles, but, unfortunately, Mingus never carried them through, either in his small-band efforts or in the big bands he toyed with in the sixties and seventies. Mingus's influence has already been wide (though rarely acknowledged), and is visible among such bassists as Scott La Faro and Steven Swallow and Gary Peacock, and among the avant-garde; his music also preserved the old beauties of jazz handed down by Lester Young and Charlie Parker. This wasn't any trouble for Mingus: he simply set himself to music.

We are in the midst of a Mingus celebration. Two recent Carnegie Hall concerts have been devoted to his music (which is just as incomplete without him as Ellington's music is without *him*), and there are four recent Mingus albums, three of them reissues. The new album, "Me Myself an Eye" (Atlantic), was made less than a year before his death in January 1979, and he does not play on it. It bears his mark, but in general it is shallow and overblown. The four numbers, two of them reworkings of old Mingus efforts, are played by twenty-five-piece bands, and little is added by the extra avoirdupois. The longest selection lasts a half hour and is called "Three Worlds of Drums." There are several series of drum solos, played by Joe Chambers, Dannie Richmond, and Steve Gadd; a couple of huge ensemble expostulations; a parade of solos (Jack Walrath, Randy Brecker, George Mraz, George Coleman, Eddie Gomez, Mike Brecker, and Larry Coryell); and, in the last three or four minutes, a beautiful, enfolding flamencan melody, played by the brass, which resolves into a dirge, backed by deep, descending organ chords. The least valuable of the reissues, "Nostalgia in Times Square" (Columbia), brings together fourteen numbers that Mingus recorded at several different sessions in 1959. Four have never been released before, and the rest restore various ensemble and solo deletions. But not much happens. "Boogie Stop Shuffle" has rhythmic intensity, and "Open Letter to Duke" has

one of Mingus's lingering, lazing melodic lines. Mingus and
Jimmy Knepper take striking solos on "Pussy Cat Dues," and
"Song with Orange" has a fine Mingus blues melody. For
whatever reasons, Mingus was not happy at Columbia, and
his best work at this time was done with Atlantic and with
Candid. Atlantic has assembled a three-record set, "Passions
of a Man," which covers the years from 1956 to 1977. Much
of Mingus's most attractive work is on it: the Gospel-blues
pieces "Wednesday Night Prayer Meeting" and "Cryin'
Blues" (but where is "Moanin' "?); the cool, melodic "Pith-
ecanthropus Erectus," "Reincarnation of a Lovebird," and
"Sue's Changes"; the multi-rhythmic "Tonight at Noon" and
"Haitian Fight Song"; and a surprise from 1974—a five-and-
a-half-minute slow blues called "Canon," in which a good
blues melody is handed back and forth, in largely unem-
bellished canon form, between two horns, a piano, and Mingus's bass. The Candid reissue (on the Barnaby/Candid label)
is "Mingus Presents Mingus," and it was made in 1960, with
the working band he had then—Ted Curson, Eric Dolphy,
and Dannie Richmond. The four men had developed a tele-
pathic understanding, a joint imaginativeness. The album includes "What Love" and "All the Things You Could Be by
Now If Sigmund Freud's Wife Was Your Mother," which
are reworkings of "What Is This Thing Called Love?" and
"All the Things You Are"; "Original Faubus Fables," Mingus's funny needling of Governor Orval Faubus; and the
twelve-minute "Folk Forms, No. 1." This last may be the
most remarkable of all Mingus's recordings. It begins with
Mingus playing a simple blueslike figure. He is joined by
Richmond, in ad-lib time. Dolphy enters (on alto saxophone),
and is almost immediately followed by Curson, who is muted.
The horns converse, the rhythm slips into four-four time and
is interrupted by breaks and out-of-tempo passages. Dolphy
and Richmond drop out, and Mingus backs Curson. Richmond and Dolphy return, and all four men swim around and

around and come to a stop. Mingus solos without backing, and Richmond reappears, pulling the horns after him. There is another stop, and Dolphy solos against broken rhythms, and the four take up their ruminations again. After a third stop, Richmond solos and he and Mingus go into a kicking, jumping, unbelievably swinging duet. Mingus falls silent, allowing Richmond to finish his solo, and there is a stop. Mingus solos briefly, and all converse intently until the rhythm slows, Dolphy moans, and they go out. It should be said that near the end of "What Love" Mingus and Dolphy (on bass clarinet) have a long and different kind of "conversation" on their instruments—apparently about Dolphy's intention of quitting the band.

June 19th

Hearing the Duke Ellington band live during its last ten years was like attending a sporting event. For the most part, the contestants were not the leader versus the orchestra (though that was sometimes the case) or members of the orchestra versus members of the orchestra (also occasionally true) but the leader and his orchestra versus the audience. The object of the game for the performers was to distract the audience so that it wouldn't notice how weary they were of much that they had to play or how badly they might play it, and the object for the audience was to get past the massed personalities onstage to the unique, exultant Ellington timbres and textures. Ellington had all kinds of weapons—his elegant verbiage, his celestial poise, his put-ons (the "I love you madly"'s, the finger-popping exercise). So did the band. Johnny Hodges feigned sleep or stony boredom. Cootie Williams strutted. Lawrence Brown oozed hauteur. Ray Nance clowned. Paul Gonsalves looked subaqueous. And there were hypnotic rituals, like the trumpet-clarinet-trombone trios that assembled solemnly at midstage to play "Mood Indigo" and "Black and Tan Fantasy." Eventually, we got through these divertisse-ments, only to realize that when Ellington and the band were gone, the jig would be up—without them we would be re-duced to memory, and to recordings. But recordings, like good portrait photographs, take on their own life: sheer availabil-ity gives them bulk and vigor, and in time they come close to supplanting their originals. Nor did we know that Elling-ton recorded constantly, and that a great deal of what he set down was unreleased. So the flood of new Ellington record-ings that have appeared during the past few years has been surprising and welcome—in particular, three small-band ses-sions done in New York and Hollywood in 1959 and 1960, and released as "The Smooth One: Johnny Hodges" (Verve) and "Duke Ellington: Unknown Session" (Columbia).

Hodges is the star of three tracks on the Columbia record-ing and of all on the Verve. It's increasingly clear that he was at the center of the Ellington firmament. His sound, style, and steadfastness (he missed only four years between 1928, when he joined the band, and 1970, when he died) were essential to Ellington's thinking and music, and so were his unique compositional gifts. Hodges's balance of emotion and coolness, intensity and ease, poetry and matter-of-fact-ness became the badge of the band. He was also a key to its curious origins. (Mercer Ellington ponders them in his book about his father.) The Ellington band was always considered a New York creation, but for a long time it was a New Or-leans band in disguise. During the twenties and thirties, it used such New Orleans musicians as Wellman Braud (bass), Lonnie Johnson (guitar), and Sidney Bechet and Barney Bigard. It used muted techniques brought forward by King Oliver, and many of its brass players reflected Louis Arm-strong. Harry Carney admired Coleman Hawkins, who, in turn, admired Armstrong. The drummer Tommy Benford remembers Hodges in Harlem in the twenties:

One Monday, at the Hoofer's Club, a kid named
Johnny Hodges sat in, and Willie the Lion Smith,
who had the band, hired him on the spot. He didn't
sound like anybody. But later Sidney Bechet put together a band and it had Hodges and me, and we
went into Herman's Inn. The first night, Hodges,
who had been playing clarinet and alto, picked up
Bechet's soprano and played it, and Bechet about
went crazy. After that, Sidney encouraged Hodges
on the soprano, and he even gave him one, which
Hodges still had when he died.

Hodges transposed Bechet's methods to the alto saxophone
and streamlined them. He eliminated Bechet's operatic vibrato
and his tendency to run the scales. He bottled Bechet's urgency and served it in cool, choice doses. He skirted Bechet's
funky tendencies—his growls and squeaks and odd, bubbling
sounds. But he kept Bechet's pouring country tone, his impeccable sense of time, and his rhapsodic approach to slow
materials. The result was two Hodges styles—one fast and
one slow. The fast style, used largely on the blues, consisted
of adroit embellishments suspended from a supply of rifflike
four- or five-note phrases that Hodges stockpiled through the
years. He would issue two or three of these figures in each
solo (his solos rarely lasted more than three choruses) and
connect them with silences, quick backstairs runs, blue notes,
and chugging single notes. He had a strong sense of dynamics, and would play his first chorus in gossiping whispers.
Then, using a loud three-note proclamation, he would start
his next chorus, drop back to a whisper for two bars, and go
up to a shout again and finish the solo. His blues solos (like
the novels of Ivy Compton-Burnett) came to sound almost
exactly alike. But this was deceptive, for he arranged his materials with ingenuity and imagination (as Compton-Burnett
did). He also had a deep well of blues emotion, and was a
legato player who unfailingly swung. His blues solos were

elegant, rocking chants, but his slow ballad numbers seemed
to be the work of a different musician. Around 1940, Ellington and/or Billy Strayhorn began writing a series of
ballads for Hodges ("Warm Valley," "Day Dream," "Passion
Flower," "Mood To Be Wooed"), and Hodges made them
into a new kind of music. It was unashamedly romantic, but
it was played with such intensity and perfection that it tran-
scended sentimentality. Hodges moved through a set of curves
in these solos. He would slide into almost every note, and use
curving ascending or descending glisses, each of them delivered with on-pitch precision. Hodges did not play nearly
enough medium-tempo standard songs. The ones he did play
were often classic (his "Sunny Side of the Street," done with
Lionel Hampton), and gave the impression that he was lob-
bing the melody back and forth from hand to hand. He was
a master of paraphrase. When he played a melody "straight,"
he would alter a note here and a note there, subtract or add
beats, and fashion an alter-melody that praised and comple-
mented the original. He was a mysterious, shrewd, monosyl-
labic man, short and oval. In the autobiography *Music Is My
Mistress*, Ellington says of Hodges, "His tonal charisma is
difficult to describe, but he always referred to it as 'the
kitchen.' If someone else played something in his style, he
would say: 'All right, come out of the kitchen.' "

"Duke Ellington: Unknown Session" is something of a jum-
ble. On hand are the leader, Ray Nance, Hodges, Lawrence
Brown, Harry Carney, Aaron Bell, and Sam Woodyard. Some
of the numbers are afterthoughts ("Mood Indigo" and "Creole Blues," in which Brown and Ellington play long duets);
one is tight and jumping in the manner of the peerless early
Ellington small-band sides ("Everything But You"); and the
rest pedal pleasantly along. Among these are a Hodges rhapsody ("Tonight I Shall Sleep") and two blues ("Dual Highway" and "Blues"). The first is credited to Hodges and is

still another demonstration of his ability to write come-hither
blues melodies. His head seems to have brimmed with them,
and certainly he must have had a hand in most of the blues
that Ellington recorded. Carney is in notable lyric shape
throughout and can be heard to excellent effect on "A Flower
Is a Lovesome Thing" and "Mighty Like the Blues." Brown,
front and center on the first side of the album, is in handsome
form, too.

Ten numbers in the Verve album (which was made without Ellington) were recorded in 1959, and have Harold Baker
(trumpet), John Sanders and Quentin Jackson (trombones),
Hodges, Ben Webster, Jimmy Hamilton, Jimmy Jones (piano), Les Spann (guitar), Ray Brown, and Jo Jones; nine
were done a year later, and have Baker and Ray Nance, Lawrence Brown and Bootie Wood (trombones), Hodges, Harold
Ashby (tenor saxophone), Hamilton, and a rhythm section
of Jones, Bell, and Woodyard. Thirteen of the numbers are
blues, twelve of them by Hodges. Each is choice, and so are
his solos, which carom and sing. Ben Webster, who rounded
off his corners under Hodges's tutelage when he was with the
Ellington band, contributes four fine statements (particularly
on "Lotus Blossom"), and Shorty Baker is limber. Hodges's
"I Told You So" is not a blues but a medium-slow ballad with
a descending melody and a turn-around ascending bridge,
and it is beautiful. Hodges plays the first chorus with the
rhythm section, and the trombones intone the melody in the
second while he marks melodic variations on its surface. It is
the sort of tune Ellington might have made a hit of.

June 22nd

The twenty-fifth Newport Jazz Festival got under way late
this afternoon at Carnegie Recital Hall with a solo performance by the pianist Al Haig. In the mid-forties, Haig, then
in his early twenties, became one of the first white musicians

to grasp the teachings of Charlie Parker and Dizzy Gillespie.
He appeared with them on Fifty-second Street and on some
of their earliest and best recordings, and he was a model for
such pianists as Hank Jones and Tommy Flanagan. It was
the high point of his musical life. Hearing him this afternoon
was like walking through an old house: there was evidence
everywhere of the people who had passed through. Haig's
billowy, indistinct attack, mostly in ad-lib tempos, was full
of Art Tatum arpeggios and harmonies, Teddy Wilson tenths,
and Nat Cole glisses. Yet there was no sign of Parker or Gillespie; nor was there any full-blown improvising. Some of
the dozen numbers that went by, stooped and vague, were
"Yesterdays," "Prelude to a Kiss," " 'Round Midnight," and
a multi-noted affair, with an ostinato bass, that sounded like
a cross between the "Bolero" and "In a Little Spanish Town."

In the evening, Dizzy Gillespie gave a bravura concert in
Carnegie Hall, in which he was accompanied by seven drummers and three percussionists. (His own quartet backed him
for one selection.) The percussionists—Luis Peralta, Tito
Puente, and Potato Valdez—formed the spine of the accompaniment, and the drummers included Grady Tate, Roy
Haynes, Max Roach, Jo Jones, Bernard Purdie, J. C. Heard,
and Art Blakey. Each drummer played a solo, accompanied
Gillespie (along with the percussionists), and gave way to
the next. Tate was inconclusive. Haynes was jumpy, using
rims and tomtoms and fretful snare-drum figures. Roach was
electrifying in a series of exchanges with Jones, who was coy.
Purdie tried to wow us. Heard exhaled a long, rustling cymbal passage that recalled Big Sid Catlett. And Blakey also
summoned Catlett, by dipping again and again into the Master's famous "Steak Face" solo, recorded in Symphony Hall
in 1947, when he was with Louis Armstrong. In fact, three
of Catlett's disciples were at the concert (Roach, Heard, and
Blakey), and one highly appreciative contemporary (Jones);
and although Catlett was never mentioned (Roach presented

Jones with a you-are-the-king award), he dominated the evening. Gillespie's playing was limited to blueslike cadenzas,
some open and some muted, and at least half were flashing.
The rest of the time, he leaned on his clichés—clichés still far
more original than most of the inventions of his descendants.
At the end of the evening, all the drummers assembled and
Gillespie conducted them, now shushing Haynes, now elevat-
ing Blakey, now calming Purdie, and it was as civilized as
any gathering of megalomaniacs can be. It should be mentioned that the audience had to swim through the lighting,
which was predominantly pale lime. At one point, Gillespie,
dressed in an ankle-length dashiki, was purple from his head
to his hips and forest green below that.

June 23rd

Betty Carter has taken jazz singing—singing in which the
voice is used for hornlike improvisation rather than as a con-
veyor of melody and lyrics—as far as it can go without
becoming abstract. Unlike most jazz singers, whose vocal
equipment barely meets their needs, she has a handsome
voice, particularly in the contralto range, and she uses it un-
erringly. At first hearing, her choice of notes seems quirky.
But the original melodic shape she draws out of her songs
demands "wrong" notes, and she chooses them with daring
and intelligence. She will hold an off note evenly for four to
six bars and, as the harmony slides away beneath, allow it to
resolve the instant she runs out of breath. She likes to tip a
note suddenly and let it fall an octave and a half, then slide
halfway up to where she began and break off. Her phrases
are often short and are shaped into lovely fragments, each
blessed with a following silence and each an inversion of part
of the original melody. She has a steady, classy sense of dynamics: her whispers brush the ear, and her occasional shouts
are belling. There is little resemblance to Charlie Parker or

Dizzy Gillespie (with whom she came up) or John Coltrane or Ornette Coleman. Transposed to a trumpet or saxophone, her creations would probably herald a new school. Music should be heard and barely seen, but Betty Carter has evolved a set of motions—flowing hands, slightly bent knees, a way of swaying irregularly to the right or left, as if she were dodging her own notes—that continually enhance her singing. Tonight, at Carnegie Hall, she did a handsome slow "What's New?," a "Trolley Song" that began fast and dissolved into a medium rock, an "Everything I Have Is Yours," and a fast scat-sung "Swing, Brother, Swing."

June 24th

Unfortunately, few of the black entertainers who have managed to work their way into the Broadway musical theatre during the past fifty or sixty years have been first-rate. With the exception of such as Bert Williams, Ethel Waters, Florence Mills, Bill Robinson, John W. Bubbles, and Fats Waller, they have often relied on their beauty, their personality, and/or the novelty of their color. (Consider black entertainers who have made their way not on Broadway but in night clubs, vaudeville, dance halls, movies, and television: Duke Ellington, Moms Mabley, Billie Holiday, Baby Laurence, Mabel Mercer, Bill Cosby, Louis Armstrong, Bessie Smith, Ray Charles, Lena Horne, Bobby Short, Nipsey Russell.) The revue held in Avery Fisher Hall tonight and called "Black Broadway" was put together by Robert Kimball, who has helped assemble books on Cole Porter and Eubie Blake, and—ironically—by Bobby Short, who read Kimball's narration and sang. Short was in good, resilient voice, and he did "Under the Bamboo Tree" (1902), "Broadway in Dahomey" (1902), "Wouldn't It Be a Dream" (1905), "The Unbeliever" (1920), and "As Long As I Live" (1934). Nell Carter, of the show "Ain't Misbehavin'," sang the title song and "I've Got a Feeling I'm Falling," in her high, brassy voice. The tap-dancer Honi Coles recalled Robinson's performance of "Doin' the New Low Down" in "Blackbirds of 1928," and did a dance of his own. Eubie Blake sang his anthems—"I'm Just Wild about Harry," "Memories of You," and "Love Will Find a Way." John Bubbles, his voice still largely intact, did "It Ain't Necessarily So," and Herb Jeffries did "Flamingo" and "The Brown-Skin Gal in the Calico Gown." The evening had two expected sensations: Adelaide Hall, who moved to England forty years ago, appeared in a shimmering white gown and white fur wrap and sang "I Must Have That Man," "Diga Diga Do," and "I Can't Give You Anything but Love" in a fine, delicate voice and with considerable charm, and Edith Wilson, who is of the same vintage, did resolute, almost swinging versions of "Black and Blue," "Yankee Doodle Blues," and "He May Be Your Man." Diahann Carroll was chosen to applaud Ethel Waters, and she went through brief Las Vegas versions of "Am I Blue," "Taking a Chance on Love," "Happiness Is a Thing Called Joe," "After You've Gone," and "Supper Time." The evening, barely watertight, all but foundered on her. Moving low and long-legged about the stage in a slinky black gown, she sang without taste and without understanding of the songs.

June 25th

Twenty pieces of jazz film were shown tonight at the Society for Ethical Culture by the collector David Chertok. We saw Sidney Bechet wrapping up an intense white French band in the early fifties, and Duke Ellington tossing off a "Caravan" with his 1952 band—Ray Nance on the violin, and mugging. Joe Turner, his voice like a canyon, sang a blues accompanied by a terrierlike group that included Bud Freeman, Max Kaminsky, and Cutty Cutshall. Errol Garner, shot mostly in soft focus, played his "Gaslight," and Charlie Parker and

Dizzy Gillespie did an all too brief "Hot House." (Parker, who skirted most of civilization, was rarely filmed.) Six pieces about women musicians were valuable for a fine Mary Osborne guitar solo on "The Man I Love" and for a 1945 duet by Dorothy Donegan and the pianist Gene Rodgers. Donegan had already assembled her dervish selves. There was a long, apathetic sequence showing Miles Davis playing "The Duke," "Blues for Pablo," and "New Rumba" with Gil Evans's band, and a long, frenetic one showing John Coltrane with McCoy Tyner, Elvin Jones, and Jimmy Garrison. Chertok's last reel began with Benny Goodman, Harry James, and Lou Mc-Garity in the fifties, and Shelly Manne with Conte Candoli and Richie Kamuca in the sixties, and went on to a stirring "I Can't Get Started" by Roy Eldridge, backed by Johnny Guarnieri and Osie Johnson. Next came "Chelsea Bridge" by Ben Webster, whose single straight-melody chorus was played with such authority it sounded like a full-scale, multi-chorus improvisation. The last bit of film was a dancing duet on "This Can't Be Love" by Buck Clayton and Charlie Shavers. Most of Chertok's material appeared to be taken from television films, whose very existence is surprising. But television has always been better than it lets on.

This afternoon, Roland Hanna gave the second of the half-dozen or so solo piano concerts to be offered during the festival at Carnegie Recital Hall. The word "recital" weighed as heavily on him as it had on Al Haig. He played six études of his own, and they had titles such as "View from an Island," "Afterglow," and "Mediterranean Seascape." They were, from this sprightly, cheerful pianist, rhapsodic, chordal, and solemn. The final number, "Silence," was by the bassist Charlie Haden. It had a lot of heavy chords, often spaced only a half tone apart, and it was bitter and unrelieved.

June 26th

None of the new, nearly epidemic improviser-composer pianists are more accomplished than Muhal Richard Abrams.
Unlike many avant-garde players, Abrams has a thorough
knowledge of the pianists who preceded him. His originality
is, in Harold Rosenberg's phrase, "emblazoned with the authority of the past." Abrams's style moves easily between
Cecil Taylor and Keith Jarrett, avoiding Taylor's pianistic
binges and Jarrett's penny emotionalism. The content of his
solos is of a high order: he establishes the plane he will move
on in his first eight bars, and he never leaves it. Abrams gave
the third Carnegie Recital Hall concert this afternoon, and he
played one nameless piece that lasted forty-eight minutes.
Nothing sagged, toppled over from exhaustion, exploded, or
ran off the road. Some of his most persuasive inventions involved a heavy ostinato bass note against which he pitted
slow, descending chords that resembled a laggard wandering
downhill; cascades of erratic, zigzagging single notes, which
emphasized that Abrams's music is high-speed not because
of its tempo, which doesn't exist, but because of the rich,
logical rapidity of its images; two melodic lines fashioned out
of chordal arpeggios and going at once, like a super George
Shearing (one also heard echoes, however muted, of Meade
Lux Lewis, Thelonious Monk, Stravinsky, Taylor, and Teddy
Wilson); several soft pools of single notes; a mountain of
dissonances that sounded as if all the notes on the keyboard
were being struck at once; and a sudden, quiet, poetic final
phrase—a garland of five ascending notes.

Count Basie, joined by his big band and by various alumni,
gave his annual Newport concert at Carnegie Hall tonight,
and his incomparable playing—a series of lucent, perfect
aphorisms—was intact.

At midday, five plaques honoring musicians who worked
in the clubs on Fifty-second Street in the forties were un-

veiled outside the CBS Building, at the west end of the block between Fifth and Sixth Avenues. The intent is to line the sidewalks with plaques on both sides of the block, which now has signs reading "Swing Street" affixed to the lampposts at either end. The first honorees are Billie Holiday, Coleman Hawkins, Dizzy Gillespie, Charlie Parker, and Lester Young. It is hard to know how such scarred, asocial creatures as Parker and Young and Holiday (dead at thirty-four, forty-nine, and forty-four) would react to such middle-class doings. Would they laugh or dance—or sit down and weep?

June 27th

What an odd, pale evening we were offered at Carnegie Hall tonight! It was a celebration for Hoagy Carmichael, who, a sly, spidery, supercharged seventy-nine, was all over the hall (he didn't sing, though), and it consisted of mechanical renditions of three dozen of his songs, among them "Skylark," "Lazy River," "I Get Along Without You Very Well," "How Little We Know," "Georgia on My Mind," "Baltimore Oriole," "Rockin' Chair," "Lazybones," "The Nearness of You," and "Two Sleepy People." Jackie Cain, Dave Frishberg, Max Morath, Marty Grosz, and Kay Starr sang, and a ten-piece band, conducted by Bob Crosby and made up of Bob Wilber, Yank Lawson, Billy Butterfield, Michael Moore, Eddie Miller, and Vic Dickenson, filled in the chinks. Carmichael's songs are often about country things, but, compared to Willard Robison's, they have a smooth, almost suburban flavor. They also have a built-in swing (he used to hang around jazz musicians a good deal)—a readiness, with the slightest push, to take off and go. Witness "Georgia on My Mind" and "Lazy River" and "Lazybones," and the uncommon number of classic recordings that have been built on his songs. So tonight was a puzzle. Jackie Cain's (purposely) flattish long notes didn't fit Carmichael's short, steadily stepping melodic lines.

Morath was empty, Grosz was adequate, and Kay Starr's lavish vibrato homogenized her songs. But Frishberg was excellent, and there were instrumental inspirations: Dickenson sneaking his way through "Lazybones"; a short, clarion Moore solo on "Baltimore Oriole"; and a duet by Butterfield and Lawson. Crosby lightened the evening with a story about the trumpeter Sterling Bose, who, when he had had too much to drink one night, attempted to solo by blowing into the bell of his horn. Getting no sound, he turned to Yank Lawson and said, "Take it, Yank. My lip is shot."

Blandness also afflicted the ten numbers the pianist Barry Harris played at Carnegie Recital Hall this afternoon. He did "We'll Be Together Again," a long slow blues, a couple of Bud Powell exercises, a Thelonious Monk medley, and "Someone To Watch Over Me." Every one of the notes had the same value, whether it stood by itself, went by in an arpeggio, was the keystone of a phrase, or ended a song. Harris was like a perfectly laid fire that refused to catch.

June 28th

The pianist Patti Bown turns up every few years—at a Newport festival for one number, at a Lexington Avenue pub for a night or two, at Bradley's for a week. But each time she leaves just enough of her brilliance behind to last until she turns up again. She has a reputation for being skittish and ungovernable, and her performance at Carnegie Recital Hall today suggested why. Much of the time, she sat at the keyboard and talked about her childhood (she was born in 1931, in Seattle), about her father's father, about her mother, about the music she heard and didn't hear when she was a child. In between these monologues, delivered in a soft, laughing way, she demonstrated a blues an elderly relative had played in a queer ragtime style (few rags have pure blues in them), a looser, windborne blues her mother had sung, a song she had written for Billie Holiday when she was eight, a gospel song, a fast jazz tune, John Coltrane's "Giant Steps," and a Swahili love song. Her style is idiosyncratic. She pushes the ryhthm around with hard left-hand offbeats and jagged right-hand figures. She likes to give the impression she has several voices going at once—one in the left hand and at least two in the right, where her restless chords seem to move side by side with her eccentric runs and connective figures. But her sense of dynamics rules the spectacular muscles in her playing, and shouldering chords are offset by delicate single-note figures. Her "Giant Steps" was an eight-minute lesson in how to make a piece of improvisation so tight and complex it would supply a dozen soloists for a week. After the Swahili love song, which was gentle and longing, Patti Bown played a blues with an exotic time signature and was gone again.

June 29th

Last February, the avant-garde trumpeter Lester Bowie, who is a founding member of the Art Ensemble of Chicago, put together a sixty-piece avant-garde band, the Sho'Nuff Orchestra, which gave a pair of concerts at the Symphony Space theatre. Most of the important members of the American avant-garde were there, and absorbed into the band were such groups as the A.E.C., Air, and the World Saxophone Quartet, along with members of Sun Ra's band. Anthony Braxton turned up, and so did the wizard trombonist George Lewis. It was a genial, cacophonic affair, in which the orchestra played some blues, a gospel piece, and "I Got Rhythm," sometimes in unison, sometimes in harmony, and sometimes free. At one point, the band marched around the theatre and then broke up into choirs, which played in the balconies, achieving a nice Berlioz effect. There were sumptuous sounds: a flute solo riding over a deep organ chord played by twenty reedmen; five drummers and two percussionists go-

ing at once; Bowie playing against two arco basses and several rolling snare drums.

The Art Ensemble of Chicago and the World Saxophone
Quartet were on hand at the Symphony Space tonight as
themselves, but the evening was opened by the Yosuke Yama-
shita Trio, from Japan. Made up of piano, drums, and alto
saxophone, the group offered deadly serious elaborations of
Cecil Taylor, Eric Dolphy, and Elvin Jones, played with a
slamming ferocity. The World Saxophone Quartet, composed
of the alto saxophonists Oliver Lake and Julius Hemphill, the
tenor saxophonist David Murray, and the baritone saxophonist Hamiet Bluiett, was an immediate antidote. It works in
the parodic tradition established more than fifteen years ago
by Charles Mingus and Archie Shepp. The W.S.Q. imitated
the Ellington reed section, using a syrupy vibrato, and they
played a fast, smeary staccato riff number that called forth
Jimmy Giuffre's "Four Brothers." They also did some Stepin
Fetchit pantomime in which they shuffled around the stage
sideways and took about an hour to pick up their instruments
for their next number. They played some smart collective
passages, and their solos were sharp and to the point. (The
opening section of their set, wherein each man appears by
himself for a meandering solo, should be dispensed with. The
group's strength is collective.) They swung hard, and it was
only at the end of their performance that one realized they
didn't have (or need) a rhythm section.

The Art Ensemble of Chicago first came together in 1968,
and it is still made up of Lester Bowie, Joseph Jarman (reeds
and percussion), Roscoe Mitchell (reeds), Famoudou Don
Moye (drums and percussion), and Malachi Favors Magous-
tous (bass). It is a musical-theatrical group, which dresses
in Oriental costumes (Bowie wears a white medical coat),
chants and recites verse, and moves about in a slow, boxlike,
ritualistic way. The music is free and achieves its kaleidoscopic, mercurial effect not so much through improvisational

skills as through the changing textures and timbres brought about by the musicians' doubling on the arsenal of instruments they carry with them. When Bowie soloed at one point tonight, this is what happened. He began with rude blats, which gave way to dying-swan sounds, which dissolved into Rex Stewart half-valved effects. There was no accompaniment. Then Bowie made sudden roaring trumpet sounds right next to the microphone and drew a fusillade of rimshots. Jarman rattled some maracas, Moye inserted a snare-drum roll, and Favors played high, scratchy chicken notes next to the bridge of his bass. Bowie went through several descending four-note phrases, breaking off the last note violently each time, as if he were being bodily pulled away from his instrument. After another spray of Moye rimshots, Bowie gave off some piercing Roy Eldridge notes, and there was silence. Two beats passed, and the silence was filled with lyricism: Bowie played a thick melody and was joined by Jarman flute and Mitchell baritone-saxophone hums. Moye took up his wire brushes, and Favors started a steady 4/4 beat that Moye began to pick at with wild and irregular rimshots and tomtom strokes. With the reeds now chanting and shouting, Bowie released an assemblage of blats and growls and yells. He slowly subsided and, finally sitting down at center stage, lowered his head while Jarman and Mitchell, on soprano and alto saxophones, worked their way into a gradually intensifying duet and Moye started exploding slowly on some gongs hung beside him. And so it went for an hour. It is not a music you simply sit and listen to. Your ears and brain turn into instruments, and before long are moving through the forest of sounds.

June 30th

The smooth, serene celebration of American song held at Carnegie Hall tonight was arranged and conducted and performed by Mel Tormé and Gerry Mulligan, who brought along Joya Sherrill, George Shearing, Jackie Cain and Roy Kral, and a band including Harry Edison, Doc Cheatham, Vic Dickenson, Mulligan, Jimmy Rowles, George Duvivier, and Oliver Jackson. Joya Sherrill sang three Ellingtons and one Strayhorn, and left them unchanged but off pitch. Jackie and Roy were streamlined and expert, and Shearing sang "Lullaby of Birdland." The rest of the evening was taken up by Tormé, who did Jerome Kern ("Nobody Else but Me," "The Folks Who Live on the Hill," "All the Things You Are," "Pick Yourself Up," "The Song Is You"), by Mulligan, who sang and/or played Kurt Weill ("Mack the Knife," "Here I'll Stay," "Speak Low"), and by the band, which did "Jive at Five," "Undecided," and an "I Want a Little Girl" that had a folksy vocal duet by Cheatham and Dickenson. Last year, Tormé and Mulligan co-chaired a similar enterprise, and it was a swift and witty interlude that stays in the mind. Tonight has already taken flight.

September 10th

Five important recordings:

Since Jimmy Rowles settled in New York in 1974, he has been recorded many times—on his own and with such as Zoot Sims, Charles Mingus, Stan Getz, Stéphane Grappelli, and Lee Konitz—but nothing has come out quite right. He has sounded bland or dispirited or uninventive, or if he appeared in promising form he hasn't been allowed to stretch out. It had begun to look as if Rowles's style would never be caught, as if we would be doomed to follow him from night club to night club (his most natural habitat), collecting a brilliant arpeggio here and a brilliant coda there, only to find, two or three days later, that they had faded and were gone. But "Al Cohn and Jimmy Rowles: Heavy Love" and "Jimmy Rowles: We Could Make Such Beautiful Music Together" (Xanadu) go a long way toward laying the fear that Rowles would never be properly recorded.

The first is a swashbuckling, eloquent, free-as-you-go duet by Rowles and his old friend the tenor saxophonist Al Cohn. (Liner notes on jazz albums are looking up. David A. Himmelstein describes Cohn's provenance this way: "Out of Lesterville, a Dexter runabout, with four brother-doors and chicken liver wheels," which means that Cohn admires Lester Young and resembles Dexter Gordon, that he was one of the famous Woody Herman saxophonists known as the Four Brothers, and that he plays with a cantorial lyricism.) Cohn and Rowles do five standards and one blues, largely in medium tempo, and they are never apart, even when they solo. Cohn's sound echoes in the mind when Rowles is alone, and when Cohn solos Rowles pulls all his accompanist stops. He supplies off-beat chords, broken chords, seesawing chords, thump-thump-thump on-the-beat chords, and crabbed single-note lines that make Cohn glint. He anticipates Cohn, duplicates him, and mischievously parodies him. Rowles's solos are often special—particularly the single-note excursions on "Them There Eyes" and "Sweet and Lovely," and his second chorus on "Taking a Chance on Love," in which he plays a series of ascending staccato notes, striking some of them two or three times to achieve a nervous stuttering effect.

On the second record, Rowles leads a trio that has George Mraz on bass and Leroy Williams on drums. The best number is a five-minute "Stars and Stripes Forever" done as a bossa nova. Rowles plays the melody in lagging single notes, improvises, and then goes into a heavy, full-orchestra section, all horns blaring, and returns to his lagging single notes, finishing with a coda made up of part of "Taps." There is also an elegant "We Could Make Such Beautiful Music," and a "Here's That Rainy Day" where, in the total-improvisation way of Lester Young, he leaves every note of the melody unturned. He does a funny version of Erroll Garner's "Shake It, but Don't Break It," and closes the record with overly long readings of "I Can't Get Started" and "In the Still of the Night."

The twelve sides on "Billie Holiday: Swing Brother, Swing" (Encore) were recorded between 1935 and 1939, and eleven have never before been released in this country on L.P. The generally anemic accompaniment (the musicians are taken from Benny Goodman, Jimmy Lunceford, Chick Webb, Fletcher Henderson, Red Norvo, Stuff Smith, and Bobby Hackett's band at Nick's) probably helps explain why they have been out of print so long. So do the songs. With the exception of "They Can't Take That Away from Me" and the good but forgotten "I Don't Know If I'm Coming or Going," "I Wish I Had You," and "You're Gonna See a Lot of Me," the material is Tin Pan Alley strudel: "Life Begins When You're in Love," "The Moon Looks Down and Laughs," "Forget If You Can," "You're So Desirable," and "Hello, My Darling." But Billie Holiday treats each song as if it were prime Gershwin or Rodgers. She carefully unfolds the lyrics and holds them up for us to see. She hand-paints each melody, concealing the nonsense and the clichés. She does her incomparable legato act, loafing along behind the beat, her shoulders hunched in mock surprise, her fingers spread in the idling air, then catches up in the last chorus, the last eight, the last measure. Teddy Wilson is on eight sides, and Claude Thornhill, who was a better pianist than he has ever been given credit for being, is on three. Listen to his things-to-come solos on "The Moon Looks Down and Laughs" and "Forget If You Can."

Red Norvo has an uncanny may of making classic recordings, and "Red & Ross" (Concord Jazz) is one. It was re-

corded at Donte's, in North Hollywood, and on hand with
Norvo are Ross Tompkins on piano, John Williams (not to
be confused with the older Johnny Williams) on bass, and
Jake Hanna on drums. Most night-club recordings are baggy
and self-indulgent, but "Red & Ross" is tight and graceful
and swinging. At least one intensely pleasing thing happens
on each of the six long tracks. On "Whisper Not," played as
a piano solo, Tompkins settles into his improvisation with a
sudden descending, skipping double-time run that is breath-
taking. "The One I Love," taken at a fast tempo, has another
exhilarating Tompkins solo, and near its end bass and drums
lay out while Norvo and Tompkins play counterpoint—a
bramble of voices moving complexly and daringly. The two
repeat their attractive act even more tellingly on "All of
Me." "How About You?" has half a dozen eight-bar breaks
by Hanna, whose admiration for Sid Catlett has worked hand-
somely for him. On "It Might As Well Be Spring," Norvo
and Hanna, using brushes on his cymbals, play a glancing,
airborne duet. "Everything Happens to Me" is very different
from the rest of the album. It is slow and is given over largely
to Norvo, who makes it into a melancholy hymn.

"The Bob Brookmeyer Small Band" (Gryphon) is a continuous and often beautiful celebration of melodic improvisation, carried out by the leader on valve trombone, Jack
Wilkins on guitar, and Michael Moore on bass, with the excellent Joe LaBarbera on drums. The recording, which has presence and clarity, was done at Sandy's Jazz Revival, a night
club in Beverly, Massachusetts, and it is made up of fifteen
numbers, ten of them standards and the rest originals or reworkings of standards by Brookmeyer, Andy Laverne, and
Art Koenig. Melodic improvisation—as opposed to abstract
improvisation—comes in several weights. The lightest is embellishment. The player alters the melody subtly, as if he
were translating it into another language, by adding grace
notes, subtracting notes, rearranging rhythms, and applying

his particular timbres. Variation is a fussier form of embellishment. Sometimes the melody vanishes altogether and the player becomes as important as the melody itself. Total improvisation, the rarest of the lot, is just that: the player, using either the melody or the chords of the tune as bedrock, builds a new and far more complex melody. If the original song is a winter tree, total improvisation is a July tree.

Brookmeyer is a master of all three forms of improvisation, but he concentrates here on the first and last. His masterly embellishments are evident on "Sweet and Lovely," "Some Day My Prince Will Come," and "You'd Be So Nice To Come Home To." The total improviser does his vanishing trick on "Smoke Gets in Your Eyes," "Body and Soul," and "I Can't Get Started." His rebuilding of the three is complete; there is no way of knowing what the original melody is without being told. Brookmeyer is a brilliant but puzzling musician who won't let the listener alone. He plays him to death. He is a lyricist, but he buries his poems in notes, smears, arpeggios, in a kind of anti-sissy bravado. It is instructive to compare Brookmeyer with Jimmy Knepper. Both are middle-aged, second-generation beboppers, but Knepper has become an aphorist while Brookmeyer is still an explainer. Wilkins, in his thirties, is a superlative guitarist who, like Jim Hall, is not hemmed in by his instrument. He likes to get off figures that suggest pianists or saxophonists or trumpeters. He uses a full tone and he prefers the upper registers and he has a good sense of dynamics. He is a wild melodist. He will throw a handful of notes into the high register, make them ring, fill the space after them with silence, and dive into his lowest register, touching each octave as he falls past. Then he will ascend and strike more urgent bells, and go into driving Django Reinhardt chords, which give way to more silence and curling, meditative middle-register single notes. His rhythmic attack accents his melodic freshness and independence. He shadows his notes, rides in

front of them, and dots their "i"s. He and Michael Moore
work together well. Moore's improvisations, often done in *his*
high registers, are pure and lofty. Moore plays over half a
dozen solos on the album, and all are superior. The album
marks the first time that Moore has been heard properly and
at length on records.

Air is made up of Henry Threadgill on reeds and hubkaphone, Fred Hopkins on bass, and Steve McCall on drums.
Like the Art Ensemble of Chicago, Air relies on subtle racial
humor and on collective abstract improvisation. Its wheels
throw off showers of timbres and textures: Threadgill plays
baritone saxophone, making Queen Mary honks, while Hopkins plays wild arco figures and McCall bounces from tomtom to tomtom; Threadgill plays flute and Hopkins supplies
delicate pizzicato runs while McCall moves through his cymbals with wire brushes; Threadgill plays his hubkaphone,
which consists of a dozen or so hubcaps strung out on a kind
of drying rack, and Hopkins and McCall go into Afro-Cuban
rhythms. "Open Air Suit" and "Lore" were made in studios,
and "Montreux Suisse" was recorded at the Montreux Jazz
Festival. Threadgill plays flute, and alto, tenor, and baritone
saxophones on the first, which has four studied pieces. They
are described this way on the back of the album: " 'Open Air
Suit' was cut and designed for Air as a five piece suit.
Whereby from a customed viewpoint Air was considered,
however it was conceived as something that Air would have
to fit itself up to or rather into. As a piece each person had
to play a hand on the basis of what they had in their hand,
secondly on the basis of what was possibly open. Remember-
ing at all times never to photograph one's entire position or
game plan prematurely." "Lore" is a conservative investiga-
tion of Jelly Roll Morton ("Buddy Bolden's Blues" and "King
Porter Stomp") and Scott Joplin ("The Ragtime Dance"),
and the approach is either gently parodic or *almost* straightforward (Threadgill does some fine embellishing), so that

one doesn't know whether to laugh at the old-timey music or weep at its suggested beauty. The group is firmly on its own ground in the festival recording. "Let's All Go Down to the Footwash" has an Ornette Coleman melody, and "Abra" is an abstract blues. The fifteen-minute "Suisse Air" is largely Threadgill bonk-bonking on his hubkaphone, with Hopkins and McCall supplying a lot of Afro-Cuban rattling. It achieves considerable momentum but near the end is blown to bits when Threadgill picks up his baritone.

October 29th

Dizzy Gillespie, under the auspices of Doubleday, has issued his memoirs, *To Be or Not To Bop.* They are in the shape of a book but consist of taped interviews with Gillespie and with relatives, musicians, singers, bandleaders, entrepreneurs, A. & R. men, and critics. These oral effusions have been arranged in rough chronological order by one Al Fraser, who says in his preface that "writing Dizzy Gillespie's personal memoirs . . . was not an easy job." The resulting gabfest takes up five hundred and two pages.

Gillespie has been a commanding trumpet player for thirty-five years, which is close to a record for an improvising wind player. (Drummers, pianists, guitarists, bassists, and vibraphonists tend to be immortal, but wind players wear out. The only consummate ones who have matched Gillespie's longevity are Roy Eldridge, Red Allen, Doc Cheatham, Vic Dickenson, Sidney Bechet, and Coleman Hawkins.) He was born in 1917, in Cheraw, South Carolina, the youngest of nine children of a harried mother and a bumptious, often cruel father, who died before his son was ten. Gillespie joined Frankie Fairfax's Philadelphia band when he was eighteen, and Teddy Hill's New York band two years later. Between 1939 and 1942, he worked with Cab Calloway, Coleman Hawkins, Benny Carter, Les Hite, Lucky Millinder, Claude Hopkins,

Charlie Barnet, Boyd Raeburn, and Earl Hines. He met Charlie Parker, wrote "Pickin' the Cabbage," "A Night in Tunisia," and "Salt Peanuts," and was married, to Lorraine Willis. And he organized his first group. By 1945, aged twenty-eight, he was on his way. Having helped Charlie Parker invent bebop, he was a leader of the first bebop band on Fifty-second Street, he took the first bebop band to the West Coast, he appeared on the first bebop recordings, and he was in the first bebop big band. He soon became a prepossessing showman, who danced well, sang like a potato, told funny jokes, and played fiery trumpet. His onstage image became sly, owlish, and slightly sardonic. But the image that emerges in the early part of *To Be or Not To Bop* is surprisingly different. He describes the treatment given him in 1937 by the older musicians in Teddy Hill's band: "Shad Collins was very nasty. During my solos, he and Dicky Wells tried to act like I was playing absolutely nothing and looked around at me sneering. They even tried to start a little protest and threatened to quit if Teddy took me to Europe. That's what they *said*, but they didn't. Today, I'm a world-renowned trumpet player and . . . Shad Collins is a cabdriver." A few pages later, he says, "One of the things that the French have never forgiven themselves for is ignoring me in Paris when I came over there in 1937. . . . Now, I'm one of the main people who has turned music all the way around, and they had a chance to catch me in my infancy and blew it."

Gillespie also liked a good fight. He describes at length the famous altercation in which he nicked Cab Calloway after Calloway accused him of shooting spitballs (he didn't) on the stand. (Calloway had good reason to suspect him, for one of Gillespie's favorite pastimes was throwing imaginary forward passes to the trombonist Tyree Glenn during Calloway's torch-song vocals.) But most of *To Be or Not To Bop* is given over to canonizing Gillespie. We are told of his kindness to younger musicians, of his pioneering use of Afro-Cuban and

South American rhythms, of his virtues as a bandleader and
composer, of his brilliance as a player, of his battles with racism, of his being the first American jazz musician to go
abroad for the State Department. It's a relief when Gillespie
gets off a good one:

> Sea to sea, America in 1945 was as backward a
> country musically as it was racially.

> A well-told lie usually contains a germ of truth.

> When the play "Othello" opened in New York
> with Paul Robeson, José Ferrer, and Uta Hagen, I
> went to the theater to see it. I was sitting way up in
> the highest balcony. Paul Robeson's voice sounded
> like we were talking together in a room. That's how
> strong his voice was coming from the stage, three
> miles away. Paul Robeson, big as he was, looked
> about as big as a cigar from where I was sitting.
> But his voice was right up there next to me.

> Musically, a square would chew the cud. He'd
> spend his money at the Roseland Ballroom to hear
> a dance band playing standards, rather than extend
> his ear and spirit to take an odyssey in bebop at the
> Royal Roost.

> The bridge in "Ain't Misbehavin'." Where did
> [Fats Waller] get that from? . . . I haven't heard
> anything in music since that's more hip, harmoni-
> cally and logically.

Little of *To Be or Not To Bop* stays in the mind. Efforts of
this kind should be listened to. The music of the voices, with
their inflections and accents, would form a counterpoint to the
meaning of the words. Perhaps *To Be or Not To Bop* should
be performed by Gillespie and his celebrators. They could sit
onstage and talk, and when they grew weary, Gillespie could
play. It would be a hip week.

It's a good time for a new history of jazz, and that's pretty much what James Lincoln Collier has put together in *The Making of Jazz*, published by Houghton Mifflin. Collier, a musician and the author of children's books, has fashioned his history not out of schools and styles but out of musical and sociological portraits of the musicians, major and minor, who have most moved him. He is particularly sharp on Fats Navarro and Clifford Brown, Miles Davis, Charles Mingus, and Ornette Coleman. He sets Benny Goodman back on the pedestal the critics knocked him off thirty-five years ago, and he gives a hand to such long-undervalued players as Buck Clayton, the trumpeter Joe Thomas, Wild Bill Davison, Bobby Hackett, and Bunny Berigan. He refurbishes Sidney Bechet and Eddie Lang and Jack Teagarden, and he gives an exhaustive summary of European jazz. His analyses of the music fall comfortably between musicology and metaphor. He can be shrewd and graceful and funny:

> Ellington was probably the finest writer of short melody in twentieth-century America. I am speaking not just of the numberless formal songs he wrote . . . but the brief snatches and fragments of melody that bob up everywhere in his compositions. An Ellington piece is afloat with little motifs, some of which are elaborated on, but many of which appear and disappear as coruscations on the surface of the music.

> Louis Armstrong was born into poverty, schooled in drudgery, and raised in ignorance. Fortunately for him and us, he happened to be a genius.

> Jazz likes to consider itself a mystery.

> Bechet was an individualist, a lone wolf, the sharp who blows into town, cleans out the locals, and disappears again.

Mingus was often successful in making the soloists stay with the idea he had laid out, and the effect gave his music an emotional unity that is lacking in a good deal of jazz, especially where strings
of soloists are at liberty to tell severally the world
what kind of day they have been having.

At times, Collier grows overly oblique; and certain important musicians are either ignored or given small attention.
He says nothing about Gerry Mulligan's experiments with
collective improvisation in the fifties (Mulligan's most valuable contribution to the music), and he skims over such fun-
damentalists as Chick Webb and Zutty Singleton. Ben Webster deserves more attention, and Collier never mentions Ray
Charles or Art Farmer or Joe Morello. But he has done his
own thinking (he is particularly good on the origin of the
blues), and he has cleared away a lot of the cant and foolish-
ness that have grown up around the music in the forty-five
years it has been written about.

Many of the photographs in Collier's book were taken by
William P. Gottlieb. Two hundred of Gottlieb's pictures have
been brought together higgledy-piggledy by Simon & Schus-
ter in *The Golden Age of Jazz*. Needless historical text and
watery captions take up space that could have been used for
larger prints. Also, some of the photographs either are pub-
licity shots or are action photographs that don't, for one reason or another, work. A hundred or so full-page pictures
would have made a classic collection. Gottlieb, who recently
retired from his own educational-film business, wrote on jazz
in the late thirties and early forties. He started taking photographs simply to enhance his stories. Many of his action
pictures are famous: a satanic Leadbelly, lit from below;
Sidney Bechet playing a looming, clublike soprano saxophone;
Muggsy Spanier's smooth, hilly Irish face awash with light;
Dave Tough, melancholy skin and bones in a shirt and tie,

practicing between sets. Taking pictures of jazz musicians
has never been easy. They work largely in semi-darkness,
and their grace is measured in seconds. But Gottlieb was not
taking pictures; he was photographing a music. Again and
again, he catches the precise moment when the musician's
face is suffused with effort and emotion and beauty: the music is *there*. Particularly intense are the pictures of Art Hodes,
in sculptured profile; of Billie Holiday, her head thrown
back, her neck arched, her open mouth full of sound; of
Charlie Parker, his burning face set off by Tommy Potter's
face and instrument; and of Baby Dodds, elegant and magis-
terial in white-on-white and a dark suit.

1980

April 7th

When jazz musicians move West, they rarely come back. Nellie Lutcher, who is at Barney Josephson's Cookery after a seven-year absence, was away twenty years before her last visit. She looks the same, which is good news and means: a luxurious ski-jump nose, snapping black-brown eyes, long, graceful fingers and scimitar thumbs, a Maillol shape, and a wide, swivelling smile. Her hands evoke wild images. When they are low and flat on the keyboard, they look like long-distance swimmers. When she suddenly lifts them, they become fighter planes peeling off. Her head moves from lower right to upper left, from side to side, from back to front, while her torso is straight as a ladderback. Her eyes blaze and droop and smile. She likes to work with a drummer (would that he were Sid Catlett, whom she stepped out with in the forties), but she has none at the Cookery—Skeeter Best is on guitar and Morris Edwards on bass—so she claps her hands when the beat weakens, making them explode on the afterbeat or on ricocheting offbeats. Out of this dervish hustle came her unique singing and her primitive, springing piano. Her playing is the child of Earl Hines, whom she idol-

ized in the early thirties, when Hines was holding forth almost nightly on the radio from the Grand Terrace in Chicago. She is a strong pianist, a broadside pianist, who likes
big-textured Hines chords in the right hand. She doesn't
much care for arpeggios or single-note melodic lines, but she
likes occasional tremolos and will slip in a glissando if she
has to get from one register to another in a hurry without
breaking sound. She uses everything in her left hand—stride
basses, tenths, offbeat notes and chords, and boogie-woogie
basses. Her playing carpets her singing. She has a robust
contralto, but she almost never uses it in a straightforward
way. She is a master of melisma: she will fill a single syl-
lable with six or seven notes. She is a master of dynamics:
whispers and shouts and crooning continually surprise one
another. Like Joe Turner, she uses words largely to hang
melody on, and what she sings is often unintelligible. She
steadily garnishes her melodic flow with squeaks, falsetto,
mock-operatic arias, yodels, and patches of talking. Yet her
singing, like Turner's and like Jack Teagarden's, is easy and
whole.

She is an encyclopedia of the black music of fifty years
ago. She grew up in the Southern Baptist church, and her
singing, with its overlay of vocal effects, is full of gospel music. She was exposed to blues singers like Ida Cox and Ma
Rainey and to the last of the minstrel shows on the T.O.B.A.
circuit, and she heard local vaudeville on the radio. She also
heard the likes of Hines and Andy Kirk on the radio, and she
heard the territory bands that roamed the South. She listened
to recordings, and somewhere she fell under the influence of
a highly specialized group of musicians who were a compound of jazz and comedy, of improvisation and clowning.
They were generally pianists, guitarists, or bassists who sang
novelty songs and used a variety of comic devices—Bronx
cheers, growls, sighs, basso profundo, falsetto, roars. They
sang scat style, and they made up their own languages and

sang them. They were expert, swinging musicians who had
discovered early in their careers that their comic gifts out-
paced their improvisational skills. Joe Venuti and Fats Waller probably got this cheerful movement started, and they
were followed by the Spirits of Rhythm, which included the
Daniels brothers on tipple, Leo Watson, and the guitarist
Teddy Bunn; Slim and Slam, who were Slim Gaillard and
Slam Stewart; the Three Peppers, led by Toy Wilson on piano and vocals; the pianist and singer Harry the Hipster
Gibson, who wore gloves when he played; Louis Jordan and
his jumping Timpany Five; Dorothy Donegan; the pianists
Loumell Morgan and Maurice Rocco, who stood while playing; and Rose Murphy, who is sometimes confused with
Nellie Lutcher. (Rose Murphy's playing is similar, but she
sings in a high, tiny Betty Boop voice decorated with buzzes
and trills and bird sounds.) These musicians performed for
the delectation of black people, and occasionally what they
did was two-edged: it made blacks laugh not only at themselves but at the Cap'n, too.

Nellie Lutcher lives in Los Angeles, and this is what an old
friend and neighbor had to say about her the other day:
"Nellie owns a fine small apartment house with six units,
and she lives in one, and Lawrence Brown, the old Ellington
trombonist, rents out part of that. He says he feels safe and
comfortable there. Nellie's apartment is big and beautiful,
and she has everything she needs or wants, including a luxurious garden. She's on the board of directors of Local 47 of
the musicians' union, and sometimes she goes over three or
four times a week. It's an elected office. She still plays, and
she never plays alone. She uses Billy Hadnott on bass and
Ulysses Livingston on guitar, and a drummer named Gene
Washington. She drives herself everywhere in her Cadillac.
She's a big woman and she needs a big car. She does a lot of
charity work, and Mayor Sam Yorty gave her a special

award. There's not a wrong one among her seven brothers and sisters still alive. Nellie is a conservative in politics, and it's the only thing we disagree on. She has an international following, but the odd thing about her music is that you care for it passionately or not at all."

Nellie Lutcher likes to loosen up between sets at the Cookery by talking. "I first worked for Barney Josephson in 1947," she said one evening. "It was the year my life turned around. I'd been plugging along in Los Angeles for over ten years when—wham!—Dave Dexter, Jr., of Capitol Records, heard me sing on a March of Dimes radio show. I did 'The One I Love,' and a couple of weeks later he signed me to a contract. I recorded 'Hurry On Down' and 'He's a Real Gone Guy,' both of which I wrote, and when I woke up I had a couple of hits. I was paid a hundred dollars a side and no royalties, so the only money I've made from the records has been from the tunes themselves. Barney Josephson brought me to New York to Café Society Downtown, and I went to Europe, where I did very well. Carlos Gastel, who handled Nat Cole and Peggy Lee, took me over. I had no trouble until the sixties, when rock knocked things out like disco's doing now. It makes me cry to think of all the musicians disco is putting out of work. But I have my little apartment house on the west side of Los Angeles, and my union position, which came my way in 1968, when I replaced Harvey Brooks after he passed. I went to Los Angeles in 1935 from Lake Charles, Louisiana, where I was born—oh, in 1915. Lake Charles is twenty-eight miles from Texas, the last little city in Louisiana going west. It's got rice fields and pecan groves, and it's on the Calcasieu River, which connects directly with the Gulf of Mexico, thirty or forty miles south. So it's a seaport town, too. Everything was segregated when I was little, but I don't thing I could have come up in a friendlier town. The Caucasian people were very considerate of the Negro people. The main trouble with Lake Charles, it has sickening humid heat

in the summer. When I stopped to see my father on his birthday a year or two before he died—he died in 1961—I discovered I couldn't tolerate that heat anymore. My father was
born in St. Joseph, in Tensas Parish, right up by the Mississippi. His mother was Nellie Johnson, and I was named after
her. My father was tall and skinny and his nickname was
Skinner. He was a truck driver and stockman for the Houston
Packing Company. He was mild-mannered but stern, and
whatever he said he wouldn't budge from. He played all the
stringed instruments but concentrated on the bass. Weekends
and some weeknights, he played in the Imperial Jazz Band,
a local group that did dances and picnics and the like. He
loved the comics, and he'd go to every minstrel show that
passed through, and just sit there and laugh and laugh. He'd
had a son by a previous marriage, and he had fifteen more
children by my mother. She lost five in infancy before I was
born, so I was the eldest. David died in infancy in the twenties, Charles died in the Second World War, and Vydha, who
was the baby, in 1971. All the rest are left: Eugenia; Florence, who married a little while ago; Florida, who designs all
my gowns; Margie, the youngest; my brother Joe, who plays
saxophone; James, who is religious and has a beauty-supply
business; and Isaac, who was named after my father—we
call him Bubba. Most of them live around Los Angeles. My
mother's desire was to play the piano, but starting a family
stopped that. She was born in Charenton, Louisiana, and she
passed in 1972. She was a beautiful lady—short and stout
and a marvellous mother. She never bothered about going
anyplace except church. We children didn't know what it
meant to have a key to our house, because Mother was always there. We had a frame house, raised up off the ground,
and she always saw to it that we were well fed and there was
enough food to share with our neighbors when they needed
it. I knew both of my grandmothers, but no grandfathers.
The grandmothers lived in a little extra house we had—Nellie,

and my mother's mother, Ellen. Nellie was even-tempered, but Ellen was cantankerous. They managed it together until they died. We had a piano, and when I started to tickling it, that thrilled my mother. I was six or seven when she arranged for me to have lessons with the wife of the junior-high-school principal—Eugenia King Reynaud. Money was short, naturally, so my mother told her, 'I'll do your laundry. I want my daughter to have the best piano lessons possible.' Mrs. Reynaud couldn't improvise one note, and if there was a fly sitting on the sheet music, she'd play that, too. She wanted me to have correct fingering, and she wanted me to learn to read. She discovered right away that I knew how to fake things, and she watched my ear all the time. If a student wasn't interested, she didn't waste time on him, but if he showed promise, she knocked herself out. She touched my life forever with her marvellous way of teaching. She was the pianist of the little Baptist church we went to, and when I was eight she allowed me to play for Sunday school. I got two dollars a month for that. I studied with her six or seven years, and eventually I was good enough for the lady who owned the Majestic Hotel in town to send word that she wanted me to play for her guests—'The Blue Danube Waltz,' and things like that. I also played for Ma Rainey, who came through town without her piano player.

"When I was fifteen or sixteen, I was asked to join the Imperial Jazz Band. Al Freeman had been the pianist, and he went home to Columbus, Ohio. They could have gotten someone to come from New Orleans, but the leader, Mr. Clarence Hart, talked to the men in the band and then he asked my father would he consent to *my* playing with them. My dad said it would be all right with him but he didn't know what my mother would say. He wasn't in the church, but she was, and at that time the church people in the South looked down on jazz music as the work of the Devil. My mother said I was too young, and this and that, but my father finally won her

over. We played mostly on weekends, because the men in the
band had jobs and families, and we travelled as far as Texas.
We played a lot of head music—improvised music—but we
also used some stock arrangements put out by Frank Skinner.
We never knew how much we were going to be paid—one or
two or maybe five dollars a night. Bunk Johnson was in the
band then. He was from New Iberia, Louisiana, about a hundred miles to the east, and he didn't have any job except to
play with the Imperial. He must have been about fifty years
old, and everyone called him Mr. Bunk. He told a lot of jokes,
and my father, who wasn't much of a joke teller, did most of
the laughing. Bunk had a staccato style. He never missed a
note or jumbled anything, and he played very clear. We
were exposed to fine music. A lot of regional bands—Don Albert, Alphonso Trent, Papa Celestin, from New Orleans—
came through town, and we listened to the radio every
chance we got. We didn't have electric lights in our house,
but a neighbor had lights and a radio and one of those two-
sided toasters, and we'd go over most nights and listen to Earl
Hines from the Grand Terrace in Chicago. I was very, very
impressed by Earl Hines's style, and I liked everything else
about him—his immaculate clothes and how much he liked
music. I love people who love what they do."

Nellie Lutcher sat down at the piano. She was dressed in a
fitted red velvet gown with puffed pink silk sleeves, and she
looked around the audience as if she were about to address a
stockholders' meeting. Then she smiled, lifted her chin,
blazed her eyes, and announced "Alexander's Ragtime Band."
It was fast and stomping, and was full of legato rhythms,
tumbling dynamics, flattened vowels, and wild Leo Watson
nonsense phrases. A medium-slow "The Lady's in Love with
You" came next, and she sang it almost straight, except that
she accompanied her piano solo with operatic humming. This
was followed by a speeding "Caravan," in which fragments

of melody raced across the room like puffs of wind across open water. She did "Hurry On Down" and "Real Gone Guy," both of them jivy and swinging and she did "St. Louis Blues" as a knocked-out blues. She got off falsetto humming and operatic high notes on her own "Lake Charles Boogie," and she didn't sing on "Mack the Knife." She sang "This Can't Be Love," and then she did a rocking, subtle "Bill Bailey, Won't You Please Come Home," stretching her vowels like rubber bands and indulging in some heavy mockturtle weeping. She made the lyrics of "A Chicken Ain't Nothing but a Bird" clear, and she sang "The Pig Latin Song" in pig Latin. She closed with a fast "Perdido" and a meditative "Fine Brown Frame."

She ordered coffee and caught her breath. Then she said, "I stayed in the Imperial five or six years. I even married one of the musicians. He was twenty years older, and my parents were bitterly opposed. It only lasted two months. I got a little bored in the Imperial, so I joined the Southern Rhythm Boys. It was a sixteen-piece group put together by Al Wilson and Paul Barnes, who had both been in the Imperial. Barnes had played with King Oliver in his last days, and Wilson had brought him into the Imperial. Al Wilson taught me arranging, which I had gotten interested in. All the musicians in the band were older and well-seasoned, and it was marvellous to be with that calibre of player. We did one-nighters all through Louisiana and Mississippi—that was all we could get. I quit and went home, and then I went to California. I knew there must be something better out there. My mother had two sisters in Los Angeles, and Mr. Clarence Hart had moved out and tried to get my daddy to follow him. I stayed with one of my aunts. A cousin knew someone at the Dunbar Hotel, on Central Avenue, in the black neighborhood, and he'd told them, 'I want you to hear my cousin, fresh in town.' I auditioned, and they hired me for the lounge, 8 P.M. to 2 A.M., two dollars a night. I didn't consider

myself much of a singer, but they kept after me, so I sang. I
admired Ethel Waters and Louis Armstrong when I was
growing up, but I don't know how much I learned from them.
I sing what I feel, I sing the story of each song. The 'St.
Louis Blues' is a sad song. The woman in it, her man is gone
and she's a little bitter. It's not a happy-feeling blues to me,
so I try and make that clear. But certain songs don't mean a
thing to me, and I won't, or can't, sing them. 'Star Dust' is
one. I love the melody, but there's nothing in the lyric for
me, and I'll never sing it. Anyway, I stayed at the Dunbar
six months. Sometimes I'd go to breakfast dances at six or
seven in the morning. They had breakfast clubs all over Los
Angeles. I married for the second time—to Leonel Lewis—
and that ended a long time ago. He was from my home town,
and we had a child, Talmadge. Talmadge lives in San Fran-
cisco, and works for Standard Oil, and we're close. After the
Dunbar, I worked in all kinds of groups. One was led by
Dootsie Williams, a trumpet player. It had trumpet, piano,
guitar, and drums, and we did vocal arrangements. We were
the intermission group at the Little Trocadero for a while,
and that was where I met Lena Horne, who was just getting
herself together. Another group had Doug and Wilbur Daniels. They'd been in the famous Spirits of Rhythm with Leo
Watson and Teddy Bunn. A man named Herman Pickett
was on piano, and he took sick and I joined them. Then the
Daniels brothers got fired, and I took over. This was at the
Club Royale. I met Sid Catlett there in 1944. He had a group
at the Streets of Paris, and I think he had Allan Eager on
tenor. Sid was a marvel. He loved people and they loved him.
Talmadge has always said that if Sid had lived he would
have tried to be a drummer, he was that crazy about the way
he played. We never got any further than the romantic department—maybe because of his gambling. He was compulsive; he'd bet on *anything*. One time, he took me out to the
track near Hollywood—I'd never been at a race track in my

life—and before I even figured out where the horses were, he'd lost two hundred dollars. Then he got real downhearted. The trouble is, I never heard of him winning. He admired Duke Ellington more than anyone, and when he was on the Coast he sat in for Sonny Greer when Sonny took a spill and hurt himself. That set Sid up.

"I love coming to New York, but it's not easy getting here. I took the train, because I won't fly, and it was fine except there was a fire and they had to move us into another car. I checked my Oshkosh trunk through in Los Angeles the day before I left. I bought it in the thirties, and it weighs about seventy-five pounds when it's empty. One side has drawers, and the other is a closet where I can hang my gowns. Everything packs in so perfectly that when I get where I'm going I never have to send anything to the dry cleaner for pressing. Of course, the days when they picked up your trunk at your door and delivered it to you at the other end are gone. Two men and a neighbor with a truck took it to the railroad station in Los Angeles, and when I got here I had to look in the directory to find someone to bring it from the Pennsylvania Station to where I'm staying, on Central Park West. When I called, they said, 'Will it fit in a van?' I said, 'No, it's too tall.' So they said, 'Can you lay it on its side?' I said, 'Yes, the clothes are packed that tightly.' So they brought it, and they charged me forty-five dollars, which wiped out any advantage I had from not using the dry cleaner. I brought clothes for all weathers. The coat I'm wearing tonight weighs eight pounds alone. So to bring down some of the weight of my clothes I'm going to mail back the heaviest things bit by bit as the weather gets warmer. Then it won't be so bad when I come to ship that trunk back the day before I leave."

June 27th

When the Whitney Museum put on its "Flowering of Amer-
ican Folk Art" show, in 1974, it acknowledged the help of
Philip Morris, Inc., in small print on the copyright page of
the catalogue. Here is how George Wein is acknowledging
the help given the Newport Jazz Festival this year by the
Brown & Williamson Tobacco Corporation: the Newport
Jazz Festival-New York has become the Kool Newport Jazz
Festival. (This offers all sorts of possibilities—the Lark Met-
ropolitan Opera, the Tareyton New York Philharmonic, the
Winston American Ballet Theatre.) The twenty-sixth edition
of the festival got under way at seven o'clock in Carnegie
Hall with a four-hour concert in honor of Charlie Parker,
who died in 1955, at the age of thirty-four. The pianist Joe
Albany played a rhapsodic blues and gave way to a group
led by Jay McShann, who had hired Parker when Parker
was eighteen. Although McShann's group had Howard Mc-
Ghee, Clark Terry, Charlie Rouse, Budd Johnson, and Cecil
Payne, the chief pleasures were his blues piano and Gus
Johnson's Sid Catlett drumming. A souped-up version of
Parker's "Yardbird Suite" was sung by Bob Dorough and
played by the alto saxophonists James Moody, Lou Donald-
son, and Lee Konitz, backed by John Lewis, Percy Heath,
and Oliver Jackson. Konitz's fleet, winding solo was full of
fine secrets. Lewis and Heath did an exquisite duet on Parker's "Billie's Bounce," and the saxophonists returned for a
look-out-I'm-passing "Cherokee." Max Roach gave a spiel
about Parker and played a drum solo. Dizzy Gillespie and
Dexter Gordon were fleshed out by Al Haig, Chuck Wayne,
Slam Stewart, and the drummer Eddie Gladden. Gordon
wandered through the gloaming, and Gillespie used his
kitchen silver. Jimmy Raney, constructing a lot of fast,
searching interior melodic figures, lifted a group led by Stan
Getz. Barry Harris and Tommy Flanagan, the yin and yang

of Detroit pianists, played two numbers, and Harris was aggressive, and even sparkling. Then Flanagan, Gus Johnson, and the bassist Gene Taylor, together with Gerry Mulligan, Zoot Sims, Al Cohn, and Jimmy Knepper, played Parker's "Ornithology" and a ballad-and-blues medley. Flanagan, full of feints, double-time dashes, and upper-register diamonds, fashioned two first-rate choruses on "Ornithology," and was matched by Knepper. On the medley, Flanagan rolled out a beautiful ballad, and Knepper, thin and tall and looking as if he might waft away, suddenly came forth with "Parker's Mood." It was a shouting, stuttering blues, and the sermon Parker meant it to be. The final group—Curtis Fuller, Jimmy Heath, Red Rodney, and Billy Mitchell, with a rhythm section of Walter Davis, George Duvivier, and Philly Joe Jones— slid down bebop mountain and came to rest on the boulders of hard-bop valley.

June 28th

At five-thirty in Carnegie Recital Hall, Dardanelle sang and played a dozen or so songs, among them "It Could Happen to You," "Spring Can Really Hang You Up the Most," "Out of This World," "It's All Right with Me," and "In the Evening." By demonstrating in her small, sweet, perfect, birdlike way just how to perform good American songs, she shamed almost all the twenty or so instrumentalists and singers gathered in Carnegie Hall tonight to celebrate Fred Astaire. (How do you celebrate Fred Astaire? Copy his dancing? Copy his singing? Copy his acting? Or, as was done tonight, perform the songs he helped make famous? Each is a poor second.) Mel Tormé began the evening at the piano, singing his own lyrics to "They Can't Take That Away from Me." Ruby Braff, aided by John Bunch, George Duvivier, and Connie Kay, did "My One and Only" and "I'm Putting All My Eggs in One Basket," and they were joined by Clark

Terry for a polyphonic "Dancing in the Dark." Braff departed, and Terry did "It's Like Looking for a Needle in a
Haystack" and was joined by Lee Konitz for a polyphonic
"All of You." Terry departed, and Konitz played "Isn't This
a Lovely Day" and "I Concentrate on You." Stan Getz did
"I'm Old-Fashioned" and "Easter Parade" and departed, for-
getting to announce Sylvia Syms—an oversight that would
have cost him his head in other days. She sang five numbers,
and sounded troubled. Her vibrato got loose and her voice
kept catching the wrong lights. George Shearing, accompanied by Brian Torff, played "Waltz in Swing Time," "You
Were Never Lovelier," and "Puttin' On the Ritz," and sang
"Change Partners." His singing has a dusty, old-dad air. The
ten final songs of the evening were done by Tormé and
Gerry Mulligan, who were first brought together at the festival three years ago. Tormé sang awhile; Mulligan sang to
Tormé's piano accompaniment; Tormé and Mulligan sang;
Tormé sang while Mulligan played and hummed organ
chords; Mulligan played. Tormé sang well, but without the
fervor he has shown in his recent New York outings, and
Mulligan carried his own weight.

June 30th

Al Cooper's Savoy Sultans, made up of two trumpets, three
saxophones, and four rhythm, was the house band at the Savoy Ballroom in Harlem from 1937 to 1945. It was a jump
band—a rhythm machine that had one purpose: to make the
customers dance their heads off. It did, and it generated such
steam that it demolished all the alternating bands. (Earl
Hines said, "The Sultans could swing you into bad health.")
It was a primitive group, which played blues and the pop
tunes of the day. The section work was offhand, the ensembles were riffs, the soloists were competent reproductions of
Roy Eldridge and Coleman Hawkins. There were a lot of

hustling black jump bands then (Sabby Lewis, Erskine Hawkins, the Mills Blue Rhythm Band), but none of their recordings capture what they sounded like in front of dancers. They were driving and free and exultant. They were showing off for the dancers, and the dancers, in return, showed off for them. It was a fervent, ritualistic relationship that made the music as close to visual as music can be. The drummer Panama Francis has resurrected the Sultans in the last year or so, and tonight he brought the band into Roseland. He had Franc Williams and Irving Stokes on trumpet, Bill Easley and Howard Johnson on alto saxophones, George Kelly, who was a member of the original Sultans, on tenor saxophone, Red Richards on piano, John Smith on guitar, and Bill Pemberton on bass. They played two sets of standards, riff blues, ballads, and old Sultan arrangements, and caused consternation and delight. Francis, a somewhat heavy Chick Webb drummer overlaid with Sid Catlett traceries, played like a madman. He pushed and roared, and one could almost see the music catapulting off the bandstand, lifting the meanest dancer, exalting the best.

The other end of the jazz rainbow appeared this afternoon at Carnegie Recital Hall. Leroy Jenkins, the elfin forty-eight-year-old violinist, violist, composer, gave a solo concert in which he played seven of his compositions. Jenkins's music occupies an unclear area. It is impossible to tell what is written and what is improvised, what is "classical" and what is jazz, what is serious and what is not. This is how "Hipnosis" went: Jenkins played two long trills, an octave apart, then produced a high, somewhat flat (conscious or not?) mosquito sound, went back to the trills, repeated the mosquito sound slightly differently, did a variation of the trills, and restated the mosquito sound. He interposed a short melodic figure, which he pored over several times, and returned to the trills and the mosquito sounds, and the piece ended. It was five minutes long. One composition had blues overtones, and one was built around a fairly direct folk-music motif, but the rest gave the impression they were scrims concealing a music in Jenkins's mind which he does not yet choose to expose. There was no sounded beat and very little of an implied one.

July 1st

Tonight at Town Hall, the jazz-film collector David Chertok showed twenty-six selections, from feature films, soundies, documentaries, and television. It was an eerie ride. Jazz recordings are blind but jazz films see, and there again were Art Tatum, Erroll Garner, Louis Armstrong, John Coltrane, Sidney Bechet, Ben Webster, Nat Cole, Billie Holiday, and Don Byas. These windows into the past showed Armstrong and Velma Middleton doing an outrageous ham-bone version of "That's My Desire"; Bechet skirling through "St. Louis Blues," backed by a straining French band; Don Byas, largely in shadow, playing a sumptuous "Don't Blame Me"; and Ben Webster, a smoke-haloed presence, clapping perfunctorily in a Danish night club after a windy Dexter Gordon performance, then turning to order another drink. Some of Chertok's clips were very funny, among them an unbelievably busy shipboard swimming-pool scene that included Bert Lahr, Red Skelton, Tommy Dorsey and his band, Eleanor Powell, and Buddy Rich; an eccentric dance done in blackface in 1929 by James Barton, his body vibrating one moment from head to foot, his legs spaghetti the next, his arms whirligigs the next; and Sammy Davis, Jr., strutting at age seven before a beautiful, overreacting Ethel Waters.

July 2nd

Almost nothing was right about "Blues Is a Woman," a celebration of female blues singing held at Avery Fisher tonight. Somewhere along the line, the event got mixed up with feminism, and that would have made Ma Rainey and Bessie

Smith and Chippie Hill hoot. The concert was presented in
the form of a history that purported to show that female
blues singing continues intact. But the great women blues
singers flourished in the twenties and early thirties, and have
since been replaced by the women gospel singers. The handful of women blues singers who have appeared since the thirties are anachronisms: Helen Humes, Julia Lee, Dinah Washington, Big Mama Thornton. The singers chosen for the
concert included Linda Hopkins, Sippie Wallace, Big Mama
Thornton, Beulah Bryant, Koko Taylor, Nell Carter, and
Adelaide Hall. Hopkins can summon up Bessie Smith, but
her stage manner is kittenish. Sippie Wallace, never a commanding blues singer, is in her eighties, and Beulah Bryant,
who has a heavy, immovable voice, is in her sixties. Mama
Thornton seemed subdued, and Koko Taylor, though full of
growls and gospel turns, was mechanical. Nell Carter, with
her sharp, elbowing voice and comic dancing, is a Broadway
person, as is Adelaide Hall. The accompaniment was supplied
by Jay McShann, Little Brother Montgomery, and a band
made up of Doc Cheatham, Vic Dickenson, Kenny Davern,
Dick Hyman, Bill Pemberton, and Panama Francis. Cheatham's and Dickenson's obbligatos shone.

The new romantic eclecticism has been on view the past
couple of afternoons at Carnegie Recital Hall. Yesterday,
Hilton Ruiz, who is twenty-eight, played four numbers in
which he revealed his fondness for McCoy Tyner, Thelonious
Monk, James P. Johnson, Albert Ammons, Cecil Taylor, and
Bill Evans. He likes to soften his edges with rhapsody, and he
avoids a sounded beat. This afternoon, Mitchel Forman, who
is twenty-four, revealed in the course of nine numbers that
he is the thinking man's Keith Jarrett: he is less maudlin
and more delicate. Martial Solal, the formidable French Art
Tatum admirer, was added after Forman. He was witty and
tough and abstract. Each number was an explosive display of
arpeggios, glisses, left-hand thunder, and locked-chording, car-

ried out with great clarity. He made Forman sound like tea
being poured.

July 3rd

The first half of "Swinging Taps," a program held at Avery
Fisher tonight and given over in part to tap-dancing, was exhilarating. The little renaissance of tap-dancing begun in the
early sixties by the late Marshall Stearns (the stunning afternoon of tap-dancing he organized for the 1962 Newport Jazz
Festival; the equally stunning appearance at the Village
Gate in 1964 of the legendary dancer Groundhog) has prob-
ably reached its height. The number of first-rate dancers is
low (Chuck Green, Sandman Sims, Honi Coles, Bunny
Briggs) and is not likely to be replenished. The competi-
tive, charged, echoing backroom environment that the great
dancers knew is gone. Tonight, the Widespread Depression
Orchestra played half a dozen numbers, several of them with
Bob Wilber, who did his unimpeachable Johnny Hodges.
Then the band began "Caravan," and there was Chuck
Green—a square, flapping scarecrow moving in half time, his
head bent forward in concentration, his arms loose. He danced
in the space of a card table, and his simplicity and elegance
were flawless. Green's dancing is designed to be heard; he is
a snare-drum dancer. Abetted by two perfectly placed and
pitched floor microphones, he filled the hall with crystalline
clicking and rattling, with square, loping four-four rhythms
from the late thirties. On "Take the A Train," he inserted
some sharp double-time patterns and some oily slide steps.
He dedicated his final number to his model, John W. Bubbles. Green has got heavier and slower in the past ten years,
but his dancing remains precise and gleaming. Sandman
Sims, who followed, is a flash dancer. He uses most of the
stage, and he is fond of hitting his heels together, opening
and closing his toes, dancing on one foot, and flinging his

legs off to one side. He aims at our eyes. He closed with a couple of sand dances, using a three-by-four board covered with fine sand. The first was shuffling and subtle, and the second an ingenious improvisation on the sounds of a steam locomotive.

After the intermission, Benny Carter, joined by Doc Cheatham, Jimmy Maxwell, Budd Johnson, Curtis Fuller, the violinist Joe Kennedy, and a rhythm section of Ray Bryant, Major Holley, and Oliver Jackson, played four interminable numbers before settling down reluctantly to accompany Honi Coles and the Copasetics—Charles Cook, Buster Brown, Bubba Gaines, Brenda Bufalino, and Debbie Mitchell. They did four or five numbers, ending with "Bugle Call Rag," but they had had to wait too long for Carter to finish, and they lacked the intensity and rhythmic press of Green and Sims.

July 4th

Max Roach has said that he learned a great deal from tap-dancers, and one can sometimes hear Baby Laurence figures in his more intricate snare-drum work. He also learned from Sid Catlett and Kenny Clarke, and they are distantly audible, too. Thirty-five years have passed since Roach, who is now fifty-five, was a neophyte, and during that time he has become the most influential modern drummer. He is spoken of as a "master," as the premier drummer of all time. He appeared at Carnegie Hall tonight with a quartet (Cecil Bridgewater on trumpet, Odean Pope on tenor saxophone, Calvin Hill on bass), and played six numbers. Two of the numbers were a cappella drum solos, and two numbers included drum solos. Roach's accompanying has changed little. He creates a "melodic" flow of broken-rhythm cymbal, snare, and bass-drum sounds. This melodic wash does not vary much (although its details are always shifting), and it has no subtlety or dynamics. (Roach has never got a good drum sound. His tightly muffled snare resembles a hatbox, and his tomtoms have no resonance.) In a short solo, he will begin with his cymbals, walking through them with both drumsticks, and then, with one hand, start a staccato series of strokes on the snare head and rims, shift both hands to the snare for a flurry of two-stroke-roll beats, make a kind of giant left-to-right triplet on his four tomtoms, double the tempo in cross-strokes between his snare and his two big right-hand tomtoms, all the while firing machine-gun bass-drum beats, walk back through his cymbals, and slow his bass drum down to a stop. Roach has what used to be called "fast wrists," and much of what he does is technically dazzling. But he doesn't swing. He leaves your feet flat on the ground, your head and hands still. What a mystery!

July 5th

This afternoon at Carnegie Recital Hall, Jimmy Rowles wiped out all the pianists who had preceded him during the week. Rowles operates on a level of intelligence and wit and skill uncommon in jazz. Many jazz musicians spend their energy on technique or on disguising their lack of originality. But Rowles, from the first bar, comes face to face with what he has to do: transform the song before him into a new song, full of wit, style, subtlety, and fresh melody. And he immediately lifts the listener to his plane. Today, he played "Remember When," which drifted into his huge repertory from a 1934 Jimmy Lunceford record; his special commingling of Billy Strayhorn's "Isfahan" and "Blood Count"; Carl Perkins's "Groove Yard"; and Cole Porter's "Dream Dancing" and "Looking at You." He did six of his own tunes, including "The Lady in the Corner" and "Pygmy Lullaby." He did "Darn That Dream," "That's All," and "How Come You Do Me Like You Do," and he closed with "Jitterbug Waltz" and Strayhorn's "Lotus Blossom." "Pygmy Lullaby" was mournful and delicate, and "The Lady in the Corner" was funny and swinging. "Jitterbug Waltz" had an improvised section in which Rowles abandoned the melody for a series of blocklike inventions. "Lotus Blossom" was an intense aside. All of Rowles's harmonic ingenuity was on view, and in almost every tune he dropped in a quick, querying arpeggio just to make sure we were listening.

July 6th

The "new music" concerts given at Town Hall during the festival, by the Art Ensemble of Chicago, the Beaver Harris-Don Pullen group, Dollar Brand, James Blood Ulmer, Archie Shepp, the World Saxophone Quartet, Robert Kraft, and Carla Bley, have not, for the most part, been very new. (Nor were fringe figures like Ulmer, Brand, and Kraft apposite.) The Art Ensemble has been around over a decade, and so have Shepp and Bley and Harris-Pullen. With the exception of Carla Bley, none of them have changed much. When Bley played the festival in 1965, her music was dour and monochromatic. Last night, it was jumping and accessible and full of singing and funny lyrics, and she demonstrated that she has become something of a comedian. Dressed in high heels and a Ginger Rogers print dress, her blond frizzed hair a thatched roof, she conducted by dancing and weaving and laughing. Would that tonight's concert had been as nimble. Called "The New Music Remembers the Old Master—Duke Ellington," it was played by a fourteen-piece group that included Frank Gordon on trumpet, Byard Lancaster on reeds, Ricky Ford on tenor saxophone, and Pat Patrick on baritone. Two numbers were arranged and conducted by Oliver Lake, one by Julius Hemphill, one by Leroy Jenkins, and three by Muhal Richard Abrams. None of what these four did to Ellington—using free ensembles, long, sometimes disquieting solos, frequent tempo changes, sly harmonies, and multiple soloists—improved or changed him. But he would have appreciated the attention.

Index